COSTING

Series Editor
Brian Coyle

PASSWORD COSTING

First edition August 1989

ISBN 1 871824 04 4

Published by
BPP Publishing Ltd
BPP House, Aldine Place,
142/144 Uxbridge Road, London W12 8AA

Printed by Dotesios Printers Ltd, Trowbridge

A CIP Catalogue reference for this book
is available from the British Library

Copyright © 1989 BPP Publishing Ltd

CONTENTS

		Page
Preface		v
How to use this book		vi

	SECTION 1: NOTES AND QUESTIONS	Page	SECTION 2: MARKING SCHEDULES AND COMMENTS	Page
1.	Materials and labour costs. Cost classification.	3		177
2.	Absorption costing.	17		185
3.	Cost control accounts.	37		196
4.	Job costing. Contract costing. Process costing.	52		203
5.	Budgets.	75		217
6.	Budgetary control. Standard costing.	98		230
7.	Marginal costing and breakeven analysis.	118		241
8.	Costs for decision-making.	139		253
9.	Joint products and by-products.	155		262
10.	Ratios and performance measurement.	164		268

PREFACE

Password is a series of multiple choice question books on business and accountancy topics. If you are studying for an examination, or would just like to test your knowledge on one of these topics, Password books have two special features which are designed to help you.

1 They contain about 300 multiple choice questions, with answers provided later in the book. You can get an objective idea of your strengths and weaknesses, and whether your standard is as high as you would like it to be.

2 We explain most solutions in some detail, to show why one answer is correct and the others are wrong. Our comments should help you to learn from any mistakes you have made, and to improve your understanding of the subject.

Objective testing is an increasingly popular method of examination. An answer is right or wrong, and there are no 'grey areas' or 'in-between answers' that are half-right or arguably correct. Multiple choice questions (MCQs) are the form of objective testing that is now most widely used. Professional bodies that have adopted MCQs for some examination papers include the Institute of Chartered Accountants in England and Wales, the Institute of Chartered Accountants of Scotland and the Chartered Institute of Management Accountants. The Chartered Association of Certified Accountants has recently taken a first step in the same direction.

MCQs offer much more than exam practice, though. They test your knowledge and understanding. And they help with learning.

- The brevity of the questions, and having to select a correct answer from four choices (A, B, C or D), makes them convenient to use. You can do some on your journey to or from work or college on the train or the bus.

- We know from experience that many people like MCQs, find them fun and enjoy the opportunity to mark their own answers exactly.

- Being short, MCQs are able collectively to cover every aspect of a topic area. They make you realise what you know and what you don't.

If you're looking for the fun and challenge of self-testing, or preparing for an examination - not just a multiple choice exam - Password is designed to help you. You can check your own standard, monitor your progress, spot your own weaknesses, and learn things that you hadn't picked up from your text-book or study manual. Most important, Password books allow you to find out for yourself how good you are at a topic, and how much better you want to be.

Good luck!

Brian Coyle
August 1989

PASSWORD. MULTIPLE CHOICE

HOW TO USE THIS BOOK

Aims of the book

This book is designed:

- to familiarise you with a type of question that you are increasingly likely to face if you are studying for examinations

- to develop your knowledge of Costing through repeated practice on questions covering all areas of the subject. There are about 300 questions in this book.

The multiple choice approach

A multiple choice question is in two parts.

- The *stem* sets out the problem or task to be solved. It may be in the form of a question, or it may be an unfinished statement which has to be completed.

- The *options* are the possible responses from which you must choose the one you believe to be correct. There is only one correct option (called the *key*); the other, incorrect, options are called *distractors*.

There are various ways in which you may be asked to indicate your chosen response. If you meet with MCQs in an examination, you should obviously read the instructions carefully. In this book, you will find that the options are identified by the letters A, B, C, D. To indicate your choice, draw a circle round the letter you have chosen.

The notes

In Section 1 of this book each chapter begins with brief notes which are designed to refresh your memory of the subject area and get you thinking along the right lines before you begin to tackle the questions.

The notes are *not* a substitute for a textbook: Password assumes that you are already broadly familiar with the topics covered in the chapter. Nor do they give you answers to all the questions.

- The notes are a *reminder* of the key points in each topic area. If your studies have left you feeling that you can't see the wood for the trees, the notes may help to bring the important issues into focus.

- They provide brief *guidance* on particularly knotty points or areas which often cause problems for students.

- Finally, they set out any *conventions* that are to be adopted in the questions. For example, there are two or more methods of costing for normal loss in process costing. But this kind of ambiguity is fatal to a successful MCQ. For this reason, you will find that the notes to chapter 4 specify which method is commonly used in examinations and is to be used in answering questions.

The questions

The questions are arranged roughly in the order of the key areas highlighted by the notes. But it is difficult, and undesirable, to keep topics completely separate: there's a great deal of overlapping.

The general principle has been for questions *on each topic* to get progressively harder. The result of this is that within a single chapter the level of difficulty will rise, and then fall back to begin rising again. So if you have trouble with two or three questions, don't assume that you have to give up on the whole chapter: there may be easier questions ahead!

If you can, try to work through a whole chapter before turning to the solutions. If you refer to the marking schedule after each question you will find it almost impossible to avoid seeing the answer to the next question, and the value of the book will be lessened.

However, the length of each chapter is variable. Some are quite short, but others are very long. We have taken the view that there is no point in dividing up longer chapters into two just for the sake of making chapters shorter, and so some chapters contain over 40 questions (for example on budgeting). In these cases you might decide to tackle the questions in a chapter in several different sessions, over a period of time, and check your answers at the end of each session.

Finally, don't rush your answers. Distractors are exactly what their name suggests: they are meant to look plausible and distract you from the correct option. Unless you are absolutely certain you know the answer, look carefully at each option in turn before making your choice. You will need a calculator and a pen, and paper for rough workings would be helpful, although you could use the blank space on each page for any rough workings that you need to do.

The marking schedules

The marking schedules indicate the correct answer to each question and the number of marks available. You should add up the marks on all the questions you got right and compare your total with the maximum marks available.

At the foot of each marking schedule there is a rating, which is intended to be helpful in indicating the amount of work you still need to do on each topic. You'll need to use your discretion in interpreting your rating, though. The book may be used by a very wide range of readers, from non-accountancy college students and students of professional, business and accountancy courses, to qualified accounts personnel with years of practical experience. A mark of 10 out of 35 might be worryingly low for an experienced cost accountant, while representing a very creditable achievement for someone at an earlier stage of his or her studies.

The comments

The answers to purely factual questions generally need no explanation, but for most other questions there is a commentary.

These comments will usually describe why a particular option is correct and (more commonly) set out the calculations leading to the correct answer. Distractors are usually chosen to illustrate common misconceptions, or plausible, but incorrect, lines of calculation. The comments will often highlight what is wrong about particular distractors and this should help in clarifying your ideas about topics that you may have misunderstood.

Conclusion

Password Costing is designed as an aid both to learning and to revision. It is not primarily aimed at those who are already expert in the subject. So don't expect to score 100%. And don't despair if your marks seem relatively low. Choosing the wrong answer to a question is not a failure, if by studying the solution and comments you learn something you did not know before. This is particularly relevant if you are using the book at an early stage in your studies, rather than in the final stages of revision.

And if you *do* score 100%? There are 14 other Password titles to get through...

SECTION 1

NOTES AND QUESTIONS

CHAPTER 1

MATERIALS AND LABOUR COSTS. COST CLASSIFICATION

This chapter covers the following topics:

- Direct costs and overheads
- Materials costs
- Stock control
- Direct labour and indirect labour costs
- Cost classification

1. Direct costs and overheads

1.1 Expenditure is commonly analysed between

- materials costs, labour costs and other expenses
- direct costs and indirect costs. A direct cost is a cost that can be identified separately in the cost of a product, service, operation or anything else for which a cost is being calculated.

1.2 The sum of indirect materials costs, indirect labour costs and indirect expenses is known as total *overhead* costs.

2. Materials costs

2.1 Stocks held by an organisation consist of

- raw materials, parts and components, and any other materials or goods purchased from external suppliers
- in production industries, part-finished work (work in progress)
- in production industries, stocks of finished goods.

2.2 The value of stocks of raw materials and components that are bought from external suppliers will usually relate in some way to their purchase price. The value of work in progress and finished goods will consist of the cost of the direct materials contained in them, the cost of the direct labour that has gone into making them and, usually, a cost for production overheads.

2.3 Materials and components have a purchase price, but stocks in hand could have been bought at several different times and at several different prices. A system must be adopted for putting a cost/value to materials when they are issued from store. Several systems might be used

1: MATERIALS AND LABOUR COSTS. COST CLASSIFICATION

- First in first out (FIFO)
- Last in first out (LIFO)
- Weighted average pricing (cumulative or periodic)
- Standard cost
- Replacement cost
- Next in first out (NIFO)
- Simple average pricing

} These try to address the problem of putting a realistic value to issued materials when the rate of inflation is high

2.4 The chosen method of materials valuation affects profits. There is an inter-relationship between (1) the cost of materials in the cost of sales and (2) the valuation of opening stocks and closing stocks.

MATERIALS	WORK IN PROGRESS	FINISHED GOODS	PROFIT AND LOSS ACCOUNT
Opening stock	Opening stock	Opening stock	Sales
+ Purchases	+ Direct materials used	+ Cost of goods made and completed	− Cost of goods sold
− Closing stock	+ Direct labour		Gross profit
Cost of materials used (direct and indirect)	+ Production overheads	− Closing stock	− Other overhead costs
	− Closing stock	= Cost of good sold	= Net profit
	= Cost of goods made and completed		

2.5 A bigger closing stock value in the balance sheet means a lower cost of materials in the cost of sales, which means a bigger profit.

3. Stock control

3.1 Stock control is the 'regulation of stock levels with respect to quantity, cost and lead time.'

> Aspects of stock control
> - recording and monitoring stock levels
> - setting target stock levels (maximum stock, minimum stock, safety stock)
> - forecasting demand for stock
> - deciding reorder quantities and when to re-order
> - reporting on slow-moving or obsolete stock
> - monitoring the cost of stocks purchased and issued
> - ensuring that goods are delivered as ordered, and issued only if properly authorised

3.2 Deciding how much to re-order of any stock item could be done using the economic order quantity (EOQ) formula.

$$EOQ = \sqrt{\frac{2cd}{h}}$$

c = cost per order
d = demand for stock item per period
h = cost of holding a unit of the stock item per period

In the absence of bulk purchases discounts, the EOQ re-order quantity for stock will minimise the combined total of stock ordering costs and stockholding costs.

4. Direct labour and indirect labour costs

4.1 The labour costs or salary costs of individuals who are only indirectly involved in making and selling a product (or service) are indirect labour costs of the product (or service).

The labour costs of a *direct worker* consist of both direct and indirect costs.

Direct labour costs	*Indirect labour costs*
• Basic pay for hours *actively worked* • Employer's National Insurance contribution • Overtime premium, where overtime is worked specifically for one job or item (direct cost of the job) • Productivity-related bonuses	• Pay for any *idle time* • Overtime premium, if overtime is not worked specifically for one job or item • Holiday pay • Sick pay • Shift allowance

5. Cost classification

5.1 Cost classification is defined in the CIMA's Official Terminology as 'the arrangement of items in logical groups having regard to their nature (subjective classification) or the purpose to be fulfilled (objective classification)'.

5.2 A cost might be a materials cost, a wages cost, or any other item of expense (rent, depreciation, charges from external suppliers for services such as office cleaning, telephone charges, electricity charges, car expenses, travel, subsistence, entertainment, postage etc). These costs describe the nature of the expense, and are subjective classifications.

5.3 A cost will be attributable/chargeable to either

- a cost unit (eg direct material cost of production), or
- a cost centre.

5.4 A *cost centre* is a location, or function or items of equipment for which costs are ascertained before relating them to cost units.

5.5 A *cost unit* is a unit of product or service or operation for which a cost is ascertained, eg

- cost per *unit of product made*
- cost per *unit of service provided*
- cost per *employee hour*
- cost per *ton/mile delivered*
- cost per *sales invoice processed*

1: MATERIALS AND LABOUR COSTS. COST CLASSIFICATION

QUESTIONS

Data for questions 1 - 2

Receipts and issues of part number 6288 for the month of August are as follows:

	Receipts units	Total value £	Issues units
3 August	2,000	6,000	
7 August	3,000	9,900	
11 August	2,000	8,000	
16 August			4,000
24 August	3,000	10,500	
30 August			5,000

Opening stocks of part number 6288 were 1,000 units, valued at £2,800.

1 Using a FIFO method of stock valuation, the cost of the issued parts in the month was

A £30,200
B £30,400
C £30,900
D £31,100

Circle your answer

A   B   C   D

2 Using a LIFO method of stock valuation, the cost of the issued parts in the month was

A £30,900
B £31,100
C £31,400
D £33,100

Circle your answer

A   B   C   D

1: MATERIALS AND LABOUR COSTS. COST CLASSIFICATION

3 Bringer Minn Ltd is a small importing company. On 1 November, it had an opening balance of 50 units of commodity X, valued at £900. On 12 November, it purchased in bulk a further 250 units of commodity X for a gross price of £5,000. It received a bulk purchase discount of 5% and a further discount of 3% on the gross price for making an early cash payment. On 29 November, it sold 200 units of commodity X for a sales value of £6,600. Using the FIFO method of valuation, the gross profit in the company's trading account for November for the sale of commodity X was

A £2,700
B £2,790
C £2,850
D £2,940

Circle your answer

A   B   C   D

Data for questions 4 - 5

Stock item 2362X

Date		Receipts Units	Receipts Price per unit £	Receipts Value £	Issues Units	Issues Price per unit £	Issues Value £
1 June	Opening stock	100	5	500			
3 June	Receipts	300	4.8	1,440			
5 June	Issues				220	?	?
12 June	Receipts	170	5.2	884			
24 June	Issues				300	?	?
30 June	Closing stock						

4 Using the weighted average price method of stock valuation, the cost of the materials issued on 5 June was

A £1,056
B £1,067
C £1,090
D £1,100

Circle your answer

A   B   C   D

5 Using the weighted average price method of stock valuation, the value of closing stock on 30 June was

A £247
B £248
C £249
D £251

Circle your answer

A   B   C   D

1: MATERIALS AND LABOUR COSTS. COST CLASSIFICATION

6 A company makes regular purchases of a particular packaging material. The price of this material has been increasing steadily during the latest period, and this trend is likely to continue into the foreseeable future. Which of the following methods will produce the lowest closing stock valuation?

A First in, first out
B Last in, first out
C Next in, first out
D Average price

Circle your answer

A   B   C   D

7 Barbarama Ltd purchases and re-sells a single item of product. Opening stock on 1 March was 400 units, valued at £1.80 each. Further receipts and sales during the month were as follows.

		Units	£ per unit
8 March	Receipts	600	2.10
14 March	Receipts	500	?
25 March	Sales	1,250	4.00

The company uses the FIFO method of stock valuation. Gross trading profit for March was £2,500. What was the cost per unit of the 500 units received on 14 March?

A £1.94
B £2.00
C £2.04
D £2.08

Circle your answer

A   B   C   D

8 One Horse Wholesaling Ltd buys and re-sells a single product, a riding helmet. On 1 May, the company had 300 helmets in stock, with a recorded cost value of £30 each. Receipts and sales of helmets during the month were as follows.

Date	Receipts units	Receipts unit cost £	Sales units
3 May	600	32	
12 May			700
17 May	300	34	
24 May	200	35	
29 May			400

The gross profit from sales for the month was calculated by the new cost accountant, Horace Ryder, to be £19,000. It has since been found that Horace used LIFO to value the cost of sales, but should have used FIFO. As a consequence, the gross profit (£19,000) has been

A understated by £1,000
B understated by £1,800
C overstated by £1,000
D overstated by £1,800

Circle your answer

A   B   C   D

1: MATERIALS AND LABOUR COSTS. COST CLASSIFICATION

9 In a period of continual price inflation for materials purchases

A the LIFO method will produce lower profits than the FIFO method, and lower closing stock values

B the LIFO method will produce lower profits than the FIFO method, and higher closing stock values

C the FIFO method will produce lower profits than the LIFO method, and lower closing stock values

D the FIFO method will produce lower profits than the LIFO method, and higher closing stock values

Circle your answer

A   B   C   D

10 Flattendale Textiles Ltd manufactures winter clothing, and its year end is 31 December. On 5 January, its cost accountant Willie Jumper carried out a physical stocktake and valuation, with the following results.

Stock item code	Quantity units	Cost per unit £	Net realisable value per unit £
206	30	12	14
357	70	7	6
429	50	8	10

The following transactions had occurred on 4 January.

Item code 206   Issued 20 units: unit price £12
Item code 357   Receipts 40 units: unit price £7

The total stock value of items as at 31 December was

A £1,180
B £1,210
C £1,380
D £2,060

Circle your answer

A   B   C   D

1: MATERIALS AND LABOUR COSTS. COST CLASSIFICATION

11 Which of the following procedures would *not* be regarded as an aspect of stock control?

  A Forecasting demand for stock items
  B Protecting stores from theft and damage
  C Determination of reorder levels
  D Deciding when and how much of a stock item to order

Circle your answer

A   B   C   D

12 A routine check of stock records shows that the current stock level of item 12788 is over $1\frac{1}{2}$ times the maximum that has been set for it. Any of the following might be causes for this high stock level EXCEPT

  A an error in the quantity of the item delivered in the month
  B an error in the re-order quantity for the item
  C a reduction in the usage rate for the item
  D an increase in the supply lead time for the item

Circle your answer

A   B   C   D

13 The following data relates to an item of raw material that is used by Marcus Highly Ltd.

Cost of raw material	£20
Usage per week	250 units
Minimum lead time	10 days
Maximum lead time	20 days
Cost of ordering material, per order	£400
Annual cost of holding stock, as a % of cost	10%

A year consists of 48 weeks of 5 days per week.

The economic re-order quantity for the raw material is

  A 2,191 units
  B 2,500 units
  C 4,899 units
  D 5,000 units

Circle your answer

A   B   C   D

1: MATERIALS AND LABOUR COSTS. COST CLASSIFICATION

14 What is the name given to a system of stocktaking, whereby a stock count is made each day of a number of items in store, and the count is checked against stock records, so that every item in store is checked at least once a year?

- A Continuous stocktaking
- B Perpetual inventory
- C ABC inventory analysis
- D Annual stock accounting

Circle your answer

A   B   C   D

15 Gross wages incurred in Department 1 in June were £54,000. The wages analysis shows the following summary breakdown of the gross pay:

	Paid to direct labour £	Paid to indirect labour £
Ordinary time	25,185	11,900
Overtime - basic pay	5,440	3,500
- premium	1,360	875
Shift allowance	2,700	1,360
Sick pay	1,380	300
	36,065	17,935

What is the direct wages cost for Department 1 in June?

- A £25,185
- B £30,625
- C £34,685
- D £36,065

Circle your answer

A   B   C   D

16 Grant Leeve is an assembly worker in the main assembly plant of Gonnaway Ltd. Details of his gross pay for the week are as follows.

	£
Basic pay for normal hours worked: 38 hours at £5 per hour	190
Overtime: 8 hours at time-and-a-half	60
Group bonus payment	12
Gross pay	262

Although paid for normal hours in full, Grant had been idle for 10 hours during the week because of the absence of any output from the machining department.

The *indirect* labour costs in his total gross pay of £262 are

- A £70
- B £72
- C £82
- D £110

Circle your answer

A   B   C   D

11

1: MATERIALS AND LABOUR COSTS. COST CLASSIFICATION

17 Bo Feeters Shoes Ltd manufactures two types of shoe in its factory, where employees are currently paid a fixed weekly wage. A suggestion has been made to switch from a basic wage method of payment to piece-rates. A typical monthly budget would be as follows.

	Shoe Type A	Shoe Type B
Monthly output	4,800 units	3,000 units
Time per unit	24 minutes	36 minutes

Unavoidable non-productive time would be 20% of productive time, and would be paid for at £4 per hour. Operatives would be paid £3.60 per unit of Shoe Type A produced and £6 per hour for work on Shoe Type B.

If the piece rate system is adopted, the monthly cost of operatives' wages in the factory would be

A £20,688
B £28,080
C £31,056
D £38,256

Circle your answer

A   B   C   D

18 The following data relates to work at the factory of Hitchin Allover Ltd.

Normal working day	8 hours
Basic rate of pay per hour	£6
Standard time allowed to produce 1 unit	2 minutes
Premium bonus	75% of time saved at basic rate

The direct labour cost for production in a day when 340 units are made will be

A £48
B £51
C £63
D £68

Circle your answer

A   B   C   D

19 Cost centres are

A units of product or service for which costs are ascertained

B amounts of expenditure attributable to various activities

C functions or locations for which costs are ascertained and related to cost units for control purposes

Cont...

1: MATERIALS AND LABOUR COSTS. COST CLASSIFICATION

D   a section of an organisation for which budgets are prepared and control exercised

Circle your answer

A   B   C   D

Data for questions 20 - 22

The computer department of Ardedge Technology Ltd has three cost centres. The department charges for the services that it provides to user departments. The budget for the department for next year is as follows.

	Software development £	Data preparation £	Mainframe operations £
Salaries	84,000	92,000	102,000
Development expenses	60,000	-	-
Maintenance	-	9,000	30,000
Materials	2,000	5,000	12,000
Power	-	4,000	8,000
Establishment costs	15,000	20,000	26,000

Budgeted hours of development work	14,000 hours
Budgeted terminal key depressions	26,000,000
Budgeted mainframe operations hours	4,000 hours

The customer liaison department has a job which requires computer department work as follows:

	Job 678
Development work	36 hours
Data preparation	120,000 key depressions
Mainframe operations	4 hours

20 In costing for the computer department's operations, an example of costs of a cost centre within the department would be

A   costs of data preparation operations
B   job 678 costs
C   cost per software development hour
D   salaries costs for the department's senior management

Circle your answer

A   B   C   D

1: MATERIALS AND LABOUR COSTS. COST CLASSIFICATION

21 In costing for the computer department's operations, an example of costs of a cost unit would be

A   costs of data preparation operations
B   cost of job 678
C   cost per key depression
D   maintenance costs

Circle your answer

A   B   C   D

22 The computer department charges user departments for its services by adding 25% to the cost of the jobs that it does. The charge to the customer liaison department for job 678 will be

A   £1,192
B   £1,366
C   £1,490
D   £1,708

Circle your answer

A   B   C   D

Data for questions 23 - 24

The overhead expenses of Parkino Fences plc, a large public company, are coded using a 7-digit coding system, as follows.

Location	Code number	Type of expense	Code number	Function	Code
London	10	Rent	410	Buying	21
Birmingham	11	Machinery depreciation	431	Production	22
Cardiff	12	Factory depreciation	432	Marketing	23
Glasgow	16	Travel	510	Finance	24
Manchester	17	Entertainment	511		
Bristol	18	Subsistence	512		

The coding for travelling expenses of a salesman from the Bristol office is 1823510.

23 The coding for the depreciation cost of the factory in Cardiff is

A   1221431
B   1222431
C   1221432
D   1222432

Circle your answer

A   B   C   D

14

1: MATERIALS AND LABOUR COSTS. COST CLASSIFICATION

24 The coding for hotel expenses incurred by the accountant of the Manchester office on a recent visit to head office in London is

A 1024512
B 1724510
C 1724511
D 1724512

Circle your answer

A   B   C   D

25 For a 4-week period, the labour availability of a full-time employee, Rhonda Bout, can be obtained from the following data

	Hours
Contractual hours	144
Annual holidays	36
Bank holidays	15
Certified absence through sickness	14
Other absences	22
Overtime hours worked	24

Rhonda is paid £5 per hour in normal time and £6.25 per hour in overtime.

Available hours are 'the number of hours for which a worker or machine is available for work' (CIMA). The cost *per available hour* of Rhonda's time in the period, direct and indirect, was (to the nearest penny)

A £5.18
B £5.37
C £7.44
D £10.74

Circle your answer

A   B   C   D

Data for questions 26 - 27

The cost items which relate to operating a fleet of transport vehicles operated by Jagger Naughton Ltd are as follows.

Item
1. Vehicle depreciation (based on straight line method)
2. Drivers' wages (one driver per vehicle)
3. Employer's National Insurance Contributions
4. Fuel
5. Oil
6. Holiday pay
7. Rent and running costs for garage and compound
8. Management salaries
9. Mechanic's wages
10. Replacement parts (vary with miles travelled)
11. Road fund licences
12. Security costs
13. Tyre replacements (once every 3 months per vehicle regardless of mileage)
14. Vehicle insurance

1: MATERIALS AND LABOUR COSTS. COST CLASSIFICATION

26 The items to include in the calculation of the direct costs (variable costs) per mile travelled would be

- A Items 1, 2, 3, 4, 5, 6, 10 and 13 only
- B Items 2, 3, 4, 5, 6, 10 and 13 only
- C Items 4, 5, 10 and 13 only
- D Items 4, 5 and 10 only

Circle your answer

A   B   C   D

27 The items to include in the calculation of the direct standing cost per year of keeping a vehicle in operation are

- A All of the items
- B All of the items except items 7, 8 and 12
- C All of the items except items 7, 8, 9 and 12
- D Items 1, 2, 3, 6, 11, 13 and 14 only

Circle your answer

A   B   C   D

CHAPTER 2

ABSORPTION COSTING

> This chapter covers the following topics:
> - Absorption costing defined
> - Allocation, apportionment and absorption of overheads
> - Fixed and variable overhead absorption
> - Over-absorbed or under-absorbed overheads

1. Absorption costing defined

1.1 Absorption costing is a method of costing whereby an amount for fixed costs as well as variable costs is included in the cost of an item. Overheads are 'absorbed' into costs per unit or per job etc.

1.2 Closing stocks of finished goods and work in progress (WIP) are valued at full production cost, which is variable production cost plus an amount of fixed production overhead.

1.3 Administration overheads and selling and distribution (marketing) overheads are sometimes absorbed into unit costs of sale, but are more commonly treated as a period charge in the profit and loss account.

2. Allocation, apportionment and absorption of overheads

2.1 Overheads are absorbed into the cost of items on the basis of a predetermined absorption rate.

$$\frac{\text{Budgeted overhead expenditure}}{\text{Budgeted or normal activity level}} = \text{Absorption rate}$$

Activity level	*Absorption rate*
• Direct labour hours	£x per direct labour hour
• Machine hours	£y per machine hour
• Units of production	£z per unit (for standard units only)
• Direct wages cost	% of direct wages cost
• Direct materials cost	% of direct materials cost
• Prime cost	% of prime cost
• Full production cost	% of full production cost
• Sales revenue	% of sales

2: ABSORPTION COSTING

2.2 The absorption rates that are used to establish the full cost of production or sales are therefore estimated/budgeted rates, not actual costs.

2.3
- Production overhead - a separate absorption rate might be used for each production department, with production overhead costs added to unit costs in each department

- Administration overhead - if absorbed into cost of sales, usually as a % of full production cost, or perhaps as a % of sales revenue

- Selling and distribution overhead - if absorbed into cost of sales, usually as a % of sales revenue.

2.4 In order to establish absorption rates, it is necessary to prepare a budget of overhead expenditures so that all overhead costs are *attributed* to one of the following

- Production departments (departments engaged directly in production work)
- Administration
- Selling and distribution.

2.5 In order to charge budgeted overhead costs in this way, overhead costs must be

- Allocated and
- Apportioned.

2.6 *Allocation* of overhead costs means charging the costs of discrete, identifiable overhead items to a cost centre. The cost centre may be

- a production department engaged directly in production

- a service department, which is a department involved indirectly in production work, such as storekeeping and machinery maintenance

- an administration department

- a sales and distribution department

- another cost centre, eg canteen, security, building costs, which cannot be classified fully as production, administration or sales and distribution.

2.7 *Apportionment* of overheads means the division of costs between two or more cost centres on a fair basis.

- The costs of cost centres such as canteen costs, security costs and general running costs such as rent and rates, heating and lighting etc, must be apportioned between production, administration and sales and distribution cost centres.

- The costs of service departments must be apportioned between production departments that are directly engaged in production work.

2: ABSORPTION COSTING

Apportionment process

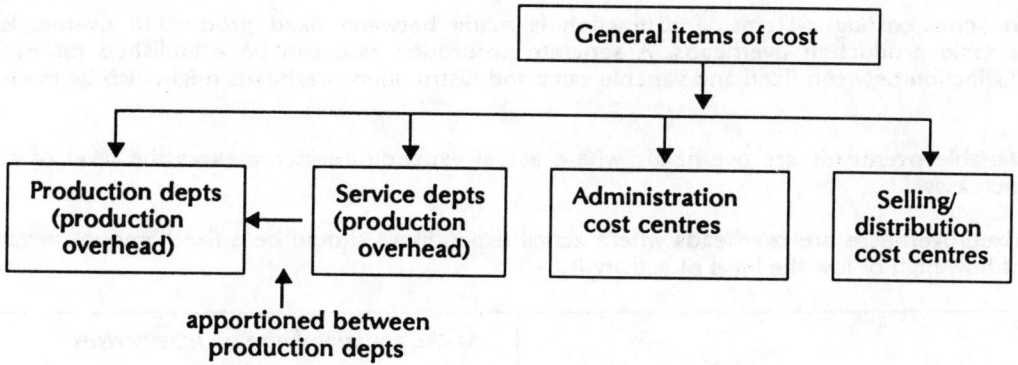

2.8 The basis of apportioning costs should be fair. For example

Cost item	*Suitable basis of apportionment*
Costs of building (rent and rates etc)	Square feet occupied by each cost centre
Machinery repairs/maintenance/depreciation	Value of machinery in each department
Canteen costs	Number of employees in each department
Storekeeping costs	Value of materials requisitioned by each department

2.9 The apportionment of service department costs between production departments may recognise the work done by service departments for each other, and the 'repeated distribution' or 'reciprocal' method of apportioning costs might be used. This is illustrated by a question which follows in this chapter.

2.10

| Production departments | Administration overheads | Selling and distribution overheads |

Overheads allocated/apportioned (attributed) to each production department → absorption rate established for each department

Overheads allocated/apportioned (attributed) and either charged to P&L as a period cost or absorbed into full cost of sale

2.11 The process of allocating and apportioning overheads is done

- for expected costs, in the budget, to establish an absorption rate *and* to establish budgeted costs and profits

- for actual costs incurred, in the cost accounts, to establish actual production overhead costs, administration overhead costs and selling and distribution overhead costs.

2: ABSORPTION COSTING

3. Fixed and variable overhead absorption

3.1 In some costing systems, a distinction is made between fixed production overheads and variable production overheads. A separate absorption rate can be established for each. (A distinction between fixed and variable sales and distribution overheads might also be made.)

3.2 Variable overheads are overheads where actual expenditure increases as the level of activity increases.

Fixed overheads are overheads where actual expenditure should be a fixed amount, regardless of how high or low the level of activity is.

	As the actual volume of activity rises	
	Fixed production overheads	*Variable production overheads*
Expenditure incurred	Should be unchanged	Will increase
Total overheads absorbed into cost of production	Will increase	Will increase

4. Over-absorbed or under-absorbed overheads

4.1 Overheads are absorbed into unit costs using a pre-determined absorption rate. Actual overhead costs incurred are likely to be different from total overheads absorbed.

	£
Absorbed overheads = Actual activity level x absorption rate	X
Actual overhead expenditure	Y
Over-absorbed/under-absorbed overhead	X-Y

- If overheads absorbed into costs are more than actual overhead expenditure, there is over-absorption of overheads.

- If overheads absorbed into costs are less than actual overhead expenditure, there is under-absorption of overheads.

- Any over-absorbed overhead is written to the P&L account as an increase to the period's profits, since overhead costs of production/sales have been overstated.

- Similarly, any under-absorbed overhead is written off as a charge to the P&L account, since overhead costs of production/sales have been under-stated.

2: ABSORPTION COSTING

4.2 Fixed overhead

	£
Absorbed fixed overhead	X
Actual fixed overhead expenditure	Y
Over-absorbed/under-absorbed fixed overhead	X-Y

This will have 2 causes

Expenditure variance

	£
Budgeted fixed overhead expenditure	P
Actual fixed overhead expenditure	Q
Fixed overhead expenditure difference	P-Q

Level of activity (volume) variance

	£
Budgeted/normal activity level	N
Actual activity level	A
Activity/volume difference	N-A
x Absorption rate R	= R(N-A)

Note: £(X - Y) = £(P - Q) + £R (N-A)

4.3 Variable overhead

	£
Absorbed variable overhead = Actual activity level x absorption rate =	X
Actual variable overhead	Y
Difference = Over-absorbed or under-absorbed variable overhead =	X-Y

2: ABSORPTION COSTING

QUESTIONS

Data for questions 1 - 3

Budgeted information relating to two departments in Rydons Tables Limited for the next period is as follows:

Department	Production overhead	Direct material cost	Direct labour cost	Direct labour hours	Machine hours
	£	£	£		
1	27,000	67,500	13,500	2,700	45,000
2	18,000	36,000	100,000	25,000	300

Individual direct labour workers within each department earn differing rates of pay, according to their skills, grade and experience.

1 What is the most appropriate production overhead absorption rate for Department 1?

A 40% of direct material cost
B 200% of direct labour cost
C £10 per direct labour hour
D £0.60 per machine hour

Circle your answer

A   B   C   D

2 What is the most appropriate production overhead absorption rate for Department 2?

A 50% of direct material cost
B 18% of direct labour cost
C £0.72 per direct labour hour
D £60 per machine hour

Circle your answer

A   B   C   D

3 During the period, job number 9287 is carried out by Rydons Tables Limited. Production data is as follows:

Direct material cost		£40
Direct labour	- department 1	4 hours at £5 per hour
	- department 2	9 hours at £4 per hour
Machine hours	- department 1	65 hours
	- department 2	1 hour

What is the total production cost of job 9287 using overhead absorption rates based on your selection in questions 1 and 2?

22

2: ABSORPTION COSTING

A £141.48
B £142.48
C £195.00
D £201.48

Circle your answer

A   B   C   D

4 What is cost apportionment?

A The charging of discrete identifiable items of cost to cost centres or cost units

B The collection of costs attributable to cost centres and cost units using the costing methods, principles and techniques prescribed for a particular business entity

C The process of establishing the costs of cost centres or cost units

D The division of costs amongst two or more cost centres in proportion to the estimated benefit received, using a proxy, eg square feet

Circle your answer

A   B   C   D

5 Tumbil and Faull Limited has been using an overhead absorption rate of £5.60 per machine hour in its machining department throughout the year. During the year the overhead expenditure amounted to £275,000 and 48,000 machine hours were used. Which one of the following statements is correct?

A Overhead was under-absorbed by £6,200
B Overhead was under-absorbed by £7,600
C Overhead was over-absorbed by £6,200
D Overhead was over-absorbed by £7,600

Circle your answer

A   B   C   D

2: ABSORPTION COSTING

6 The following budgeted and actual data relate to production activity and overhead costs in Severn Windows of the World Ltd.

		Budget	Actual
Production overhead:	fixed	£36,000	£39,000
	variable	£9,000	£12,000
Direct labour hours		18,000	20,000

The company uses an absorption costing system and production overheads are absorbed on a direct labour hour basis.

Production overhead during the period was

A Under-absorbed by £1,000
B Over-absorbed by £1,000
C Under-absorbed by £5,000
D Under-absorbed by £6,000

Circle your answer

A   B   C   D

Data for questions 7 - 9

The annual costs listed below have been budgeted for Isabel Ringing Ltd, a company which manufactures fire alarm equipment.

	£000
Energy and water costs (for the building as a whole)	10
Electricity for machines	5
Building rental and rates	90
Building repairs and maintenance	10
Machine repairs and maintenance	8
Direct materials	350
Direct wages	171
Machinery depreciation	52
Security	30
Carriage inwards for raw materials	30
Carriage outwards	70
Indirect production wages and salaries	50
Salesmen's salaries and expenses	76
General administration and management	38
Advertising	30

	Area occupied: square metres
Production	6,000
Sales and distribution	1,000
Administration	3,000

Costs related to the building are apportioned between production, sales and administration overheads on the basis of floor area.

2: ABSORPTION COSTING

7 The budgeted total of allocated and apportioned production overhead costs for the year is

- A £199,000
- B £229,000
- C £255,000
- D £299,000

Circle your answer

A   B   C   D

8 Sales and distribution overheads are absorbed into the cost of sales as a percentage of sales value. Given budgeted sales of £4,000,000, the sales and distribution overhead absorption rate for the year will be

- A 3.00% of sales value
- B 4.00% of sales value
- C 4.75% of sales value
- D 5.45% of sales value

Circle your answer

A   B   C   D

9 Administration overheads are absorbed into the cost of sales as a percentage of full production cost. The administration overhead absorption rate for the year will be (to one decimal place)

- A 10.7% of full production cost
- B 11.1% of full production cost
- C 14.5% of full production cost
- D 14.7% of full production cost

Circle your answer

A   B   C   D

10 The budgeted absorption rate for variable production overhead in Department X of Wiggipen Ltd's factory is £2.50 per direct labour hour and for fixed overhead is £4 per direct labour hour. Actual direct labour hours worked fell short of budget by 1,000 hours. If expenditures were as expected for variable and fixed overheads, the total under-absorbed overhead for the period would be

- A £0
- B £2,500
- C £4,000
- D £6,500

Circle your answer

A   B   C   D

25

2: ABSORPTION COSTING

Data for questions 11 - 14

A manufacturing company, Leyton Friday Ltd, has three production departments X, Y and Z. A predetermined overhead absorption rate is established for each department on the basis of machine hours at normal capacity. The overheads of each department consist of the directly allocated costs of each department plus a share of the service department's overhead costs, apportioned in the ratio 5 : 2 : 3 to departments X, Y and Z respectively. All overheads are fixed costs.

The following incomplete information is available, relating to the period just ended.

	Production department		
	X	Y	Z
Budgeted directly allocated overhead expenses	£74,000	£44,000	£61,500
Budgeted service department apportionment	(?)	(?)	£42,000
Normal machine capacity (hours)	(?)	6,000 hrs	(?)
Pre-determined absorption rate per machine hour	£7.2	(?)	(?)
Actual machine utilisation (hours)	21,200 hrs	(?)	10,000 hrs
Over/(under) absorption of overhead	(?)	£(6,720)	£(11,500)

Actual overhead expenditure incurred in each department was as per budget.

11 The absorption rate per machine hour in Department Y is

A £7.33
B £11.20
C £12.00
D £19.00

Circle your answer

A B C D

12 Actual machine hours worked in Department Y were

A 5,400 hrs
B 5,440 hrs
C 6,560 hrs
D 6,600 hrs

Circle your answer

A B C D

2: ABSORPTION COSTING

13 Normal capacity and the over- or under-absorbed overhead in Department X were

	Normal capacity	Overhead over/ (under) absorbed
A	20,000 hours	£8,640
B	20,000 hours	£(8,640)
C	22,400 hours	£8,640
D	22,400 hours	£(8,640)

Circle your answer

A   B   C   D

14 Normal capacity and the absorption rate per hour in Department Z were

	Normal capacity	Absorption rate per hr
A	11,111 hours	£10.35
B	11,111 hours	£9.20
C	11,250 hours	£10.35
D	11,250 hours	£9.20

Circle your answer

A   B   C   D

15 The following statements relate to the effects or advantages of using a pre-determined overhead absorption rate, rather than calculating overhead costs on the basis of actual costs and actual activity levels.

Statement

A   SSAP9 requires the absorption of production overhead to be based on normal levels of activity rather than actual levels of activity

B   Using a pre-determined absorption rate avoids fluctuations in unit costs caused by abnormally high or low overhead expenditure or activity levels

C   The net profit each year, allowing for the under- or over-absorbed overhead adjustment to profit, will be the same with pre-determined overhead rates as with actual rates

D   Using a pre-determined absorption rate offers the administrative convenience of being able to record full production costs sooner.

All of these statements are correct EXCEPT

A   Statement A
B   Statement B
C   Statement C
D   Statement D

Circle your answer

A   B   C   D

2: ABSORPTION COSTING

16 Nye Fedge Ltd makes two products, P and Q, each of which passes through two production departments. In order to calculate an overhead cost per unit using separate departmental overhead rates, the following budgeted data is available.

	Department 1	Department 2
Allocated and apportioned fixed overhead	£360,000	£90,000
Variable overhead	£0.5 per direct labour hour	£1 per direct labour hour
Direct labour hours per unit		
P	2 hrs	1.2 hrs
Q	1 hr	0.3 hrs

Budgeted production is 10,000 units of each product. Fixed overheads are absorbed on the basis of direct labour hours.

The budgeted overhead cost per unit of product P is

A £31.2
B £33.4
C £34.2
D £47.2

Circle your answer

A   B   C   D

17 Chris Court-Volley, cost accountant of Backe and Smash Ltd, has produced the following budgeted data for next year.

Sales		6,000 units
Finished goods:	opening stock	500 units
	closing stock	1,000 units
Work in progress:	opening stock	500 units, 40% complete
	closing stock	1,000 units, 60% complete
Budgeted production overheads		£187,680
Budgeted production time per unit		2 direct labour hours

In a system of absorption costing, using a direct labour hour basis for absorbing overhead, the production overhead absorption rate per direct labour hour would be

A £12.68
B £13.60
C £13.80
D £14.44

Circle your answer

A   B   C   D

2: ABSORPTION COSTING

Data for questions 18 - 19

Hammerexia Ltd is a manufacturing company operating two production departments, and making two products, M and R. Next year's budgeted manufacturing costs per unit are as follows

	Product M £	Product M £	Product R £	Product R £
Direct materials		18		30
Direct labour				
Department 1	8		15	
Department 2	6		15	
		14		30
Production overheads				
Department 1	16		10	
Department 2	12		30	
		28		40
		60		100

The company operates a full absorption costing system, and absorbs overheads on a machine hour basis in Department 1 and as a percentage of direct labour cost in Department 2.

Absorption rates (fixed and variable overheads combined)
Department 1   £2 per machine hour
Department 2   200% of direct wages costs

Budgeted direct labour costs, Department 2
Product M   £180,000
Product R   £600,000

Stocks of work in progress are not carried.

18 Total budgeted overheads for the company next year are, in £000,

A 1,200
B 1,560
C 2,320
D 2,440

Circle your answer

A   B   C   D

2: ABSORPTION COSTING

19 Assume that, next year, actual results are exactly as those predicted in the budget except that production of M is 3,000 units higher than budgeted. As a consequence, over-absorbed overhead was £42,000 in Department 1 and £30,000 in Department 2. The variable overhead cost per machine hour in Department 1 is therefore

- A £0.25
- B £0.50
- C £1.75
- D £2.00

Circle your answer

A   B   C   D

Data for questions 20 - 21

Budgeted data for Contraflow Ltd, a manufacturing company which makes two products, for next year is as follows.

	Product S	Product T
Sales	6,000 units	8,000 units
Opening stock of finished products	2,000 units (value £56,000)	3,000 units (value £107,000)
Closing stock of finished products	1,000 units	5,000 units
	£ per unit	£ per unit
Direct materials cost	10	10
Direct labour cost (£5 per hour)	10	15
Budgeted production overheads (all fixed costs)		£180,000

Production overhead costs are absorbed on a direct labour hour basis.

The company prices stock issues on a FIFO basis.

20 The budgeted full production cost of sales for the year is

- A £471,500
- B £482,000
- C £483,000
- D £500,000

Circle your answer

A   B   C   D

2: ABSORPTION COSTING

21 If actual production of product T exceeded budget by 2,000 units, but in all other respects, actual output, sales, unit direct costs and fixed costs were as budgeted, the company's actual profit for the year would be

A   the same as budgeted
B   £23,480 higher than budgeted
C   £27,000 higher than budgeted
D   £30,000 higher than budgeted

Circle your answer

A   B   C   D

22 Ali Pali Ltd is a small jobbing company. Budgeted direct labour hours for the current year were 45,000 hours and budgeted direct wages costs were £180,000.

Job number 34679, a rush job for which overtime had to be worked by skilled employees, had the following production costs

	£	£
Direct materials		2,000
Direct wages		
Normal rate (400 hrs)	2,000	
Overtime premium	500	
		2,500
Production overhead		4,000
		8,500

Production overhead is based on a direct labour hour rate.

If production overhead had been based on a percentage of direct wages costs instead, the production cost of job number 34679 would have been

A   £8,500
B   £9,500
C   £10,250
D   £10,750

Circle your answer

A   B   C   D

23 Mason Limited has two production cost centres, X and Y, and two service cost centres, stores and maintenance. Before apportionment of the service department costs, the overhead allocations were:

Cost centre	Overhead allocation £
Production dept X	5,015
Production dept Y	4,485
Stores	5,000
Maintenance	4,000

2: ABSORPTION COSTING

The apportionment of the service department costs is on the following basis:

	Proportion of work done for			
Work done by	Dept X	Dept Y	Stores	Maintenance
Stores	30%	50%	-	20%
Maintenance	80%	10%	10%	-

What is the total overhead of cost centre X after the apportionment of service department costs, to the nearest £? Use the repeated distribution/reciprocal method of service department cost apportionment.

A £10,445
B £10,750
C £10,960
D £11,127

Circle your answer

A   B   C   D

Data for questions 24 - 25

Knott Wright plc started to make and sell a new product which was sold for £30 per unit. In the first year, production was 80,000 units, the normal level of activity. Sales were 60,000 units. Actual costs were the same as budgeted, which were

	Variable	Fixed
Direct costs	£10 per unit produced	-
Factory overhead	£2 per unit produced	£240,000
Selling expenses	£5 per unit sold	£120,000

Any under- or over-absorption was written off to the profit and loss account for the year.

24 Using absorption costing, the value per unit of closing stock was

A £12
B £15
C £16
D £23

Circle your answer

A   B   C   D

25 Using absorption costing, the profit for the year was

A £420,000
B £480,000
C £540,000
D £680,000

Circle your answer

A   B   C   D

2: ABSORPTION COSTING

Data for questions 26 - 27

Budgeted and actual data for Korman and Gowan Ltd for the year to 31 December 19X1 is as follows

	Budget	Actual
Fixed production overhead		
Department P	£78,000	£81,000
Department Q	£114,000	£112,000
Direct labour hours		
Department P	1,500	1,000
Department Q	8,000	10,000
Machine hours		
Department P	2,500	2,000
Department Q	500	600

Fixed production overhead is absorbed on a machine hour basis in Department P and a direct labour hour basis in Department Q.

26 In the year to 31 December 19X1, absorbed fixed production overhead was

A £194,500
B £199,600
C £200,665
D £204,900

Circle your answer

A   B   C   D

27 Fixed overhead in the year was

A under-absorbed by £1,000
B over-absorbed by £7,600
C over-absorbed by £11,900
D over-absorbed by £12,900

Circle your answer

A   B   C   D

2: ABSORPTION COSTING

28 Revon Engines Ltd absorbs production overhead into product costs on the basis of direct labour hours.

Budgeted and actual data for the year to 31 December 19X1 were as follows.

	Budget	Actual
Product X	2,000 units	1,500 units
Product Y	3,000 units	4,000 units
Direct labour hours		
per unit of X	3 hrs	4 hrs
per unit of Y	3 hrs	2½ hrs
Idle time	1,000 hrs	2,000 hrs
Fixed production expenditure	£144,000	£150,000

The fixed overhead absorbed during 19X1 was

- A £144,000
- B £153,600
- C £158,400
- D £172,800

Circle your answer

A   B   C   D

Data for questions 29 - 30

Trapdoor Ltd has the following budgeted and actual data for the year ended 31 December 19X0.

	Budget	Actual
Production (units)	8,000 units	9,000 units
Variable production overhead, per unit	£3	£3
Fixed production overheads	£360,000	£432,000
Sales (units)	6,000 units	8,000 units

Absorption basis for fixed overheads: per unit, based on budgeted output and expenditure.

29 The production overhead absorbed during 19X0 was

- A £384,000
- B £387,000
- C £405,000
- D £432,000

Circle your answer

A   B   C   D

2: ABSORPTION COSTING

30 Production overhead was

  A under-absorbed by £27,000
  B under-absorbed by £72,000
  C under-absorbed by £90,000
  D over-absorbed by £45,000

Circle your answer

A   B   C   D

31 The following data for the year just ended relates to Bumblebee Ltd, which absorbs fixed overhead costs on a unit basis.

	Budget	Actual
Fixed overhead expenditure	£150,000	£148,000
Activity level (production units)	30,000	29,000

Which one of the following statements is correct?

  A Fixed overheads were under-absorbed by £5,000, being the difference between budgeted expenditure and 29,000 units at £5 per unit

  B Fixed overheads were under-absorbed by £5,000, being the difference between budgeted and actual production at £5 per unit

  C Fixed overheads were over-absorbed by £3,000, being partly the difference between budgeted and actual expenditure and partly the production shortfall of 1,000 units

  D Fixed overheads were under-absorbed by £3,000, being partly the difference between budgeted and actual expenditure and partly the production shortfall of 1,000 units

Circle your answer

A   B   C   D

2: ABSORPTION COSTING

Data for questions 32 - 33

Arthur Leetsfoot Ltd has estimated its annual production overheads to be as follows.

An output of	Production overhead cost
20,000 units	£100,000
30,000 units	£114,000

Normal output per annum 25,000 units

32 The fixed production overhead absorption rate next year, as a rate per unit, should be

A £2.88
B £3.80
C £4.28
D £5.00

Circle your answer

A B C D

33 Actual production overhead costs for the year turn out to be £102,000 and actual production is 28,000 units. The under- or over-absorbed overhead for the year is

A Under-absorbed £21,360
B Over-absorbed £ 4,400
C Over-absorbed £17,840
D Over-absorbed £38,000

Circle your answer

A B C D

CHAPTER 3

COST CONTROL ACCOUNTS

> This chapter covers the following topics:
> - Control accounts
> - Interlocking accounts
> - Memorandum reconciliation account
> - Integrated accounts

1. Control accounts

1.1 In cost bookkeeping, a record is kept of costs. There are accounts for stores items, for work in progress (jobs, processes, contracts etc) and for finished goods. Cost records are kept for wages and overhead expenses, and so on, and a fixed assets register may be kept. Other cost accounts will also be kept, depending on the nature of the business, and whether interlocking or integrated accounts are used.

1.2 Control accounts are summary accounts or total accounts. The balance on a control account should equal the total of the balances on the individual accounts in the subsidiary ledger or section of accounts for which it is the total account.

1.3 A simplified system of control accounts is shown in the diagram on the next page.

- This diagram ignores administration, selling and distribution overheads, for simplicity. It also avoids itemising production overhead expenses (eg provision for depreciation).

- There will be opening stocks (debit item brought forward) and closing stocks (credit item carried forward) in the stores ledger control account, work in progress control account and finished goods control account.

- The diagram is not complete, because the debits into the stores, wages and production overhead accounts, and the credit for sales in the sales account, do not have a corresponding credit/debit entry in another account. Just what these credit/debit items are depends on whether interlocking or integrated accounts are used.

3: COST CONTROL ACCOUNTS

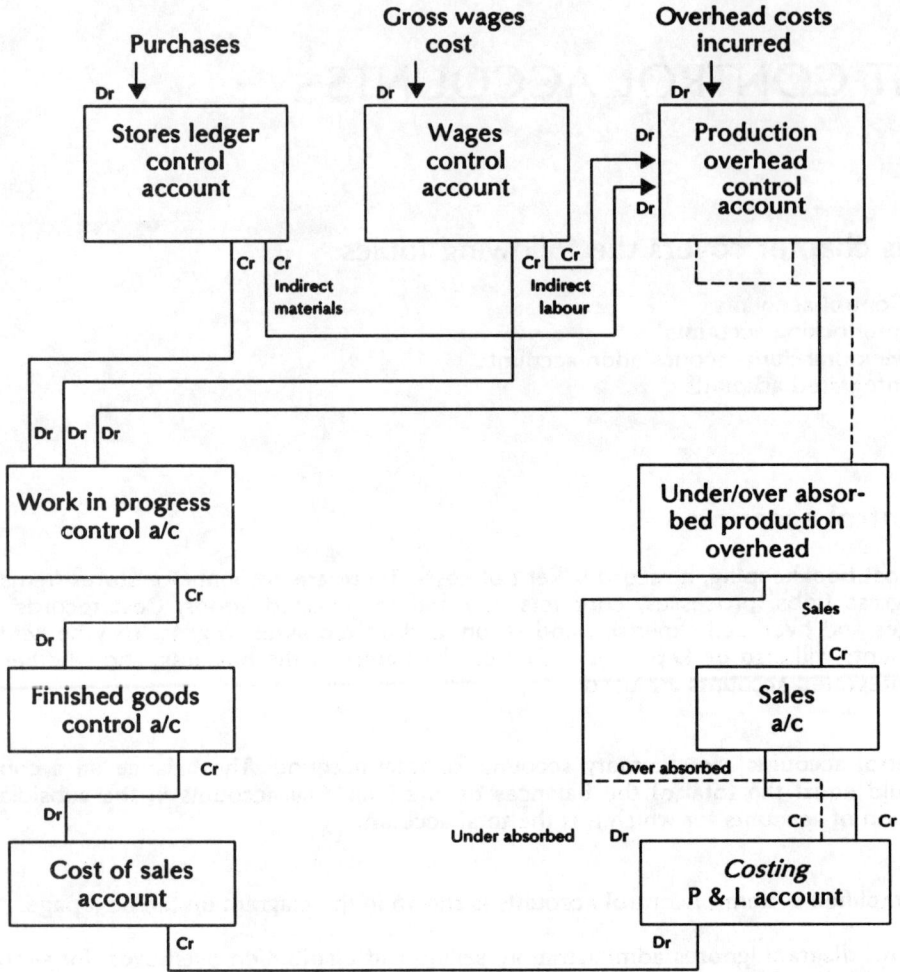

- This diagram ignores administration, selling and distribution overheads, for simplicity. It also avoids itemising production overhead expenses (eg provision for depreciation).

- There will be opening stocks (debit item brought forward) and closing stocks (credit item carried forward) in the stores ledger control account, work in progress control account and finished goods control account.

- The diagram is not complete, because the debits into the stores, wages and production overhead accounts, and the credit for sales in the sales account, do not have a corresponding credit or debit entry in another account.

2. Interlocking accounts

2.1 A company might maintain separate financial accounts and cost accounts. This is an *interlocking* cost accounting system. The financial ledger accounts and the cost ledger accounts are self-balancing, and must be reconciled at the end of a period.

2.2 The cost ledger will contain some accounts that the financial ledger won't. These include

- stores ledger control account, work in progress control account, finished goods control account, cost of sales account

- costing profit and loss account

- production overhead control account, sales and distribution overhead account, administration overhead account, under/over absorbed overhead account.

2.3 The financial ledger will contain many accounts that aren't in the cost ledger. These include

- creditors
- debtors
- cash
- discounts received/allowed
- interest received/paid
- dividends received/paid

2.4 When a corresponding double entry for a transaction in the cost accounts should be to an account that is not in the cost ledger, the double entry is recorded in a cost ledger control account (sometimes called a financial ledger control account). For example

- *Credit* Sales account
  Debit Cost ledger control account (instead of debtors or cash)

- *Debit* Production overhead account
  Credit Cost ledger control account (instead of creditors or cash).

2.5 To make the cost ledger self-balancing, we also have the entry

- *Debit* Costing P&L account
- *Credit* Cost ledger control account } with the profit recorded for the period.

2.6 At the end of a period, the closing balance on the cost ledger control account will be equal to the sum of the closing balances on all the other cost accounts, usually just the three stock accounts - ie the stores ledger control account, WIP control account and the finished goods control account.

3. Memorandum reconciliation account

3.1 With interlocking accounts, the profit or loss recorded in a set of financial accounts for a period will differ from the costing profit or loss. The financial accounting profit and cost accounting profit can be reconciled in a memorandum reconciliation account.

3: COST CONTROL ACCOUNTS

	£
Financial accounting profit	X

(1) Differences in profit caused by differences between the valuation in the financial accounts and the cost accounts of:

- Opening stock balances and
- Closing stock balances of
  - raw material/components stores
  - work in progress
  - finished goods   X or (X)

(2) Items in the financial accounts which affect profit, and which are not recorded in the cost accounts - eg interest received/paid, dividends received/paid, discounts for early settlement   X or (X)

Cost accounting profit   X

3.2 Stock differences can be confusing. It helps to remember

```
  Opening stock
+ Purchases/costs incurred
- Closing stock
= Cost of sales
```

A higher opening stock value adds to the cost of sales
A higher closing stock value reduces the cost of sales

4. Integrated accounts

4.1 Integrated accounts combine the financial accounts and the cost accounts into a single set of accounting records, with common input of data for all accounting purposes. There is no need for a cost ledger control account.

3: COST CONTROL ACCOUNTS

QUESTIONS

1 The following data relates to the stores ledger control account of Duckboard Ltd, a manufacturing company, for the month of October 19X2.

	£
Opening stock	18,500
Closing stock	16,100
Deliveries from suppliers	142,000
Returns to suppliers	2,300
Cost of indirect materials issued	25,200

The issue of direct materials would have been recorded in the cost accounts as

A *Debit* Stores ledger control account £112,100
   Credit Work in progress control account £112,100

B *Debit* Work in progress control account £112,100
   Credit Stores ledger control account £112,100

C *Debit* Stores ledger control account £116,900
   Credit Work in progress control account £116,900

D *Debit* Work in progress control account £116,900
   Credit Stores ledger control account £116,900

Circle your answer

A   B   C   D

2 Rypoll Dage Ltd has recorded the following wages costs for direct production workers in the month of November 19X1.

	Direct workers £	
Basic pay	63,000	
Overtime premium	2,000	- overtime not worked for any specific job
Holiday pay	500	
	65,500	
Income tax	(12,000)	
Employees' National Insurance	(4,000)	
Cash wages	49,500	
Employer's National Insurance	7,800	

41

3: COST CONTROL ACCOUNTS

The accounting entries for these wages costs would be

A *Debit*   Wages control account   £49,500
   Credit Work in progress control account
                                           £47,000
   Credit Production overhead control
            account   £2,500

B *Credit* Wages control account   £57,300
   Debit   Work in progress control account
                                           £54,800
   Debit   Production overhead control
            account   £2,500

C *Credit* Wages control account   £65,500
   Debit   Work in progress control account
                                           £63,000
   Debit   Production overhead control
            account   £2,500

D *Credit* Wages control account   £73,300
   Debit   Work in progress control account
                                           £70,800
   Debit   Production overhead control
            account   £2,500

Circle your answer

A   B   C   D

3 Brixon Morter Ltd is a manufacturing company, which is based in a single factory location. In its cost accounts, it uses an absorption costing system. 70% of the building is taken up by the production divisions, with the remainder of the space taken up by general administration (20%) and marketing (10%). The rental cost for the premises in the year just ended was £40,000.

Which one of the following bookkeeping entries would have been recorded in the company's integrated cost/financial accounts for the period?

A *Debit*   Rent account   £28,000
   Credit Production overhead control
            account   £28,000

B *Debit*   Cash   £40,000
   Credit Rent account   £40,000

C *Debit*   Production overhead control
            account   £28,000
   Credit Rent account   £28,000

D *Debit*   Production overhead control
            account   £40,000
   Credit Rent account   £40,000

Circle your answer

A   B   C   D

3: COST CONTROL ACCOUNTS

Data for questions 4 - 5

Underfoot Ltd is a manufacturing company that uses absorption costing and has a system of interlocking cost accounts. It has two production departments, for which the budgeted overhead data for the year was as follows.

	Budgeted overhead expenditure	Normal capacity	Basis of absorption
Department X	£90,000	30,000 direct labour hours	Direct labour hours
Department Y	£80,000	20,000 machine hours	Machine hours

Total production overhead expenditure for the year turned out to be £195,000. 35,000 direct labour hours were worked in Department X and 25,000 machine hours were worked in Department Y.

4 The expenditure of production overhead would be recorded in the cost accounts as

A *Debit* Production overhead control account £195,000
   Credit Cost ledger control account £195,000

B *Debit* Production overhead control account £195,000
   Credit Creditors £195,000

C *Debit* Cost ledger control account £205,000
   Credit Production overhead control account £205,000

D *Debit* Production overhead control account £205,000
   Credit Cost ledger control account £205,000

Circle your answer

A   B   C   D

3: COST CONTROL ACCOUNTS

5 The under- or over-absorbed overhead would be recorded in the production overhead control account as

- A   *Debit*   Under/over absorbed overhead account   £10,000
    Credit   Production overhead control account   £10,000

- B   *Debit*   Production overhead control account   £10,000
    Credit   Under/over absorbed overhead account   £10,000

- C   *Debit*   Under/over absorbed overhead account   £25,000
    Credit   Production overhead control account   £25,000

- D   *Debit*   Cost ledger control account   £45,000
    Credit   Under/over absorbed overhead account   £45,000

Circle your answer

| A | B | C | D |

Data for questions 6 - 7

Curly Wigg Ltd is a manufacturing company that uses an absorption costing system in its cost accounts. The factory overhead absorption rate for the year just ended was £2 per direct labour hour. 30,000 direct labour hours were worked. Factory overhead expenses incurred were £67,000.

The direct costs of goods produced in the year were £131,000. There were no opening or closing stocks.

6 In the company's cost control accounts, the costs of goods produced would be recorded as

- A   *Debit*   Finished goods account   £191,000
    Credit   Work in progress account   £191,000

- B   *Debit*   Work in progress account   £191,000
    Credit   Finished goods account   £191,000

Cont...

3: COST CONTROL ACCOUNTS

    C *Debit* Finished goods account £198,000
       Credit Work in progress account
                                      £198,000

    D *Debit* Work in progress account
                                      £198,000
       Credit Finished goods account £198,000

Circle your answer

A   B   C   D

7 The over- or under-absorbed factory overhead in the period would have been recorded as

    A *Debit* Under/over absorbed overhead account
       Credit Cost of sales account

    B *Debit* Cost of sales account
       Credit Under/over absorbed overhead account

    C *Debit* Under/over absorbed overhead account
       Credit Profit and loss account

    D *Debit* Profit and loss account
       Credit Under/over absorbed overhead account

Circle your answer

A   B   C   D

8 The following data relates to Knalebiter Ltd for the year to 31 December 19X1.

	£
Sales	500,000
Opening stocks of finished goods	30,000
Closing stocks of finished goods	35,000
Direct materials costs of production	120,000
Direct labour costs	80,000
Production overhead expenses incurred	140,000
Other overhead expenses incurred	60,000

Production overhead absorption rate = 200% of direct labour costs. There were no opening or closing stocks of raw materials or work in progress.

The profit for the year would be recorded in a system of interlocking accounts as

3: COST CONTROL ACCOUNTS

A *Debit* Costing P&L account   £85,000
   Credit Cost ledger control account
                                      £85,000

B *Debit* Cost ledger control account
                                      £85,000
   Credit Costing P&L account   £85,000

C *Credit* Costing P&L account   £95,000
   Debit Cost ledger control account
                                      £95,000

D *Credit* Cost ledger control account
                                      £105,000
   Debit Costing P&L account   £105,000

Circle your answer

A   B   C   D

Data for questions 9 - 13

Ava Kardo Ltd operates a job costing system fully integrated with the financial accounts. The following data relates to May 19X2.

	£
Balances at the beginning of the month	
Stores ledger control account	8,000
Work in progress control account	15,000
Finished goods control account	22,000
Prepayments of production overheads, brought forward from April 19X2	1,000
Transactions during the month	
Materials purchased	75,000
Materials issued to production	34,000
Materials issued to factory maintenance	4,000
Materials transferred between jobs	3,500
Total wages of direct workers	23,000
Recorded non-productive time of direct workers	2,500
Direct wages incurred on installation of new manufacturing equipment	5,000
Wages of indirect production workers (total)	11,000
Other production overheads incurred	16,000
Selling and distribution overheads incurred	12,000
Sales	110,000
Cost of finished goods sold	65,000
Cost of finished goods damaged and scrapped in the month	2,000
Value of work in progress at 31 May 19X2	18,000

Production overhead absorption rate: 200% of direct wages. It is company policy to include a share of production overheads in the cost of capital equipment installed in the factory.

3: COST CONTROL ACCOUNTS

9 The closing balance at 31 May 19X2 in the stores ledger control account was

  A £37,000
  B £45,000
  C £48,500
  D £49,000

Circle your answer

A B C D

10 If there was no stock loss in production, the recorded transfer of finished goods from the work in progress control account to the finished goods control account would be

  A £77,500
  B £81,000
  C £83,500
  D £85,000

Circle your answer

A B C D

11 The under- or over-absorbed production overhead in the month was

  A £6,500 under-absorbed
  B £3,500 under-absorbed
  C £6,500 over-absorbed
  D £9,000 over-absorbed

Circle your answer

A B C D

12 The closing balance on the finished goods control account at 31 May 19X2 was

  A £32,500
  B £34,500
  C £44,500
  D £46,500

Circle your answer

A B C D

13 The profit reported in the profit and loss account for May 19X2 was

  A £22,000
  B £24,000
  C £31,000
  D £33,000

Circle your answer

A B C D

3: COST CONTROL ACCOUNTS

14 Locke and Hunter Ltd is a manufacturing company that operates an interlocking system of accounts, with the financial accounts separate from the cost accounts. Data for the year to 31 March 19X2 are as follows.

Sales for the year	£300,000
Profit for the year	£50,000
Materials in store at 31.3.X2	£25,000
Work in progress at 31.3.X2	£15,000
Finished goods at 31.3.X2	£80,000

The balance on the cost ledger control account at 31 March 19X2 was

A £70,000
B £120,000
C £130,000
D £170,000

Circle your answer

A   B   C   D

---

15 Innes Stead Ltd recorded the following items in its cost accounts for 19X1.

	Prepayments	Accruals
Production overhead expenses at		
1 January 19X1	£8,000	£20,000
31 December 19X1	£5,000	£30,000

Transactions during the year	
Depreciation of plant and machinery	£25,000
Indirect wages	£40,000
Indirect materials	£15,000
Invoices received for production expenses	£60,000

The production overhead absorption rate for the year is £5 per direct labour hour.

Given that 30,000 direct labour hours were worked in the year, the under/over-absorbed overhead in 19X1 was

A £3,000 (under-absorbed)
B £20,000 (under-absorbed)
C £7,000 (over-absorbed)
D £27,000 (over-absorbed)

Circle your answer

A   B   C   D

---

16 Plowden Scatter Ltd, a company which manufactures farming equipment, has two factories. It rents the factory at site X but owns the factory at site Y. As a consequence, Sid Drill, the chief cost accountant, makes a notional rental charge of £30,000 for the site Y factory in the company's cost accounts.

Which of the following accounting entries would be appropriate, given that the company operates a system of interlocking accounts (ie with cost accounts and financial accounts separate)?

3: COST CONTROL ACCOUNTS

> A *Debit*   Notional rent account   £30,000
>   *Credit* Production overhead account
>   £30,000
>
> B *Debit*   Notional rent account   £30,000
>   *Credit* Costing Profit and loss account
>   £30,000
>
> C *Debit*   Notional rent account   £30,000
>   *Credit* Cost ledger control account
>   £30,000
>
> D *Debit*   Cost ledger control account
>   £30,000
>   *Credit* Notional rent account   £30,000

Circle your answer

| A | B | C | D |

17 Houseboxes Ltd uses a standard costing system, and values all its stocks of raw materials at standard price. Stocks are issued to work in progress at standard price. Data for July 19X2 are as follows

Opening stock:	Nil
Goods received:	400 units of Material X
Goods subsequently issued to production:	300 units of X
Standard price per unit of X:	£2
Actual price per unit of X:	£2.50

The cost accounting entry for the material price variance would be

> A *Debit*   Price variance account   £150
>   *Credit* Stores account   £150
>
> B *Debit*   Stores account   £150
>   *Credit* Price variance account   £150
>
> C *Debit*   Price variance account   £200
>   *Credit* Stores account   £200
>
> D *Debit*   Stores account   £200
>   *Credit* Price variance account   £200

Circle your answer

| A | B | C | D |

3: COST CONTROL ACCOUNTS

18 Luke Don Touch Ltd maintains separate cost and financial accounts. The only difference between these accounts, however, is the valuation of stocks. The following information is available for the year ended 30 June 19X1.

	Financial accounts £	Cost accounts £
Raw materials opening stock	53,000	55,400
Raw materials closing stock	36,000	34,000
Finished goods opening stock	83,500	78,600
Finished goods closing stock	74,200	75,900
Work in progress, opening and closing stock	0	0

The profit recorded in the cost accounts for the year was £95,000. The profit recorded in the financial accounts was

A £92,200
B £92,800
C £97,200
D £97,800

Circle your answer

A B C D

---

19 Kane Furniture Ltd maintains separate cost and financial accounts. The cost accounts do *not* include fixed asset records. The profit in the financial accounts for the year ended 31 December 19X1 was £40,000.

The following information is also available for the year, showing the differences between the cost accounts and the financial accounts.

(1) Opening stocks: financial accounts £26,000
                     cost accounts £21,000
(2) Closing stocks: financial accounts £23,000
                     cost accounts £19,000
(3) Dividends received by the company £2,500
(4) A machine with a net book value of £7,000 was sold for £3,000 during the year.

The profit recorded in the cost accounts was

A £37,500
B £39,500
C £40,500
D £42,500

Circle your answer

A B C D

---

20 Walkden Bye Ltd maintains separate cost and financial accounts. The profit in the financial accounts for the year ended 31 December 19X1 was £80,000.

The following data are also available for the year.

	£
Notional interest on plant and machinery	5,000
Opening stocks: financial accounts	32,000
cost accounts	36,000
Closing stocks: financial accounts	18,000
cost accounts	24,000

3: COST CONTROL ACCOUNTS

Notional interest on plant and machinery is charged to production overhead and credited to the cost accounting profit and loss account.

The cost accounting profit for the year was

    A   £73,000
    B   £77,000
    C   £78,000
    D   £82,000

Circle your answer

    A   B   C   D

21 Decoupled Ltd maintains interlocking cost and financial ledgers. There was a balance of £105,000 in the cost ledger control account in the cost accounts at the end of the period.

A further investigation showed that:

(1) Raw materials costing £7,000 had been received into store and recorded in the cost ledger, but the transaction had not yet been entered in the financial ledger.

(2) Depreciation of £18,000 had been provided for in the financial ledger, but no provision had been made in the cost accounts.

(3) The factory overhead account in the cost accounts shows an over-absorbed balance of £10,000. Any under/ over absorbed overhead is to be taken to the costing P & L account at the end of a period, although this has not yet been done.

The closing balance on the cost ledger control account in the cost accounts should be adjusted, to take account of these items, to

    A   £95,000
    B   £105,000
    C   £108,000
    D   £115,000

Circle your answer

    A   B   C   D

CHAPTER 4

JOB COSTING. CONTRACT COSTING. PROCESS COSTING

> This chapter covers the following topics:
> - Definitions: job, contract, batch and process costing
> - Job costing
> - Contract costing
> - Process costing: introduction
> - Process costing: normal loss, abnormal loss, abnormal gain
> - Process costing: disposal value of loss
> - Process costing: opening and closing WIP: equivalent units

1. Definitions: job, contract, batch and process costing

1.1 Job costing is a form of costing in which costs are aggregated for a single customer order (of short duration) or a specific task. The cost unit is the job. The job is a continually identifiable unit.

1.2 Contract costing is a form of job costing where the job or contract is of a long duration. It is commonly applied to construction work. The cost unit is the contract, and the contract is separately identifiable.

1.3 Batch costing is a form of costing that is similar to job costing, except that costs are aggregated for a batch of items collectively. The cost unit is the batch. A cost per unit is calculated by dividing the number of units in the batch into the total batch cost.

1.4 Process costing or continuous operation costing is a costing method which is applied to continuous or repetitive operations or processes. It is not usually possible to identify a separate batch, and costs are charged to the process as a whole. A cost per unit is derived by dividing units produced into the total process costs. It is usual to have unfinished opening WIP brought forward and unfinished closing WIP carried forward.

2. Job costing

2.1 Businesses which carry out small jobs to customer specifications will often base their prices on an estimate of full job cost plus a mark-up for profit.

4: JOB COSTING. CONTRACT COSTING. PROCESS COSTING

2.2 Job costing can be used to control costs of production, and to encourage cost-awareness and responsibility among managers. In some organisations, job costing is applied to work done internally by one department for another (eg repair jobs, and capital expenditure jobs such as machinery installation).

3. Contract costing

3.1 With contract costing, there are several problems and difficulties.

- Contracts will take two or more years to complete. Should some of the profits be taken for a contract before it is completed, or should the profits be taken only when the contract has been finished?
- How should contract work in progress be valued at the end of an accounting period?
- How should foreseeable losses on a contract be dealt with?

3.2 For any contract, *provided that* its outcome can be assessed with reasonable certainty, a 'prudently calculated' attributable profit can be recognised in the P & L account, even when the contract has not yet been completed.

3.3 Foreseeable *losses* on a contract should be taken to the P & L account, even though the losses have not yet arisen and might not arise.

		£
3.4	Cumulative turnover on a contract (perhaps the value of work certified)	X
	minus the cost of this work	Y
	equals cumulative gross profit on the contract	X-Y

The gross profit for an accounting period is the cumulative gross profit minus the profit taken already in earlier years.

3.5 Payments received from a contractee will not be the same as turnover on the contract. Often, the contractee will hold back some payments, referred to as *retentions*, until the contract has been satisfactorily completed.

3.6

		Illustrative figures	
		£'000	£'000
Turnover		200	250
minus	Cumulative payments on account	160	280
equals	Amounts recoverable on contracts	40	
or	Excess payments on account		30

Amounts recoverable on contracts appear as debtors in the balance sheet (SSAP 9).

4: JOB COSTING. CONTRACT COSTING. PROCESS COSTING

3.7 *SSAP 9 on contract balances/creditors*

Illustrative figures

		£'000	£'000
Total costs incurred to date		180	160
less Costs transferred to cost of sales		120	140
		60	20
less Excess payments on account (if any)		30	25
equals Closing WIP in balance sheet		30	-
or Creditor in balance sheet (payment received on account)			5

4. Process costing: introduction

4.1 Process costing is one of the most difficult subjects to learn in costing. This is because it calls for a thorough understanding of the principles of apportionment, as well as the treatment of losses.

4.2 The main problems with process costing are:

- losses
- losses which have a disposal value, or a disposal cost
- unfinished work in process at the beginning and end of a period.

5. Process costing: normal loss, abnormal loss, abnormal gain

5.1 Normal loss is loss in production that is expected to occur in the normal course of events. It is a well accepted principle that the cost of normal loss should be shared out between other units of production.

5.2 Sharing the costs of normal loss can be done by dividing the process costs by the *expected* number of units of production

> Example: Process costs, say £1,800
> Input 1,000 units
> Normal loss 100 units
> Expected output 900 units
>
> Cost per unit of output = £1,800 ÷ Expected output 900 units
> = £2 per unit

Normal loss (assuming no disposal value or scrap value) therefore has a nil value.

4: JOB COSTING. CONTRACT COSTING. PROCESS COSTING

5.4 Expected loss (normal loss) and actual loss might differ. The difference is abnormal loss or abnormal gain.

	Example 1	Example 2
Input 1,000 units		
Normal loss 10%		
Actual output	870 units	920 units
Normal loss	100 units	100 units
	970 units	1,020 units
Input	1,000 units	1,000 units
Abnormal (loss)/gain	(30) units	20 units

Abnormal gain is given a value. Abnormal loss is given a cost.

5.5
> Cost per unit of output (ignoring disposal value or disposal cost of loss)
>
> $= \dfrac{\text{Total process costs}}{\text{Expected output}}$

This cost per unit is applied to finished output and also to units of abnormal loss or abnormal gain.

- Abnormal loss is a cost, credited to the process account
- Abnormal gain has a value, which is debited to the process account.

6. Process costing: disposal value of loss

6.1 When loss (eg scrapped units) has a disposal value, the disposal value of normal loss units and the disposal value of abnormal gain/loss units are accounted for differently.

6.2 The disposal value of *normal loss* units is deducted from the total costs of the process (and more specifically, from the direct materials costs of the process).

> A cost per unit produced $= \dfrac{\text{Process costs minus disposal value of normal loss}}{\text{Expected units of output}}$

The disposal value of normal loss is credited to the process account:

Credit Process account
Debit Scrap/disposals account

6.3 The disposal value of units of abnormal loss is subtracted from the cost of abnormal loss, and the net cost is written off to the P & L account.

Similarly, the disposal value of units of abnormal gain is subtracted from the value of abnormal gain, and the net amount is credited to the P & L account.

This setting off is done in an abnormal loss account or abnormal gain account within the cost bookkeeping system.

4: JOB COSTING. CONTRACT COSTING. PROCESS COSTING

7. Process costing: opening and closing WIP: equivalent units

7.1 A further complication arises with the costing of opening and closing stocks of WIP.

- Opening stocks need a bit more work doing on them to finish them
- Closing stocks have been only part-completed.

How should process costs be apportioned so that opening and closing stocks receive a fair share of the process costs for the accounting period?

7.2 Equivalent units are the concept on which the apportionment of process costs is based. Equivalent units are similar to expected units of output. If a unit of closing WIP is 50% complete, the unit counts as ½ an equivalent unit.

A distinction is often made between equivalent units of materials (often introduced in full at the start of processing) and equivalent units of conversion costs (direct labour and production overheads).

$$\text{Cost per equivalent unit} = \frac{\text{Total process costs minus disposal value, if any, of normal loss}}{\text{Equivalent units of output}}$$

7.3 Units of *normal loss*, are usually worth no equivalent units.

Units of *abnormal loss* and *abnormal gain* are *usually* one equivalent unit each.

7.4 Closing WIP is valued at

Equivalent units of direct material x Cost per equivalent unit of material

plus Equivalent units of conversion cost x Cost per equivalent unit of conversion cost

7.5 The method of stock valuation in process costing may be FIFO, weighted average pricing or standard costing (not dealt with in this chapter)

FIFO	Weighted average pricing
• Process costs for the period exclude value of opening WIP b/fwd	• Process costs for the period include value of opening WIP b/fwd
• Units of opening WIP are valued at the number of equivalent units of work needed to complete them in the period	• Units of opening WIP are valued at a full equivalent unit of work done

The cost per equivalent unit will differ according to the method of stock valuation used.

4: JOB COSTING. CONTRACT COSTING. PROCESS COSTING

QUESTIONS

1 The following information relates to job 2468, which is being carried out by Soxon Feet Ltd to meet a customer's order.

	Department A	Department B
Direct materials consumed	£5,000	£3,000
Direct labour hours	400 hrs	200 hrs
Direct labour rate per hour	£4	£5
Production overhead per direct labour hour	£4	£4
Administration and other overhead	20% of full production cost	
Profit mark-up	25% of sales price	

What is the selling price to the customer for job 2468?

A £16,250
B £17,333
C £19,500
D £20,800

Circle your answer

A   B   C   D

2 The following information relates to job 3579, which is being carried out by Mittenson Hands Ltd to meet a customer's order.

Materials issued to job 3579	£5,000
Materials transferred to job 2456	£400

Grade X labour (direct labour): 200 hours at £3 per hour basic rate. 100 of these hours were worked in overtime, at the request of the customer, in order to complete the job earlier.

Overtime premium is £1 per hour.
Production overhead : £5 per direct labour hour.

A supervisor, Wat Chover, recorded on his job sheet that 20 hours of his time was spent on this job. He is paid £5 per hour, and the cost of his time is treated as a direct labour cost in the company's cost accounts.

What is the full production cost of job 3579?

A £6,300
B £6,400
C £6,500
D £6,900

Circle your answer

A   B   C   D

4: JOB COSTING. CONTRACT COSTING. PROCESS COSTING

Data for questions 3 - 5

Twist and Tern Ltd is a company that carries out jobbing work. One of the jobs carried out in February was job 1357, to which the following information relates.

Direct material Y: 400 kilos issued from stores at a cost of £5 per kilo
Direct material Z: 800 kilos issued from stores at a cost of £6 per kilo
60 kilos returned. A further 20 kilos were damaged in Department Q and had to be disposed of: this was treated as an abnormal loss.
Department P: 300 hours of labour, of which 100 hours were done in overtime
Department Q: 200 hours of labour, of which 100 hours were done in overtime

Overtime work is carried out normally in Department P, where basic pay is £4 per hour plus an overtime premium of £1 per hour. Overtime work was done in Department Q in February because of a request by a customer for another job to complete his job quickly. Basic pay in Department Q is £5 per hour and overtime premium is £1.50 per hour.

Department P had to carry out rectification work which took 20 hours in normal time. These 20 hours are additional to the 300 hours above. This rectification work is normal for a job such as job 1357, and since it was expected, is included in direct costs of the job.

Overhead is absorbed at the rate of £3 per direct labour hour in both departments.

3 What was the direct material cost of job 1357?

A £6,320
B £6,440
C £6,680
D £6,800

Circle your answer

A   B   C   D

4 What was the direct labour cost of job 1357?

A £2,200
B £2,280
C £2,530
D £2,600

Circle your answer

A   B   C   D

4: JOB COSTING. CONTRACT COSTING. PROCESS COSTING

5 What was the full production cost of job 1357?

   A £10,100
   B £10,160
   C £10,280
   D £10,335

Circle your answer

A   B   C   D

6 Which one of the following statements is *incorrect*?

   A Job costs are collected separately, whereas process costs are averages

   B In job costing, the progress of a job can be ascertained from materials requisition notes and job tickets or time sheets

   C In process costing, information is needed about work passing through a process and work remaining in each process

   D In process costing, but not job costing, the cost of normal loss will be incorporated into normal product costs

Circle your answer

A   B   C   D

7 Brixon Mortar plc began a major construction contract on 1 January 19X1, which is expected to take 8 years to complete. Cost data for the second year of the contract work, 19X2, include the following.

	Accrued at 31.12.X1 £	Prepayment 31.12.X1 £	Cash paid in 19X2 £	Accrued at 31.12.X2 £
Site wages	15,000	-	400,000	22,000
Contract expenses	-	8,000	200,000	5,000

What are the costs for site wages and contract expenses for the contract in 19X2?

   A £566,000
   B £580,000
   C £604,000
   D £620,000

Circle your answer

A   B   C   D

4: JOB COSTING. CONTRACT COSTING. PROCESS COSTING

Data for questions 8 - 11

Arthur Quake Constructions plc has four long-term contracts in progress at the end of 19X1. Data for these contracts are as follows.

	Contract 1 £	Contract 2 £	Contract 3 £	Contract 4 £
Cumulative turnover as at end of 19X1	270,000	150,000	300,000	120,000
Cumulative cost of sales for the contract as at end of 19X1	200,000	110,000	210,000	140,000
Cumulative payments received on account	220,000	175,000	330,000	80,000
Total costs incurred on contract as at end of 19X1	200,000	120,000	260,000	140,000
Provision for foreseeable loss on contract	-	-	-	15,000

The company applies the principles of SSAP 9 to accounting for long-term contracts.

8 What is the amount of work in progress on Contract 1, and what is the amount recoverable on the contract, to be included in balance sheet debtors, as at 31 December 19X1?

	Closing WIP	Amount recoverable £
A	0	50,000
B	0	70,000
C	20,000	50,000
D	20,000	70,000

Circle your answer

A B C D

9 What amount should be included in the company's balance sheet at 31 December 19X1 as 'payment received on account' in respect of Contract 2?

A £15,000
B £25,000
C £55,000
D £65,000

Circle your answer

A B C D

4: JOB COSTING. CONTRACT COSTING. PROCESS COSTING

10 What amount should be included in the company's balance sheet at 31 December 19X1 in stocks (WIP), under long-term contract balances, in respect of Contract 3?

- A £120,000
- B £70,000
- C £50,000
- D £20,000

Circle your answer

A   B   C   D

11 What amounts should be included in the company's balance sheet as debtors and as gross loss in respect of Contract 4, as at 31 December 19X1.

	Debtors £	Gross loss £
A	0	20,000
B	0	35,000
C	40,000	20,000
D	40,000	35,000

Circle your answer

A   B   C   D

Data for questions 12 - 14

Landy Stroyers plc is a construction company. Data relating to one of its contracts, XYZ, for the year to 31 December 19X2, are as follows.

	£'000
Value of work certified to 31 December 19X1	500
Cost of work certified to 31 December 19X1	380
Plant on site b/f at 1 January 19X2	30
Materials on site b/f at 1 January 19X2	10
Cost of contract to 1 January 19X2 b/f	370
Materials issued from store	190
Sub-contractors' costs	200
Wages and salaries	200
Overheads absorbed by contract in 19X2	100
Plant on site c/f at 31 December 19X2	15
Materials on site c/f at 31 December 19X2	5
Value of work certified to 31 December 19X2	1,200
Cost of work certified to 31 December 19X2	950

No profit has been taken on the contract prior to 19X2.

4: JOB COSTING. CONTRACT COSTING. PROCESS COSTING

12 What was the total cumulative cost of contract XYZ to the end of December 19X2?

- A £1,040,000
- B £1,060,000
- C £1,070,000
- D £1,080,000

Circle your answer

A B C D

13 Turnover on the contract is taken as the value of work certified. The gross profit for the contract for the year to 31 December 19X2 will be

- A £120,000
- B £130,000
- C £230,000
- D £250,000

Circle your answer

A B C D

14 What will be the value of the contract work in progress at 31 December 19X2, applying the principles of SSAP 9? (Ignore plant on site and materials on site).

- A £10,000
- B £90,000
- C £130,000
- D £210,000

Circle your answer

A B C D

15 Changing Ltd manufactures a product which goes through three consecutive processes, Process 1, Process 2 then Process 3. Data for March is as follows.

	Process 1 £	Process 2 £	Process 3 £
Opening stock of WIP	8,000	13,000	2,000
Added materials	20,000	4,000	5,000
Conversion costs	10,000	10,000	16,000
Closing stock of WIP	6,000	9,000	4,000

What was the value of output transferred from Process 3 to the finished goods account in March?

- A £63,000
- B £65,000
- C £67,000
- D £69,000

Circle your answer

A B C D

4: JOB COSTING. CONTRACT COSTING. PROCESS COSTING

Data for questions 16 - 17

Dotsun Dashes Ltd manufactures a product in a process operation. Normal loss is 5% of input, and is not costed. Loss is assumed to occur at the end of processing.

Data for May are as follows.

Opening stock of WIP	Nil
Input materials	6,000 units, cost £13,060
Direct labour	£5,000
Production overhead	300% of direct labour cost
Closing stock of WIP	Nil
Output to finished goods	5,800 units

16 What was the full cost of output to finished goods in May?

A £28,060
B £31,958
C £33,060
D £33,640

Circle your answer

A   B   C   D

17 What would be the appropriate double entry in the cost accounts to record the abnormal loss or gain in May?

A Debit   Process account   £570
   Credit   Abnormal loss/gain account   £570

B Debit   Abnormal loss/gain account   £570
   Credit   Process account   £570

C Debit   Process account   £580
   Credit   Abnormal loss/gain account   £580

D Debit   Abnormal loss/gain account   £580
   Credit   Process account   £580

Circle your answer

A   B   C   D

4: JOB COSTING. CONTRACT COSTING. PROCESS COSTING

> **Data for questions 18 - 19**
>
> Hatton Head Ltd manufactures a product in a single process operation. Normal loss, which is 10% of output, is not costed. Loss is assumed to occur at the end of processing. Data for June are as follows.
>
> | | |
> |---|---|
> | Opening and closing stocks of WIP | Nil |
> | Costs of input materials (3,300 units) | £59,100 |
> | Direct labour and production overhead | £30,000 |
> | Output to finished goods | 2,750 units |

18 The full cost of finished output in June was

- A £74,250
- B £81,675
- C £82,500
- D £89,100

Circle your answer

A   B   C   D

19 The entry for the abnormal loss or abnormal gain in the cost accounts will be.

- A Debit   Abnormal loss/gain account   £6,600
     Credit Process account   £6,600

- B Debit   Process account   £6,600
     Credit Abnormal loss/gain account   £6,600

- C Debit   Abnormal loss/gain account   £7,425
     Credit Process account   £7,425

- D Debit   Process account   £7,425
     Credit Abnormal loss/gain account   £7,425

Circle your answer

A   B   C   D

Data for questions 20 - 21

Birdseed Ltd manufactures a certain product, product Jay, in two consecutive processes. Data for September are as follows.

Process 1

Opening stock	Nil
Input	
Direct materials	2,200 units
Production cost	£43,560
Output to Process 2	2,000 units
Closing stock	Nil

Process 2

Opening stock	Nil
Input from Process 1	2,000 units
Production cost	
(labour and overhead)	£6,760
Output to finished goods store	1,700 units
Closing stock	Nil

At a quality control inspection at the end of Process 1, 10% of items are normally rejected. Input from Process 1 is added to Process 2 in full at the start of the process. Normal loss in Process 2 is 10% of input, and loss occurs at the end of the process.

Normal loss is not costed. Scrapped units have no value.

20 What was the cost of output transferred from Process 1 to Process 2 in September?

- A £39,600
- B £43,120
- C £43,560
- D £44,000

Circle your answer

A   B   C   D

21 The cost of output transferred to finished goods store in September was

- A £42,772
- B £47,800
- C £47,940
- D £50,320

Circle your answer

A   B   C   D

4: JOB COSTING. CONTRACT COSTING. PROCESS COSTING

Data for questions 22 - 24

Odson Ends Ltd produces a small standard component in a process operation. There is a quality control check at the end of processing. Items which fail this check are sold off as scrap for £1.80 per unit. The expected rate of rejection is 10%. Normal loss is not given a cost, except that its scrap value is credited to the process account. The cost/value of abnormal loss or gain, net of scrap value, is written off to the profit and loss account. Data for July are as follows.

Opening stock and closing stock of WIP	Nil
Materials input	1,000 units cost £5,100
Direct labour and overhead cost	£3,000
Output to finished goods	800 units

22 What was the full cost of finished output that passed the quality control check in July?

- A £7,040
- B £7,200
- C £7,740
- D £8,100

Circle your answer

A   B   C   D

23 What was the write-off to the profit and loss account for abnormal loss in July?

- A £700
- B £720
- C £880
- D £1,360

Circle your answer

A   B   C   D

24 If the scrap value of loss were credited directly to the profit and loss account, as sundry sales revenue, what would have been the cost of the finished goods that passed the quality control check in the month?

- A £7,040
- B £7,200
- C £7,740
- D £8,100

Circle your answer

A   B   C   D

4: JOB COSTING. CONTRACT COSTING. PROCESS COSTING

25 Patacake Ltd produces a certain food item in a manufacturing process. On 1 November, there was no opening stock of work in process. During November, 500 units of material were input to the process, with a cost of £9,000. Direct labour costs in November were £3,840. Production overhead is absorbed at the rate of 200% of direct labour costs. Closing stock on 30 November consisted of 100 units which were 100% complete as to materials and 80% complete as to labour and overhead. There was no loss in process.

The full production cost of completed units during November was

- A £10,400
- B £13,600
- C £16,416
- D £16,800

Circle your answer

A   B   C   D

Data for questions 26 - 27

Sludge Ltd produces a single product from one process. At the beginning of December, 3,000 completed units were still in process, awaiting transfer to finished goods. They were valued as

	£
Direct material	2,920
Conversion costs	2,800

During December, a further 40,000 units were put into the process, and the costs charged to the process in December were

	£
Direct material	42,180
Conversion costs	37,100

36,000 units were transferred to finished stock and 5,000 units remained in work in process at the end of the month, complete as to material but only 40% complete as to conversion costs. A loss of 2,000 units, being normal, occurred during the process.

The company uses the average method of stock pricing.

26 What was the cost of output transferred to finished goods stock in December?

- A £71,610
- B £76,670
- C £77,330
- D £77,400

Circle your answer

A   B   C   D

67

4: JOB COSTING. CONTRACT COSTING. PROCESS COSTING

27 What was the value of work in process as at the end of December?

A £7,600
B £7,670
C £10,750
D £10,850

Circle your answer

A B C D

28 Collymules Ltd manufactures a product in a process operation. Materials are introduced in full at the start of operations. There is occasionally some loss in process, and this occurs half-way though processing, at a quality control inspection. The cost of loss is written off to the profit and loss account. Data for October are as follows.

Opening stock	Nil
Materials introduced	4,000 units, cost £29,640
Labour and overhead cost	£74,100
Closing stock	Nil
Finished and transferred to warehouse	3,800 units

The cost of loss written off to the profit and loss account in October was

A £3,382
B £3,420
C £5,187
D £5,460

Circle your answer

A B C D

Data for questions 29 - 30

Hick Cups Ltd manufactures small standard tea cups in a single process. The following data relates to August.

Opening stock of work in process	Nil
Direct materials cost	£13,500
Direct labour cost (2,070 hours)	£6,210
Production overhead	£6 per direct labour hour
Closing stock of work in process	5,000 cups, 60% complete as to material and 10% complete as to labour
Finished output	20,000 cups

During the month, 5,000 teacups were scrapped in the middle of processing, when it was estimated that they were 80% complete as to materials and 40% complete as to labour.

4: JOB COSTING. CONTRACT COSTING. PROCESS COSTING

29 What was the full cost of scrap in August, which was written off to the profit and loss account?

A £3,105
B £3,460
C £3,620
D £4,760

Circle your answer

A   B   C   D

30 The value of closing work in progress at 31 August was

A £2,310
B £3,060
C £3,105
D £3,570

Circle your answer

A   B   C   D

Data for questions 31 - 33

Dringweed, an agricultural fertiliser, is manufactured in a single continuous process. Opening stock on 1 March was 200 units, which were valued at £30,095, which consists of £25,200 in materials cost and £4,895 in conversion cost. This was 100% complete as to materials and 25% complete as to conversion cost. 1,200 units were added to production during March, and these had a materials cost of £168,000. Closing stock of 200 units on 31 March was 100% complete as to materials and 50% complete as to conversion cost. Conversion costs during March were £158,125.

There was no loss in process

31 What were the equivalent units of production in March?

	Materials	Conversion costs
A	1,400 units	1,350 units
B	1,200 units	1,100 units
C	1,200 units	1,150 units
D	1,200 units	1,250 units

Circle your answer

A   B   C   D

4: JOB COSTING. CONTRACT COSTING. PROCESS COSTING

32 Using the FIFO method of stock valuation, what was the cost of finished goods completed during March?

    A   £315,570
    B   £335,095
    C   £341,845
    D   £349,985

Circle your answer

A   B   C   D

33 Using the weighted average method of stock valuation, what was the value of closing stock of work in process at 31 March?

    A   £40,140
    B   £40,650
    C   £47,020
    D   £52,680

Circle your answer

A   B   C   D

Data for questions 34 - 36

Fissiozim, a chemical compound, is manufactured from two consecutive processes. Details for the second process, Process 2, for the month of June are as follows.

Opening stock of WIP	Nil
Materials transferred from Process A	10,000 kilos value £309,600
Direct labour cost	£103,500
Overheads	100% of direct labour cost
Output transferred to finished goods	7,600 kilos
Closing stock of WIP	1,000 kilos

Quality control checks at the end of Process 2 normally lead to a rejection rate of 10% of the number of units *input* to the process in the period. Rejected items have no scrap value. Normal loss is not given any cost.

Closing work in process is 100% complete for material content and 70% complete for labour and overhead content.

Full absorption costing is used. The cost per equivalent unit of production is calculated to the nearest penny.

4: JOB COSTING. CONTRACT COSTING. PROCESS COSTING

34 The equivalent units of production in June were

	Materials	Labour and overhead
A	8,600 units	8,300 units
B	9,000 units	8,600 units
C	9,000 units	8,700 units
D	9,000 units	9,000 units

Circle your answer

A   B   C   D

35 The cost of abnormal loss in June, written off to the profit and loss account, was

- A £22,960
- B £23,276
- C £23,388
- D £24,376

Circle your answer

A   B   C   D

36 The value of closing work in process at the end of June was

- A £50,940
- B £51,053
- C £51,249
- D £58,190

Circle your answer

A   B   C   D

Data for questions 37 - 39

Bloch Kade Ltd manufactures a product in two consecutive processes. Data for Process 1 in September are as follows.

Opening stock of work in process 2,000 units

	Degree of completion	Cost £
Direct materials	100%	80,000
Direct labour and overhead	40%	20,000
		£100,0000

Added to Process 1 in the month
   Direct materials 5,000 units cost   £189,200
   Direct labour and overhead   £160,160

Closing stock of work in process   Nil
Transferred to Process 2   6,000 units

Cont...

4: JOB COSTING. CONTRACT COSTING. PROCESS COSTING

> It is expected that there will be wastage equal to 10% of units completed.
>
> Scrapped or wasted units have a scrap value of £4.40 each, and the scrap value of normal loss is set off against the cost of materials in the process account. Loss is assumed to occur at the end of the process. Full absorption costing is used.

37 Using a FIFO method of valuation, what was the number of equivalent units of work in the month to be used for apportioning process costs?

	Materials	Labour/overhead
A	4,000 units	5,200 units
B	4,400 units	5,200 units
C	4,400 units	5,600 units
D	4,500 units	5,700 units

Circle your answer

A B C D

38 Using the FIFO method of valuation, what was the cost of the work transferred to Process 2 in the month?

A £313,245
B £384,000
C £418,320
D £420,720

Circle your answer

A B C D

39 The cost of abnormal loss, net of its scrap value, which was written off to the profit and loss account in the month was

A £26,640
B £28,400
C £32,627
D £34,827

Circle your answer

A B C D

4: JOB COSTING. CONTRACT COSTING. PROCESS COSTING

Data for questions 40 - 41

Ruffles Ltd manufactures a product in two consecutive operations. Data for Process 2 for the month of October are as follows.

Opening work in process	Nil
Materials transferred from Process 1	10,000 kg value £38,880
Labour and overhead cost	£50,337
Output transferred to finished goods	7,900 kg
Closing work in process	1,500 kg, 100% complete as to materials and 60% complete as to labour and overhead

Normal loss is 10% of input, and loss is assumed to be complete for materials, labour and overhead content.

Ruffles Ltd has an accounting policy of calculating a cost for its normal loss, and attributing this cost to completed output in the month, so that abnormal loss or gain, and closing work in process, are not attributed with any normal loss costs.

40 The cost of normal loss in October was

- A £8,535
- B £8,922
- C £9,243
- D £10,313

Circle your answer

A B C D

41 What is the value of closing stocks of work in process at 31 October?

- A £9,841
- B £10,651
- C £11,873
- D £13,864

Circle your answer

A B C D

4: JOB COSTING. CONTRACT COSTING. PROCESS COSTING

Data for questions 42 - 44

Turner Green Ltd produces an industrial cleansing fluid in a process. Data for February are as follows.

Opening and closing work in process	Nil
Direct materials input	10,000 kilos, cost £50,000
Conversion costs	£31,000
Output: Finished production	8,800 kilos
Toxic waste	900 kilos

Toxic waste must be disposed of at a cost of £3 per kilo.

Normal output per 100 kilos input to the process is as follows:

Finished production	90 kilos
Toxic waste	6 kilos
Loss through evaporation	4 kilos

42 What was the value of abnormal loss or abnormal gain from evaporation loss in February?

- A £900
- B £920
- C £2,700
- D £2,760

Circle your answer

A   B   C   D

43 What was the value of finished units completed in February?

- A £79,200
- B £80,960
- C £81,000
- D £82,800

Circle your answer

A   B   C   D

44 What was the amount written off to the profit and loss account for abnormal toxic waste in February?

- A £1,800
- B £1,860
- C £2,700
- D £3,660

Circle your answer

A   B   C   D

CHAPTER 5

BUDGETS

> This chapter covers the following topics:
> - Preparing budgets
> - Sales, production and purchase budgets
> - Cash budgets
> - Learning curve: budgeting labour costs
>
> Flexible budgets, budgetary control, and budget limiting factors are dealt with in later chapters.

1. Preparing budgets

1.1 The main purposes of budgeting are
- formal *planning*. Managers are compelled to make forecasts and plans
- *co-ordination*. Activities of all departments are co-ordinated into a single master plan
- to establish a system of *control*, often by comparing actual results against budget targets
- to *communicate* the organisation's policies and targets
- arguably, to *motivate* individuals.

1.2 Budgets are prepared for a budget period, typically one year, sub-divided into shorter control periods, typically one month. Responsibility for compiling the budget may be given to a budget committee. Procedures for preparing departmental budgets etc should be set out in a budget manual, which managers can use.

1.3 Budget preparation involves a lot of number-crunching, with frequent revisions when estimates are changed. The use of microcomputers and spreadsheet packages (Lotus 123, Supercalc, Quattro etc) have eased this task greatly. However, for cost accounting students, learning about budgets often calls for detailed computational work.

2. Sales, production and purchase budgets

(1)		(Hypothetical numbers)
		units
	Budgeted sales	50,000
Plus	Budgeted closing stocks of finished goods	6,000
Minus	Budgeted opening stocks of finished goods	(4,000)
Equals	Budgeted transfer of completed goods to finished goods stock	52,000

	(2)	Equivalent units
	Budgeted transfer of completed goods to finished goods stock	52,000
Plus	Budgeted closing stocks of WIP	1,000
Minus	Budgeted opening stocks of WIP	(2,000)
	Budgeted production	51,000

	(3)	Kilograms
	Raw materials usage budget (production units x raw materials per unit)	153,000
Plus	Closing stocks of raw materials	16,000
Minus	Opening stocks of raw materials	(14,000)
	Raw materials purchase budget	155,000

3. Cash budgets

3.1 Cash budgets or cash flow forecasts are budgets of

- cash receipts, cash payments, and net cash inflows/outflows in a period
- cash balance/overdraft at the end of a period

3.2 *Budgeted receipts from debtors.* These are calculated from

- budgeted sales
- the budgeted payments pattern (eg cash/credit sales split; % who pay after 1 month, 2 months etc)
- estimates of discounts allowed for early payment, if any
- estimated bad debts, if any

3.3 You can use the formula

> Opening debtors plus sales minus closing debtors = Cash receipts

However, adjustments will be needed for any early settlement discounts and bad debts.

3.4 *Budgeted payments to materials suppliers.* These are calculated from

- budgeted purchases
- the budgeted period of credit taken
- estimates of discounts receivable for early payment, if any

3.5 You can use the formula

> Opening creditors plus purchases minus closing creditors = Payments to creditors

However, make an adjustment for any early settlement discounts.

3.6 *Budgeted payments for fixed overheads*. To budget monthly cash payments for fixed overheads, it is necessary to

- establish total budgeted overheads for the year
- subtract non-cash expenditures, such as depreciation
- subtract one-off cash payments - ie cash payments that do not occur monthly, but just once or a few times each year, eg rent, interest on loans
- divide the remaining expenditure by 12, to arrive at regular monthly spending on fixed overhead items
- add back one-off cash payments as expenditures in the month when they are expected to occur.

Illustration

	£
Budgeted fixed overheads for the year	200,000
less: Annual depreciation	40,000
Cash expenditures in fixed overheads	160,000
less: Occasional one-off expenditures: rent	28,000
Regular expenditures	132,000

Monthly expenditure on regular items (÷ 12) £11,000.

4. Learning curve: budgeting labour costs

4.1 In some companies, a significant amount of work goes into manufacturing products which have not been made in large numbers before, and where labour skills are important. Where this happens, there is likely to be a learning effect, whereby the work force as a whole gains more experience at making the product as it manufactures each extra item, and the time to make each extra unit is less than the time needed for the previous unit.

4.2 As a consequence, direct labour costs per unit and labour-related overhead costs per unit will fall as more units are produced.

4.3 The *learning curve* is an expression of this phenomenon, which is known to exist in industries such as aircraft manufacture and defence equipment manufacture.

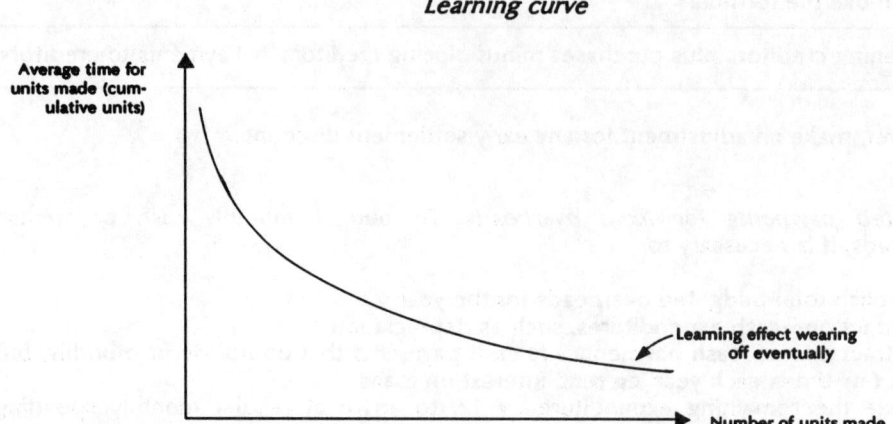

Learning curve

4.4 If an 80% learning curve applies, then *every time that total cumulative output doubles* the cumulative average time per unit (the average unit time for all units made so far) drops to 80% of what it was previously.

Similarly, if a 90% learning curve applies, then every time that total cumulative output *doubles*, the cumulative average time per unit drops to 90% of what it was previously.

An 80% learning curve reflects a bigger saving in time and costs than a 90% learning curve.

4.5 For industries where a learning curve applies, estimating the learning rate can have enormous significance for budgeting

- direct labour costs
- labour-related overhead costs
- factory output capacity/capability .

5: BUDGETS

QUESTIONS

1 Which of the following is NOT a functional budget?

A   Research and development budget
B   Purchasing budget
C   Cash budget
D   Direct labour cost budget

Circle your answer

A   B   C   D

2 For a company that does not have any production resource limitations, in what sequence would the following budgets be prepared?

Budget

1. Cash budget
2. Sales budget
3. Stocks budgets
4. Production budget
5. Purchases budget

A   Sequence 2, 3, 4, 5, 1
B   Sequence 2, 3, 4, 1, 5
C   Sequence 2, 4, 3, 5, 1
D   Sequence 4, 3, 2, 1, 5

Circle your answer

A   B   C   D

3 Each unit of product Alpha requires 3 kgs of raw material. Next month's production budget for product Alpha is as follows:

Opening stocks:
   raw materials   15,000 kg
   finished units of Alpha   2,000 units
Budgeted sales of Alpha   60,000 units
Planned closing stocks:
   raw materials   7,000 kg
   finished units of Alpha   3,000 units

The number of kilograms of raw materials that should be purchased next month is:

A   172,000
B   175,000
C   183,000
D   191,000

Circle your answer

A   B   C   D

5: BUDGETS

4 Each unit of product Bravo uses 6 kg of raw material. The production budget and stock budgets for December are as follows:

Opening stocks	- raw materials	21,000 kg
	- finished goods	15,000 units
Closing stocks	- raw materials	24,400 kg
	- finished goods	11,400 units

Budgeted sales of Bravo for December are 18,000 units. During the production process it is usually found that 10% of production units are scrapped as defective and this loss occurs after the raw materials have been input.

What will raw materials purchases be in December?

A 89,800 kg
B 96,000 kg
C 98,440 kg
D 99,400 kg

Circle your answer

A   B   C   D

5 Each unit of product Charlie requires 5 kilograms of raw material. Next month's sales budget and stock budgets for Charlie are as follows.

Opening stocks:	
raw materials	9,000 kg
finished goods	3,000 units
Budgeted sales of Charlie	40,000 units
Planned closing stocks	
raw materials	5,000 kg
finished goods	5,000 units

What is the budgeted raw materials usage quantity for the production of Charlie in the month?

A 190,000 kilograms
B 200,000 kilograms
C 205,000 kilograms
D 210,000 kilograms

Circle your answer

A   B   C   D

6 Each unit of product Delta requires 6 kilograms of raw material. Next month's sales budget and stock budgets for Delta are as follows.

Opening stocks	
Raw materials	16,000 kg
Work in progress (75% complete as to material content)	2,000 units
Finished goods	4,000 units
Planned closing stocks	
Raw materials	12,000 kg
Work in progress (25% complete as to material content)	3,000 units
Finished goods	1,000 units

Budgeted sales of Delta are 80,000 units.

The quantity of raw materials that should be purchased next month is

- A 453,500 kg
- B 459,500 kg
- C 462,750 kg
- D 475,500 kg

Circle your answer

A   B   C   D

7 Each unit of product Echo takes 5 direct labour hours to make. Quality standards are high, and 8% of units are rejected after completion as sub-standard. Next month's budgets are as follows.

Opening stocks of finished goods	3,000 units
Planned closing stocks of finished goods	7,600 units
Budgeted sales of Echo	36,800 units

All stocks of finished goods must have successfully passed the quality control check.

What is the direct labour hours budget for the month?

- A 198,720 hours
- B 200,000 hours
- C 223,560 hours
- D 225,000 hours

Circle your answer

A   B   C   D

8 Each unit of product Foxtrot requires 4 direct labour hours of work. A quality control check of all units takes place on completion of production, when 5% of inspected units are normally rejected. Of these rejected units, one half can be re-worked. Re-working of units takes 2 hours per unit, and the rejection rate at a further quality control check is nil.

Budgeted data for next year is as follows.

Opening stock of finished goods	2,000 units
Planned closing stock of finished goods	3,950 units
Budgeted sales of Foxtrot	90,675 units

What is the direct labour hours budget for next year?

- A 375,131 hours
- B 380,000 hours
- C 384,750 hours
- D 394,875 hours

Circle your answer

A   B   C   D

5: BUDGETS

9 The following information is available about the budgets for next year of Roger Handout Ltd.

	Opening stocks £	Closing stocks £
Raw materials	23,200	17,300
Work in progress	4,700	8,200
Finished goods	16,600	18,800

Raw materials purchases budget	£140,000
Direct labour hours budget (30,000 hrs)	£120,000
Production overhead absorption rate	£5 per direct labour hour
Administration overhead	£80,000
Sales and distribution overhead	£120,000
Sales budget	£620,000

What is the company's budgeted profit for the year?

A £6,300
B £7,600
C £9,800
D £10,200

Circle your answer

A   B   C   D

10 Sayles Tork Ltd is preparing next year's budget, using the current year's figures as a basis for forecasting next year's results.

Current year data includes:

Sales volume: 100,000 units
Price of raw materials: £2 per kg

There is a wastage rate of 20% of output produced, so that each unit of output requires 1.2 kg of materials input.

Data for next year

A reduction in selling price for the finished product is expected to increase sales volume by 25%.

The wastage rate on materials is expected to be reduced to 10% of output produced. The price of raw materials will go up by 10%, but a bulk purchase discount of 5% should be obtained, whereas none was obtained in the current year.

There are expected to be no opening and no closing stocks of raw materials, work in progress or finished goods.

What is the raw materials purchase budget for next year?

A £256,500
B £280,500
C £287,375
D £288,750

Circle your answer

A   B   C   D

5: BUDGETS

11 Hall Thumms Ltd manufactures Product Y. Budgeted data for next year is as follows.

Sales	9,000 units
Opening stock of finished goods (inspected and passed)	3,000 units
Closing stock of finished goods (inspected and passed)	4,800 units
Opening and closing work in progress	Nil
Standard direct labour hours per unit	10 hrs
Budgeted productivity (or efficiency) ratio	90%
Normal rejection rate of output as scrap on inspection after production completed	20% of inspected items

What is the budgeted quantity of direct labour hours required for Product Y next year?

A 100,000 hrs
B 121,500 hrs
C 144,000 hrs
D 150,000 hrs

Circle your answer

A   B   C   D

12 A manufacturing company wishes to reduce the direct labour cost per unit for its products. Its direct labour employees are paid an agreed rate for the hours they work. Completed units are inspected before transfer to finished goods store, and about 15% of inspected items are rejected.

Which of the following would enable the company to reduce its budgeted direct labour costs per unit of product transferred to finished goods store?

Measure

1. Improve direct labour productivity
2. Increase the number of hours worked
3. Reduce the rate of rejections

A Measures 1 and 2 only
B Measures 1 and 3 only
C Measures 2 and 3 only
D Measure 1 only

Circle your answer

A   B   C   D

13 Heighway Rubbery Ltd manufactures a range of products, and its results for the year just ended included the following.

	£
Direct labour costs (7,200 hrs)	36,000
Variable production overheads	7,200
Fixed production overheads	52,500

The company uses full absorption costing in its cost accounts, and absorbs production overhead on a direct labour hour basis. Stan Dandeliver, the company's cost accountant, remarked that although expenditure had been kept under control, and actual spending

83

equalled what should have been expected, there was under-absorbed production overhead of £2,100 because the actual number of direct labour hours worked was 300 less than budgeted.

What were the total budgeted production overheads for the year and what was the total production overhead absorption rate?

	Overheads	*Absorption rate per hour*
A	£57,600	£7
B	£59,700	£7
C	£60,000	£8
D	£61,800	£8

Circle your answer

A B C D

Data for questions 14 - 16

Lawrie Load Ltd manufactures a single product, Product Z. Budgeted data for the next four-week budget period is as follows.

Raw materials 6kgs of Material P and 5 kgs of Material Q are needed to produce 10 kgs of Z.

Direct labour The direct labour work force consists of 100 operatives who each work 36 hours in a normal working week. Normal time is paid at the rate of £4 per hour, and overtime is paid at time-and-one half. Overtime will be worked if required.

Production rate 600 kg of Z per plant hour

Budgeted sales 90,000 kg of Product Z, at a price of £4 per kilogram

Stocks

	Opening stocks kg	Opening stocks value £	Planned closing stocks kg
Material P	50,000	50,000	60,000
Material Q	30,000	60,000	60,000
Work in progress	Nil	-	Nil
Finished goods, Product Z	58,000	174,000	64,000

Closing stocks of finished goods will be valued at £3 per kilogram. Raw material purchase prices are expected to reflect the average price of goods currently in stock.

Budgeted indirect expenses (excluding overtime premium)
    Production   £63,000
    Administration and marketing   £80,000

5: BUDGETS

14 What is the budgeted cost of direct labour for the period, *including* the cost of the premium for any overtime worked?

- A £65,200
- B £67,200
- C £88,800
- D £96,000

Circle your answer

A   B   C   D

15 What is the raw materials purchases budget for the period, in £?

- A £101,600
- B £153,600
- C £214,000
- D £223,600

Circle your answer

A   B   C   D

16 What is the budgeted profit or loss for the period?

- A Loss of £11,800
- B Profit of £10,000
- C Profit of £11,400
- D Profit of £14,200

Circle your answer

A   B   C   D

Data for questions 17 - 19

Extracts from next year's budget for Millstone Ltd are shown below.

Product X
Sales   37,500 units. Selling price £20 per unit
Opening stock   4,000 units, value £16 per unit
Budgeted closing stock   2,500 units

	£
Direct material cost per unit	4
Direct labour cost per unit (2 hours)	8

Budgeted annual overheads	£
Variable production overheads	28,080
Fixed production overheads	140,400
Other overheads (administration, selling etc)	120,000

The company operates a full absorption costing system using a direct labour hour absorption rate and prices stock issues on the FIFO basis of valuation.

Production is budgeted to occur evenly throughout the year, but monthly sales are expected to vary. Budgeted sales of Product X in month 1 are 5,000 units. Overhead expenses will occur at an even monthly rate.

5: BUDGETS

17 What is the budgeted value of closing stocks of Product X at the end of month 1?

A £32,640
B £33,360
C £40,800
D £41,700

Circle your answer

A   B   C   D

18 What is the budgeted profit for month 1?

A £8,600
B £9,320
C £18,600
D £19,320

Circle your answer

A   B   C   D

19 The effect on budgeted profit in month 1, if actual results are as predicted, except that actual production of Product X is 50 units higher than the budget, would be an increase in profit over budget by

A £180
B £195
C £216
D £234

Circle your answer

A   B   C   D

20 What is the name given to the method of budgeting whereby all activities are re-evaluated each time a budget is prepared, and the incremental costs of activities compared with their incremental benefits?

A Incremental budgeting
B Rolling budgets
C Zero base budgeting
D Flexible budgets

Circle your answer

A   B   C   D

Data for questions 21 - 23

Hetty Kett Ltd plans to produce and sell 5,000 units of its product, the Manna, for which the selling price is £25 per unit.

1 unit of Manna requires 3 units of Material X and 4 units of Material Y. Opening stocks of raw materials are as follows.

Cont...

5: BUDGETS

	Units value £	Total
Material X	8,000	16,000
Material Y	10,000	5,000

The closing stock of raw materials is to be a level which is sufficient to produce 3,000 units of Manna.

There are no opening stocks or planned closing stocks of Mannas.

Hugo First, the company's cost accountant, has made the following estimates.

(1) Purchase prices for all raw materials next year will be 10% higher than the prices reflected in the opening stock values

(2) Sales and purchases are all on credit. The opening balances at the beginning of the year will be
   Debtors   £80,000
   Trade creditors   £29,000

(3) Expected receipts from debtors in the year are £86,000 and expected payments to trade creditors are £26,000

21 What is the budgeted cost of raw materials purchases for the year?

A £41,900
B £43,000
C £44,300
D £47,300

Circle your answer

A B C D

22 What is the budgeted closing balance for debtors, given no bad debts and no discounts allowable?

A £119,000
B £122,000
C £125,000
D £131,000

Circle your answer

A B C D

5: BUDGETS

23 The budgeted amount for trade creditors at the end of the budget period, given no discounts receivable, is

A £40,000
B £44,300
C £46,000
D £50,300

Circle your answer

A   B   C   D

Data for questions 24 - 26

Actual sales of a retail company, Markup Ltd, for November and December 19X1, together with budgeted monthly sales for January-June 19X2, are shown below.

		Sales £	
19X1	November	160,000	(actual)
	December	210,000	(actual)
19X2	January	80,000	
	February	60,000	
	March	100,000	
	April	90,000	
	May	120,000	
	June	150,000	

The company sells food products with a very short shelf life, and so it carries no stocks of goods beyond the end of any day. All goods purchased on any day are resold during the day.

The purchase price of the goods for Markup Ltd is 75% of their retail price. Purchases are on 1½ months' credit. Sales are 50% for cash and 50% on credit. One half of credit customers pay after 1 month and the other half pay after 2 months.

There are no bad debts. Sales and purchases occur at an even rate throughout each month.

24 What are the budgeted cash receipts in February 19X2?

A £77,500
B £102,500
C £132,500
D £175,000

Circle your answer

A   B   C   D

25 What are the budgeted cash receipts in the six month period January - June 19X2?

    A £600,000
    B £615,000
    C £625,000
    D £650,000

Circle your answer

A   B   C   D

26 What are the budgeted cash payments to suppliers in the six month period January - June 19X2?

    A £450,000
    B £495,000
    C £510,000
    D £680,000

Circle your answer

A   B   C   D

Data for questions 27 - 29

The following budgeted data relates to Holden Tite Ltd.

At 1.1.X2

Debtors	£60,000 (2 months' sales)
Stocks	£24,000 (1 month's cost of goods sold)
Creditors for materials purchases	£24,000 (1 month's purchases)

The cost of goods sold consists entirely of materials, and amounts to 80% of sales value. Sales in 19X1 occurred at an even rate of £30,000 per month, and this same rate is budgeted to continue throughout 19X2. No discounts are currently offered to customers.

There has been a proposal by the budget committee to improve working capital management, and from 1 January 19X2 the following changes will be made.

Debtors   25% of sales will be for cash, with a discount of 5% now offered for cash payment. Of the 75% credit sales, one half would be expected to pay after 1 month and one half after 2 months.

Stocks   Stock turnover will be reduced to ½ month

Creditors   Credit taken from suppliers will be extended to 2 months

5: BUDGETS

27 What are the budgeted payments to suppliers of raw material purchases in 19X2?

- A £252,000
- B £264,000
- C £276,000
- D £315,000

Circle your answer

A   B   C   D

28 What are the budgeted receipts from cash and credit sales for 19X2?

- A £368,250
- B £370,500
- C £381,750
- D £386,250

Circle your answer

A   B   C   D

29 Compare the budgeted cash flows in 19X2 with what the cash flows would have been if debtors continued to pay after 2 months, stock turnover remained at 1 month and suppliers continued to be paid after 1 month. In comparison, the changes in working capital management will improve the net cash inflow in 19X2 by:

- A £34,500
- B £45,750
- C £57,750
- D £62,250

Circle your answer

A   B   C   D

Data for questions 30 - 33

On 1 January, the summary balance sheet of Curran Bunn Ltd was as follows.

	£		£
Share capital	60,000	Machinery: at cost	170,000
Reserves	64,250	Accumulated depreciation	(70,000)
Creditor for loan interest	3,750		
10% loan	50,000		100,000
Proposed dividend			
(payable 20 January)	20,000	Stocks	35,000
Overdraft	17,000	Debtors	80,000
	215,000		215,000

50% of sales are on credit, with payment after 1 month. 50% of sales are for cash, with a discount of 5% given for cash settlement. Payments for purchases are made in the month of purchase, to benefit from a 10% prompt settlement discount. Stock levels are expected to remain constant throughout the period.

5: BUDGETS

The following are expected during the next 3 months.

	Sales £	Purchases £	Expenses £
January	90,000	60,000	20,000
February	150,000	120,000	25,000
March	240,000	200,000	25,000

Sales and purchases figures are before deduction of discounts. The expenses figure includes depreciation on machinery of £2,000 per month: the remaining expenses are all cash items and paid for in the month in which they are charged. Loan interest for a whole year is payable at the end of March. Overdraft interest should be ignored.

30 What is the budgeted net cash inflow in January?

- A £28,750
- B £30,750
- C £33,000
- D £50,750

Circle your answer

A   B   C   D

31 What is the budgeted net cash outflow in February?

- A £1,000
- B £11,000
- C £12,750
- D £14,750

Circle your answer

A   B   C   D

32 What is the budgeted net cash outflow in March?

- A £15,250
- B £19,000
- C £20,000
- D £21,000

Circle your answer

A   B   C   D

5: BUDGETS

33 What is the budgeted profit for the period January - March?

A £51,000
B £54,750
C £60,750
D £77,000

Circle your answer

A   B   C   D

34 Wally Tempty Ltd has made the following budget forecasts for next year.

Opening cash balance, 1 January	£24,000
Net profit from trading for the year, before tax	£100,000
Payment of tax	£25,000
Payment of dividends	£20,000
Purchases of new fixed assets	£70,000
Annual depreciation charge	£22,000

	1 January £	31 December £
Stocks	32,000	35,000
Debtors	41,000	28,000
Creditors	16,000	31,000

This is no other relevant information.

What is the company's budgeted cash holding at 31 December next year?

A £6,000
B £26,000
C £34,000
D £56,000

Circle your answer

A   B   C   D

35 Czech Stubbs Ltd allows its credit customers up to 3 months to pay their debts, and the normal pattern of payment from credit customers, which the company uses for budgeting, is as follows.

After 1 month	20%
After 2 months	50%
After 3 months	25%
Uncollectable	5% - written off after 3 months
	100%

The company's debtors at 31 December are £194,400. Actual sales in October - December in the current year and budgeted sales for January next year are as follows.

		£
Actual sales	October	40,000
	November	80,000
	December	140,000
Budgeted sales	January	60,000

92

10% of sales are for cash and 90% of sales are on credit. There are no other sources of cash receipts other than sales revenue.

What are the budgeted cash receipts for January next year?

A £76,200
B £78,000
C £83,000
D £84,000

Circle your answer

A   B   C   D

Data for questions 36 - 37

Letdown Ltd is having difficulty with its bad debts. Its normal pattern of payment from debtors which the company uses for budgeting is as follows.

In the month of sale	15%
After 1 month	50%
After 2 months	25%
Uncollectable	10%

Bad debts are written off after 2 months.

The company is preparing its budgets for next year, and the following data is relevant.

Actual sales in the current year

November	£50,000
December	£55,000

Budgeted sales next year

January - June	£60,000 per month
July - December	£70,000 per month

The provision for bad debts is to be increased from £15,000 at 1 January to £21,000 at 31 December. Sales revenue is the only source of cash receipts for the company, and all sales are on credit.

36 What are the budgeted cash receipts in January of next year?

A £49,000
B £50,000
C £54,000
D £60,000

Circle your answer

A   B   C   D

5: BUDGETS

37 What are the budgeted cash receipts for the whole of next year?

A £676,250
B £679,750
C £682,250
D £685,750

Circle your answer

A B C D

Data for questions 38 - 40

The following actual and budgeted data relates to Windswept Ltd, a manufacturing company.

Actual sales, current year
    December   £70,000
Budgeted sales, next year (1st 6 months)
    January   £80,000
    February   £40,000
    March   £50,000
    April   £60,000
    May   £100,000
    June   £120,000

The cost of the raw material content in goods sold is 30% of sales value. The company has a policy of maintaining stocks of raw materials at a level equal to the raw materials content in the next 3 months' sales, and maintaining stocks of finished goods at a level equal to the quantity needed for the next 2 months' sales. One month's credit is taken from raw material suppliers.

38 What is the budgeted cost of raw material purchases for the 3 month period January - March next year?

A £45,000
B £51,000
C £84,000
D £96,000

Circle your answer

A B C D

39 What is the budgeted payment to raw materials suppliers in January next year?

A £6,000
B £9,000
C £15,000
D £24,000

Circle your answer

A B C D

5: BUDGETS

40 What is the budgeted payment to raw materials suppliers for the 3-month period January - March next year?

A £45,000
B £51,000
C £84,000
D £96,000

Circle your answer

A B C D

Data for questions 41 - 43

The following extract is from the balance sheet of Justin Casings Ltd as at 31 December 19X1.

	£
Fixed assets at cost	360,000
less: Accumulated depreciation	120,000
Net book value	240,000

Depreciation is charged by the straight line method, at the rate of 20% of cost per annum. Depreciation is charged from the time a fixed asset is acquired until the time of its disposal.

Budgeted data for 19X2 includes the following.

Fixed production asset purchased on 1 April 19X2, cost £108,000
Fixed production asset disposal on 1 October 19X2, for cash. The fixed asset cost £24,000 originally, and will have accumulated depreciation of £14,400 at the time of sale. There is expected to be a profit of £2,300 on the sale.

Depreciation is included in fixed production overhead, and fixed production overhead (allowing for the fixed asset acquisition and disposal) is budgeted to be £693,000 in total for the year. Variable production overheads are £2 per direct labour hour, and paid for in the month that they occur. All overheads are cash expenditures (with the exception of depreciation). They are paid for in the month in which they arise with the exception of the following two items.

Rent (fixed cost) Paid in April, cost £80,000
Factory insurance (fixed cost) Paid in July, cost £16,000

41 What is the expected cash receipt from the fixed asset disposal?

A £7,300
B £11,900
C £12,100
D £16,900

Circle your answer

A B C D

95

5: BUDGETS

42 What is the budgeted fixed production overhead expenditure for the year, *excluding depreciation?*

  A £601,200
  B £606,000
  C £608,400
  D £609,600

Circle your answer

A   B   C   D

43 What is the budgeted cash payment for production overheads in April, a month when budgeted production is 20,000 direct labour hours?

  A £162,500
  B £162,800
  C £170,500
  D £170,800

Circle your answer

A   B   C   D

44 Brainbox Ltd has produced a new product for the first time. The costs for the first unit were:

	£
Materials	6,000
Direct labour (1,000 hours @ £4)	4,000
	10,000

A customer has ordered 2 units of the new product and will accept the first unit as part of the order.

If Brainbox Ltd experiences an 80% learning rate, what will be the direct production cost of the order?

  A £16,000
  B £18,000
  C £18,400
  D £19,200

Circle your answer

A   B   C   D

45 Loganberry Ltd has been making a new product and the time taken to produce successive units has been recorded:

Cumulative output (units)	Total hours taken
2	500
3	635
4	750
6	951
8	1,125

Which one of the following learning rates is the company experiencing?

A 50%
B 60%
C 70%
D 75%

Circle your answer

A   B   C   D

46 Bedder and Bedder Ltd has just made the first unit of a new product. The costs were:

	£
Materials (1,000 kg at £3)	3,000
Labour (200 hrs at £4)	800
Variable overheads (200 hrs at £1)	200
	4,000

Bedder and Bedder Ltd will experience a 90% learning effect with making the product.

A customer has asked the company to supply 3 units of the new product. The first unit made cannot be sold as it is only a prototype.

What will be the total variable production cost to the company of making the *additional 3 units* for the customer's order?

A £11,240
B £11,520
C £12,240
D £14,240

Circle your answer

A   B   C   D

47 Slim Margins is the cost estimator for Tightrope Ltd, a company which has just received an inquiry about an order for 7 units of a recently introduced product. So far only one unit has been made and sold to another customer.

Details of the first unit were:

	£
Materials	900
Labour (100 hrs x £5)	500
Production overheads (100 hrs x £10)	1,000
Fixed production cost	2,400

The company is experiencing an 80% learning curve on this product.

Slim has decided to quote a price to the customer which gives a profit margin (sales minus full production cost) which is 25% of sales value. The price to be quoted for the order for 7 units is therefore:

A £14,592
B £14,774
C £16,592
D £16,640

Circle your answer

A   B   C   D

CHAPTER 6

BUDGETARY CONTROL. STANDARD COSTING

> This chapter covers the following topics:
> - Budgetary control and flexible budgets
> - Standard costs
> - Variances

1. Budgetary control and flexible budgets

1.1 Budgetary control is a method of reporting to management for control purposes, whereby actual results in a period (or sometimes forecast results based on revised current estimates) are compared with the budget.

1.2 In order to compare actual results against the budget, the budget is flexed. A flexible budget is one in which budgeted revenues and costs are adjusted according to the level of activity. For budgetary control, the level of activity will usually be the volume of production/sales achieved in the period.

> Unless you are given information to suggest that different circumstances apply (eg a different budgeted selling price at a different volume of sales) you should assume that
>
> - the sales price per unit is the same at all volumes of sales
> - variable costs per unit are the same at all volumes of production/sales.

1.3 Variances are differences between actual and budgeted results. With the exception of the sales volume (profit margin or contribution margin variance) they compare actual results with a budget that has been flexed to the same level of activity.

6: BUDGETARY CONTROL. STANDARD COSTING

Illustrative figures

	Master budget		Flexed budget		Actual		Difference between flexed budget and actual	
Sales/production volume	10,000 units		11,000 units		11,000 units			
	£000	£000	£000	£000	£000	£000	£000	
Sales revenue		200		220		218	2(A) =	Sales price variance
Direct materials costs	30		33		32		1(F) =	Direct materials cost variance
Direct labour costs	40		44		47		3(A) =	Direct labour cost variance
Variable overheads	10		11		8		3(F) =	Variable overhead cost variance
Fixed overheads (see note 1.4)	60		60		64		4(A) =	Fixed overhead expenditure variance
Total costs		140		148		151		
Profit		60		72		67	5(A)	

Difference = sales volume contribution variance (12F)

(F) denotes a favourable variance
(A) denotes an adverse variance. (U) is sometimes used instead, denoting an unfavourable variance.

1.4 *Fixed overheads in the flexed budget*. There are two different methods of treating fixed *production* overheads in a flexed budget.

- *Method 1*, used in the illustration above, is for budgeted fixed overheads to be the same as in the original master budget. This is because fixed overhead spending, unlike variable cost spending, does not vary with the level of activity. The difference between budgeted and actual fixed overhead spending is a fixed overhead *expenditure variance*.

- *Method 2*, which might be used with absorption costing systems, is to show in the flexed budget the amount of fixed production overhead *absorbed*, rather than what fixed overhead expenditure should be. The difference between actual fixed overheads incurred and the absorbed overheads in the flexed budget is then a fixed overhead *total cost* variance, which can be sub-analysed into an expenditure and a volume variance, as described in the earlier chapter (Chapter 2) on absorption costing.

1.5 If you are given sufficient information, total cost variances (for direct materials, direct labour etc) can be sub-analysed in flexible budgeting in the same way as for standard costing variance calculations. (Standard costing variance analysis is simply one form of budgetary control system.)

2. Standard costs

2.1 A standard cost is a predetermined unit cost. It might be established for

- a unit of product,
- a unit of work, such as a direct labour hour or a machine hour.

2.2 A standard cost will be established for

(1) **direct materials**, analysed into quantity of material multiplied by standard price per unit of material

(2) **direct labour**, analysed into number of hours of work multiplied by a standard rate of pay per hour

(3) **overhead** (variable/fixed) analysed into number of hours multiplied by a standard or budgeted rate per hour.

2.3 A standard can be set at any level or target of achievement, and might be

- a current standard
- an attainable standard
- an ideal standard
- a basic standard

3. Variances

3.1 The calculation of variances can be taught and learned by several different methods. Just the formula method is shown here in the notes. The formulae show the principles on which variances are calculated, and suggest, in broad terms, the meaning or cause of each variance.

3.2 *Direct materials variances*

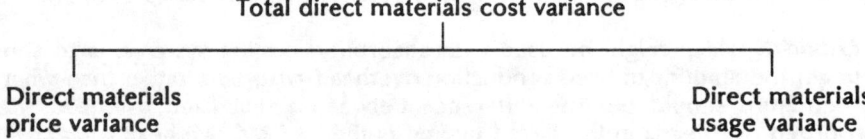

- Direct materials price variance = (AQM x AP) - (AQM - SP)

    AQM = actual quantity of direct materials

    - Take actual quantity *purchased* in the period if closing stocks are valued at standard price
    - Take actual quantity *used* in the period if closing stocks are valued at actual price (ie on a FIFO, weighted average or LIFO basis etc)

AP = actual price per unit of material
SP = standard price per unit of material

- Direct materials usage variance = (AQSM x SP) - (SQM x SP)

  This is the difference between the actual quantity of materials *used* (AQM) and the standard quantity that should have been used to produce the actual output of units (SQM), valued at the *standard* direct materials price per unit.

3.3 *Direct labour variances*

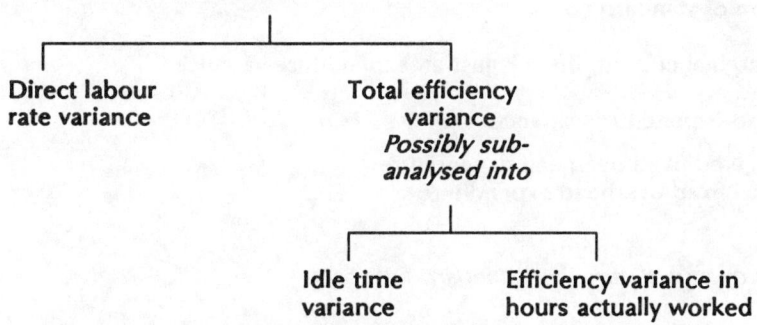

- Total direct labour cost variance = (AQ x AC) - (AQ x SC)

  AQ = actual quantity of units produced
  AC = actual direct labour cost per unit
  SC = standard direct labour cost per unit

- Direct labour rate variance = (ALH x AR) - (ALH x SR)

  ALH = actual (direct labour hours) paid for
  AR = actual direct labour hour rate of pay
  SR = standard direct labour hour rate of pay

- Direct labour efficiency variance = (ALH x SR) - (SLH x SR)

  This is the difference between the actual labour hours taken to produce the actual output units (ALH) and the standard direct labour hours (SLH) which is the time that should have been taken. This is valued at the standard direct labour rate of pay per hour (SR).

3.4 *Variable overhead variances*

- Total variable overhead cost variance = (AQ x AC) - (AQ x SC)

  AQ = actual quantity quantity of units produced
  AC = actual variable overhead cost per unit
  SC = standard variable overhead cost per unit

- Variable overhead expenditure variance = (AH x AR) - (AH x SR)

  AH = actual hours worked (usually, direct labour hours)
  AR = actual variable overhead rate of expenditure per hour
  SR = standard variable overhead rate of expenditure per hour

- Variable overhead efficiency variance in *hours* as for direct labour (usually excluding any idle time variance) valued at the standard variable overhead rate of expenditure per hour.

3.5 *Fixed production overhead variances: standard marginal costs*

Fixed production overhead variances differ between an absorption costing system and a marginal costing system of standard costs.

With standard marginal costing, there is just an expenditure variance.

- Fixed overhead expenditure variance = BFO - AFO

  BFO = Budgeted fixed overhead expenditure
  AFO = Actual fixed overhead expenditure

3.6 *Fixed production overhead variances: standard full costs*

With an absorption costing system:

- Fixed production overhead total variance = the under- or over-absorbed fixed production overhead = AFO - (AQ x SFC)
  AFO = actual fixed overhead expenditure
  AQ = actual quantity of units produced
  SFC = standard fixed production overhead cost per unit

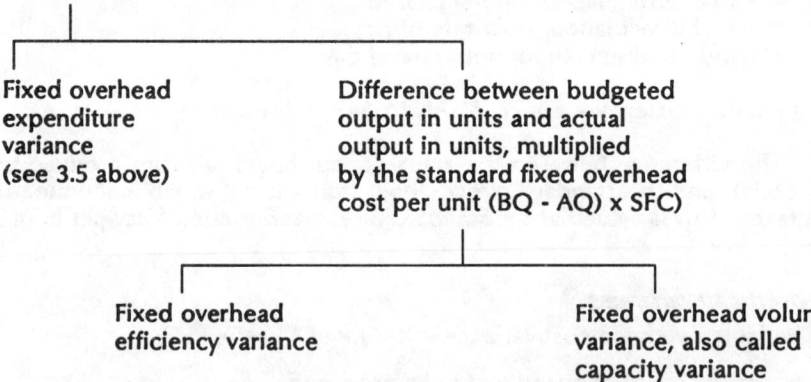

- Fixed overhead efficiency variance = (ALH x SFR) - (SLH x SFR)

  This is the same as the direct labour efficiency variance (excluding any idle time variance) and the variable overhead efficiency variance *in hours*, but valued at the standard fixed overhead rate per hour (SFR).

- Fixed overhead volume/capacity variance = (BLH - ALH) x SFR

    This is the difference between the budgeted labour hours (BLH) and actual hours worked (ALH), valued at the standard fixed overhead rate per hour (SFR).

3.7 *Sales price variance.* This is not shown in the cost accounts, where sales revenue is recorded at actual value. It *is* shown in management reports, such as operating statements.

Sales price variance = (AQS x AP) - (AQS x SP)

AQS = actual quantity sold
AP = actual sales price per unit
SP = standard sales price per unit

3.8 *Sales volume variance.* This is not shown in the cost accounts. It is valued as either a profit margin or a contribution margin.

Sales volume variance = (BQS x SM) - (AQS x SM)

BQS = budgeted quantity of sales
AQS = actual quantity of sales
SM = standard margin on sales, which will be a standard *profit* margin in the case of an absorption costing system, and a standard *contribution* margin in the case of a standard marginal costing system.

> Try not to confuse favourable and adverse variances, by remembering the simple rules that:
>
> (F) - favourable variances mean that actual results have turned out better than expected - lower costs, higher sales, higher output, higher selling prices;
>
> (A) - adverse variances mean the opposite, that actual results are worse than standard or budget.
>
> It might seem easy to remember this, but it is surprisingly easy to make mistakes!

6: BUDGETARY CONTROL. STANDARD COSTING

QUESTIONS

1 Crack Tribb Ltd manufactures a single product and has drawn up the following flexed budget for the year

	Level of activity		
	70%	80%	90%
	£	£	£
Direct materials	31,990	36,560	41,130
Direct labour	58,100	66,400	74,700
Production overhead	75,600	77,400	79,200
Other overhead	60,000	60,000	60,000
Total cost	225,690	240,360	255,030

What would be the total cost in a budget that is flexed at the 55% level of activity?

A £179,185
B £189,015
C £190,185
D £203,685

Circle your answer

A   B   C   D

Data for questions 2 - 3

The annual budget of Grays D'Elbo Ltd was as follows.

	£	£
Sales		400,000
Direct materials	60,000	
Direct labour (20,000 hours)	70,000	
Variable production overhead	5,000	
Fixed production overhead	90,000	
Administration overhead	60,000	
Selling and distribution overhead	80,000	
		365,000
Profit		35,000

Direct materials and direct labour are variable costs. Administration, selling and distribution overheads are fixed costs, with the exception of sales commission, which is 5% of invoiced sales. Revenue is considered to be variable with direct labour hours worked.

6: BUDGETARY CONTROL. STANDARD COSTING

2 If actual sales were £480,000, what amount of profit would be expected?

A £84,000
B £85,000
C £88,000
D £104,000

Circle your answer

A   B   C   D

3 Suppose that the actual direct labour hours worked amounted to 23,000 hours, and that actual direct materials costs were £67,000 and that selling and distribution overhead costs were £85,500. What would be the direct materials cost variance and the selling and distribution overhead cost variance?

	Direct materials cost variance	Selling and distribution cost variance
A	£2,000 (F)	£2,500 (A)
B	£2,000 (F)	£5,500 (A)
C	£2,000 (A)	£2,500 (A)
D	£7,000 (A)	£5,500 (A)

Circle your answer

A   B   C   D

4 What is the name given to a standard that can be achieved, allowing for normal shrinkage, wastage and machine breakdowns, if a standard unit of work is performed efficiently, a machine is properly operated or materials are properly used?

A Attainable standard
B Basic standard
C Current standard
D Ideal standard

Circle your answer

A   B   C   D

Data for questions 5 - 6

Rooney Nose Ltd, which manufactures product Z, uses a standard costing system and values its stocks at standard cost. The standard cost of raw materials in product Z is

    3 kilos of material R at £5 per kilo = £15 per unit of Z.

During April, Rooney Nose Ltd purchased 28,300 kilos of material R at a cost of £148,575, or £5.25 per kilo. It manufactured 8,500 units of product Z, using 26,200 kilos of R.

6: BUDGETARY CONTROL. STANDARD COSTING

5 What was the raw materials price variance for material R in April?

A £3,500 (A)
B £6,550 (A)
C £7,075 (A)
D £10,050 (A)

Circle your answer

A   B   C   D

6 What was the raw materials usage variance for material R in April?

A £3,500 (A)
B £3,675 (A)
C £10,050 (A)
D £14,000 (A)

Circle your answer

A   B   C   D

Data for questions 7 - 8

Stefan Sore Ltd manufactures product M. The company uses a standard costing system and the standard direct materials cost per unit of M is 6 litres of liquid L at £1.50 per litre = £9 per unit.

However, stocks of materials are valued at 'actual' cost, using the FIFO method of valuation. The stores records for May contain the following data for Liquid L.

		Litres	Price per litre £	Total value £
Opening stock	1 May	2,000	1.40	2,800
Purchases	15 May	4,500	1.55	6,975
Purchases	26 May	3,500	1.75	6,125
Closing stock	31 May	1,800	?	?

There were no losses of stock through deterioration or theft etc in the month, when 1,400 units of product M were manufactured. There were no opening or closing stocks of work in progress.

6: BUDGETARY CONTROL. STANDARD COSTING

7 What was the price variance for liquid L in the month?

A £450 (A)
B £650 (A)
C £900 (A)
D £1,100 (A)

Circle your answer

A   B   C   D

8 What was the usage variance for liquid L in the month?

A £300 (F)
B £350 (F)
C £900 (F)
D £1,050 (F)

Circle your answer

A   B   C   D

9 Hake and Legge Ltd manufactures Product T and uses a standard costing system. Closing stocks of direct materials are valued at actual cost. Data for the production of product T in June include the following.

Direct materials used:	21,600 kg of material V
Cost of direct materials used	£128,304
Direct materials price variance (material V)	£1,296 (F)
Direct materials usage variance (material V)	£2,880 (A).

4,800 units of Product T were manufactured in June.

What is the standard direct materials cost of Product T?

A 4.6 kg of V at £5.88 per kg
B 4.5 kg of V at £5.94 per kg
C 4.5 kg of V at £6.00 per kg
D 4.4 kg of V at £6.00 per kg

Circle your answer

A   B   C   D

10 A manufacturing company revises its standard costs at the beginning of each year. Because of inflation, it sets its standard price for materials at the estimated price level for the middle of the year. During one control period early in the year, a fairly large favourable direct materials price variance was reported. Which one of the following would *NOT* help to explain this variance?

6: BUDGETARY CONTROL. STANDARD COSTING

- A The control period was early in the year
- B Direct materials were purchased in greater bulk than normal
- C An alternative source of supply for materials was found and used
- D Discounts were taken from suppliers for early settlement of invoices

Circle your answer

A B C D

11 Which one of the following would NOT help to explain a favourable direct materials usage variance?

- A Using a higher quality of materials than specified in the standard
- B Achieving a lower output volume than budgeted
- C A reduction in quality control checking standards
- D A reduction in materials wastage rates

Circle your answer

A B C D

12 Paul Damstring Ltd manufactures Product W. It employs a standard costing system, and the standard direct labour cost for Product W is 2 hours per unit at £3.60 per hour = £7.20.

In July, 5,000 units of W were manufactured. The direct labour costs totalled £36,400, and of the 9,700 direct labour hours worked in July, 200 hours were in overtime.

What were the direct labour rate variance and the direct labour efficiency variance in July?

	Rate variance	Efficiency variance
A	£400 (A)	£1,080 (F)
B	£400 (A)	£1,800 (F)
C	£1,480 (A)	£1,080 (F)
D	£1,480 (A)	£1,800 (F)

Circle your answer

A B C D

6: BUDGETARY CONTROL. STANDARD COSTING

13 Neil Igament Ltd manufactures a product for which the standard time to make one unit is 4 minutes. The standard rate of pay is £3.50 per hour.

During December, the performance of one direct labour operative was as follows.

Actual rate of pay	£3.75 per hour
Output by the employee:	2,340 units of the product
Actual hours paid	160 hours*

* All of this time was spent on production activities, with the exception of 4 hours spent waiting for repairs on his machine and 15 hours spent waiting for work to come in.

The company uses a standard costing system, and records idle time variances separately.

What was the direct labour efficiency variance for the operative in December and what was his idle time variance?

	Efficiency variance	*Idle time variance*
A	£14 (A)	£66.5 (A)
B	£15 (A)	£71.25 (A)
C	£52.5 (F)	£66.5 (A)
D	£56.25 (F)	£71.25 (A)

Circle your answer

A B C D

14 Carter Ledge Ltd manufactures product Q, and uses a standard costing system. During September, the following results were recorded for the Carter Ledge operations.

Number of units of Q produced:	2,200 units
Direct labour hours worked	4,840 hours
Direct labour cost	£14,520
Direct labour rate variance	£968 (A)
Direct labour efficiency variance	£1,232 (F)

What is the standard direct labour cost for product Q?

A 2   hours at £2.80 per hour
B 2.1   hours at £3.20 per hour
C 2.24 hours at £3.00 per hour
D 2.4   hours at £2.80 per hour

Circle your answer

A B C D

15 Which one of the following terms best describes the rate of output which qualified workers can achieve as an average over the working day or shift, without over-exertion, provided they adhere to the specified method of working and are well-motivated in their work?

A Standard time
B Standard performance
C Standard hours
D Standard unit

Circle your answer

A B C D

6: BUDGETARY CONTROL. STANDARD COSTING

16 Which one of the following would NOT explain an adverse direct labour efficiency variance?

- A Poor scheduling of direct labour workers
- B Setting standard efficiency at a level that is too low
- C Unusually lengthy machine breakdowns
- D A reduction in direct labour training

Circle your answer

A   B   C   D

17 Good Elf Insurance Ltd uses standard costing for its insurance-selling operations. Its 19X1 budget was to sell 8,000 policies. Labour costs of underwriting staff were budgeted at £56,000, and these are regarded as direct costs that vary with activity. Actual results in 19X1 were to sell 6,250 policies, and underwriting staff costs were £51,700. The underwriting staff would have been paid exactly at the budgeted rate, except that they received a pay award of 10% which was back-dated to 1 January, but had not been included in the budget.

Taking the original budget as a basis for comparison, what were the underwriting staff rate variance and the underwriting staff efficiency variance in 19X1?

	Rate variance	*Efficiency variance*
A	£4,700 (A)	£3,250 (A)
B	£4,700 (A)	£7,950 (A)
C	£5,170 (A)	£2,780 (A)
D	£5,170 (A)	£7,950 (A)

Circle your answer

A   B   C   D

Data for questions 18 - 19

Hanklin Plaster Ltd uses a standard process costing system. The standard direct materials cost and standard direct labour cost for 1 litre of output of product J is as follows.

		£
Direct materials	1.2 litres at £5 per litre	6
Direct labour	0.25 hours at £4 per hour	1
		7

Data for October is as follows.

Opening stock of work in process 400 litres.   Degree of completion 100% materials
                                                                      25% labour

Input to the process in October: 6,000 litres
Direct labour hours   1,350 hours
Closing stock of work in process 800 litres   Degree of completion 100% materials
                                                                      75% labour

Output of product J transferred to finished goods store: 4,700 litres.

The loss of materials in process occurs as soon as the direct materials are input to the process.

110

6: BUDGETARY CONTROL. STANDARD COSTING

18 What is the direct materials usage variance in October?

    A   £500 (F)
    B   £600 (F)
    C   £3,000 (F)
    D   £6,000 (F)

Circle your answer

A   B   C   D

19 What is the direct labour efficiency variance in October?

    A   £200 (A)
    B   £300 (A)
    C   £400 (A)
    D   £700 (A)

Circle your answer

A   B   C   D

Data for questions 20 - 21

The budgeted sales of Product X in August were 2,400 units. Bruce Chinn Ltd, the company that manufactures Product X, uses a standard costing system, and the standard cost per unit of Product X is £21. The company recorded the following variances for the month.

Sales price variance	£300 (A)
Sales volume profit variance	£1,200 (F)

During August 2,700 units of Product X were actually sold.

20 What was the budgeted profit for Product X in August?

    A   £6,300
    B   £7,200
    C   £9,600
    D   £10,800

Circle your answer

A   B   C   D

6: BUDGETARY CONTROL. STANDARD COSTING

21 What was the actual sales revenue for Product X in August?

A £57,600
B £67,200
C £67,500
D £68,400

Circle your answer

A B C D

Data for questions 22 - 24

Ed Lice Ltd manufactures a single product, Product F, for which the standard production overhead cost is 4 hours per unit at £6 per hour = £24 per unit.

This standard overhead cost is based on a budgeted absorption rate per direct labour hour. All production overheads are fixed costs.

Data for the year's operations are as follows.

    Actual production of F: 4,500 units
    Actual production overhead expenditure £126,000
    Budgeted production of F: 4,800 units
    Direct labour hours worked 18,800 hrs

22 What was the production overhead expenditure variance for the year?

A £7,200 (A)
B £10,800 (A)
C £13,200 (A)
D £18,000 (A)

Circle your answer

A B C D

23 What was the production overhead efficiency variance for the year?

A £4,800 (A)
B Nil
C £2,400 (F)
D £4,800 (F)

Circle your answer

A B C D

6: BUDGETARY CONTROL. STANDARD COSTING

24 What was the production overhead volume variance for the year? (This variance is sometimes known as the fixed overhead capacity variance).

A £18,000 (A)
B £4,800 (A)
C £2,400 (A)
D £2,400 (F)

Circle your answer

A   B   C   D

Data for questions 25 - 27

Burr Steerdrum Ltd uses a standard full costing system. It manufactures product V for which the following budgeted and actual data for the year are available.

Budgeted production of V: 6,000 units
Standard production overhead cost:

	£
Variable overhead (3hrs x £0.50 per hr)	1.50
Fixed overhead (3 hrs x £5 per hr)	15.00
	16.50

Actual production of V: 6,200 units
Production time taken: 17,700 hours
Actual variable overhead expenditure: £9,200
Actual fixed overhead expenditure: £92,800

25 What was the total production overhead variance for the year?

A £300 (A)
B £200 (A)
C £200 (F)
D £300 (F)

Circle your answer

A   B   C   D

26 What was the total production overhead expenditure variance for the year?

A £300 (A)
B £2,800 (A)
C £3,150 (A)
D £4,650 (A)

Circle your answer

A   B   C   D

6: BUDGETARY CONTROL. STANDARD COSTING

27 What were the total overhead efficiency variance and the overhead volume variance for the year? (The overhead volume variance is sometimes known as the fixed overhead capacity variance).

	Efficiency variance	Volume (capacity) variance
A	£4,500 (F)	£1,500 (F)
B	£4,950 (F)	£1,500 (A)
C	£4,950 (F)	£1,650 (A)
D	£4,950 (F)	£3,000 (F)

Circle your answer

A   B   C   D

Data for questions 28 - 31

Hitchin Parts Ltd, which manufactures a single product, used the following standard cost for the year 19X2.

	£ per unit
Direct materials	4
Direct labour	6
Variable production overhead	1
Fixed production overhead	6
	17
Standard selling price	20
Standard profit	3

Actual results in 19X2, when actual sales were 16,000 units, included the following.

	£
Direct materials cost variance	1,700 (A)
Direct labour cost variance	1,200 (F)
Variable production overhead total variance	600 (F)
Fixed production overhead total variance	9,000 (F)
Sales price variance	2,700 (A)
Sales volume profit variance	4,500 (F)

The fixed production overhead expenditure variance was £3,000 (A)

There were no opening stocks in 19X2, and no closing stocks of direct materials or work in progress. Closing stocks of finished goods were budgeted to be nil. Actual closing stocks are valued at standard full cost.

---

28 What was the budgeted profit in 19X2?

A   £43,500
B   £47,325
C   £48,000
D   £52,500

Circle your answer

A   B   C   D

6: BUDGETARY CONTROL. STANDARD COSTING

29 What was the actual profit in 19X2?

- A £45,400
- B £51,400
- C £54,400
- D £58,900

Circle your answer

A   B   C   D

30 What was the value of closing stocks at the end of 19X2?

- A £5,500
- B £8,500
- C £11,000
- D £17,000

Circle your answer

A   B   C   D

31 What were actual sales revenue and actual fixed overhead expenditure in 19X2?

	Sales revenue	Fixed overhead expenditure
A	£317,300	£81,000
B	£317,300	£90,000
C	£317,300	£99,000
D	£322,700	£99,000

Circle your answer

A   B   C   D

Data for questions 32 - 33

Pinzon Needles Ltd, a manufacturing company, uses a standard full absorption costing system. The standard production overhead cost is based on the following budget.

Fixed overhead budgeted	£720,000
Standard hours of work budgeted	120,000 hours
Variable overhead budget	£1.50 per hour

The year is divided into 12 monthly control periods with budgeted fixed costs apportioned equally between each control period. During January, 11,200 standard hours of output were produced, and these took 10,900 actual hours of work. Total production overhead costs in January were £78,200.

6: BUDGETARY CONTROL. STANDARD COSTING

32 What was the total production overhead variance in January?

A £3,200 (A)
B £2,250 (F)
C £5,800 (F)
D £6,750 (F)

Circle your answer

A   B   C   D

33 What was the production overhead expenditure variance in January?

A £1,400 (A)
B £1,850 (A)
C £3,200 (A)
D £2,250 (F)

Circle your answer

A   B   C   D

Data for questions 34 - 36

Armenia Sling Ltd manufactures and sells a single product. Shown below is a summary of the budget for the previous year (19X1) and actual results.

	Budget		Actual	
	£	£	£	£
Sales		500,000		600,000
Direct materials costs	200,000		300,000	
Other costs (all fixed)	250,000		250,000	
		450,000		550,000
Profit		50,000		50,000

Fanny Bone, the company's owner, made two decisions on 1 January 19X1.

(1) She reduced the sales price of the product by 25% for all units sold in the year.

(2) She switched to a different supplier for direct materials, purchasing a lower quality material but obtaining a 20% reduction on the budgeted price. There were no stocks of direct materials, work in progress or finished goods on either 1 January 19X1 or 31 December 19X1.

It is be assumed that the original budget shown above was an accurate estimate of the likely results for 19X1 before these two decisions were made.

The original budget is to be taken as a basis for comparison with actual results, for budgetary control purposes.

6: BUDGETARY CONTROL. STANDARD COSTING

34 Contribution is the difference between sales price and variable cost. What were the sales volume contribution variance and the sales price variance in 19X1, in £000?

	Sales volume variance	Sales price variance
A	£60 (F)	£150 (A)
B	£150 (F)	£200 (A)
C	£180 (F)	£150 (A)
D	£180 (F)	£200 (A)

Circle your answer

A B C D

35 What was the direct materials price variance in 19X1 in £000?

- A £20 (F)
- B £50 (F)
- C £60 (F)
- D £75 (F)

Circle your answer

A B C D

36 The direct materials usage variance in 19X1 in £000 was

- A £60 (A)
- B £55 (A)
- C £25 (A)
- D £20 (F)

Circle your answer

A B C D

CHAPTER 7

MARGINAL COSTING AND BREAKEVEN ANALYSIS

> This chapter covers the following topics:
>
> - Profit reporting: marginal costing and absorption costing methods
> - Cost behaviour graphs. Breakeven charts
> - Cost estimation: high-low method
> - Breakeven arithmetic (CVP arithmetic)

1. Profit reporting: marginal costing and absorption costing methods

1.1 Either marginal costing or absorption costing might be used as a method for measuring trading profits.

No matter what method of costing is used, trading profits can be measured as follows:

				£
(1)		Sales		X
(2)		Opening stock b/fwd	X	
(3)	plus	Actual costs *incurred* in the period	X	
			X	
(4)	minus	Closing stock c/fwd	(X)	
(5)	equals	Cost of sales		(X)
(6)		Profit		X

1.2 Sales and actual costs incurred (items 1 and 3) are exactly the same, no matter whether marginal costing or absorption is used.

1.3 The only difference in (5) cost of sales and (6) profit between absorption costing and marginal costing is due to differences in items 2 and 4 - ie differences in the valuation of opening stock brought forward and closing stock carried forward. With absorption costing, stock values include an amount for fixed production overhead. With marginal costing, stock is valued at marginal production cost only.

1.4 If there is no opening stock and no closing stock, reported profit will be the same using either marginal costing or absorption costing.

1.5 Comparing reported profitability between a marginal costing method of accounting and an absorption costing method therefore boils down to a comparison of differences in stock valuations.

7: MARGINAL COSTING AND BREAKEVEN ANALYSIS

2. Cost behaviour graphs. Breakeven charts

2.1 You need to be able to recognise
- the meaning of various cost behaviour graphs and
- different ways of presenting a breakeven chart.

2.2 A cost behaviour graph shows, for any individual cost item, how *either* the total cost of the item *or* the cost per unit of output or sale changes as the total volume of output or sale (or the level of activity) increases. Your knowledge of some of these graphs is tested in the questions that follow.

2.3 *Breakeven charts*

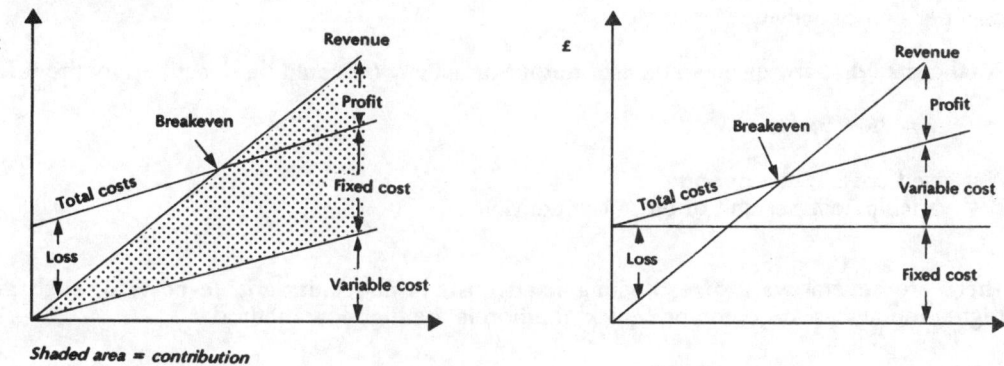

The charts shown here assume no step costs and no change in unit variable costs or unit sales prices.

2.4 *Profit/volume chart*

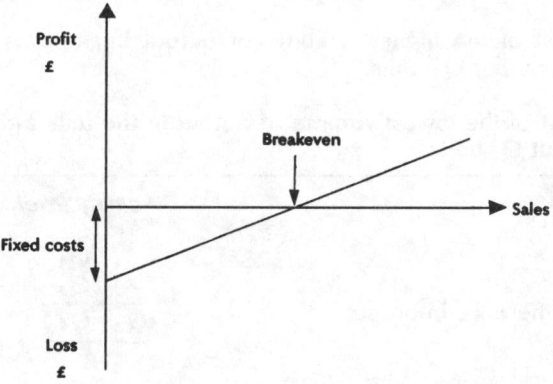

7: MARGINAL COSTING AND BREAKEVEN ANALYSIS

> **Assumptions in 'traditional' breakeven charts:**
>
> - variable costs vary directly with output/sales;
> - fixed costs incurred are the same at all output levels;
> - unit sales prices are the same for all units sold;
> - if more than one product is sold, there is a constant sales mix;
> - production and sales are the same in volume terms.

3. Cost estimation: high-low method

3.1 'Cost estimation' is a term used to refer to the analysis of costs into fixed costs and a variable cost per unit of activity.

Total costs (y) at any given volume of output or activity (x) could be described by the formula

$y = A + Bx$

A = fixed costs in the period
B = variable cost per unit of output or activity.

3.2 There are several ways of estimating fixed costs A and unit variable costs B, such as linear regression analysis. A common 'quick' method is the high-low method.

3.3 The high-low method uses historical cost data.

- Where necessary because of price inflation, costs should be adjusted to a common price level.

- Two historical costs are selected

    (1) The total cost of the highest volume of output in the data available. Suppose this is Cost £C_1 for output Q_1 units.

    (2) The total cost of the lowest volume of output in the data available. Suppose this is cost £C_2 for output Q_2 units.

	Activity level	Cost
		£
Highest output	Q_1	C_1
Lowest output	Q_2	C_2
Variable cost of difference in output	$(Q_1 - Q_2)$	$C_1 - C_2$
Variable cost per unit	=	$\dfrac{(C_1 - C_2)}{(Q_1 - Q_2)}$

7: MARGINAL COSTING AND BREAKEVEN ANALYSIS

4. Breakeven arithmetic (CVP arithmetic)

4.1 Breakeven arithmetic involves the use of marginal costing principles to calculate (1) breakeven point, or (2) the sales volume needed in order to achieve a target profit figure. Alternatively, problems might ask about the effect on profits of a change in certain variable costs or fixed costs, or about the incremental profit from a proposed new activity.

4.2 The key to dealing with breakeven arithmetic problems is usually **total contribution**.

4.3 *Calculation of breakeven point*

- Let S = Sales revenue
       F = Fixed costs
       V = Variable costs
       P = Target profit

- At breakeven point,   P = 0

  and so   S - V - F = 0

  ∴   S - V = F
  ie
  Total contribution = Fixed costs

  ∴ Breakeven point in units

  = F ÷ Contribution per unit

- Alternatively, given a contribution/sales ratio = C/S,

  Breakeven in £ revenue = $\dfrac{F}{C/S}$

4.4 *Sales required to achieve a target profit P*

- S - V - F = P
  S - V   = F + P

  ie Total contribution =
       Fixed costs + Target profit

  ∴ Sales required in units
    = (F + P) ÷ Contribution per unit

- Alternatively,

  In £ revenue = $\dfrac{F + P}{C/S}$

121

7: MARGINAL COSTING AND BREAKEVEN ANALYSIS

4.5
> *Total contribution* is simply **Contribution per unit x Sales volume**
>
> $$= (S_u - V_u) Q$$
>
> where S_u and V_u are sales price and variable cost per unit respectively, and Q is the sales volume.

4.6
> The total sales revenue and the sales price per unit required to achieve a target profit.
>
> - Target sales $\quad S = P + F + V$
> $\qquad\qquad\qquad = (P + F) + (Q \times V_u)$
>
> - Sales price per unit = Target sales revenue ÷ sales volume Q

4.7 When there is a change in the unit variable cost, fixed costs, sales price or sales volume, breakeven arithmetic is based on similar calculations.

4.8 *Margin of safety.* This is sometimes calculated to assess the possible risk of failing to break even. It is the difference between budgeted sales and breakeven sales, expressed as a % of budgeted sales.

7: MARGINAL COSTING AND BREAKEVEN ANALYSIS

QUESTIONS

Data for questions 1 - 2

The accountant of Katten Mousse plc has calculated the company's breakeven point from the following data:

	£
Selling price per unit	6.00
Variable production cost per unit	1.20
Variable selling cost per unit	0.40
Fixed production costs per unit, based on a budgeted 10,000 units pa	4.00
Fixed selling costs per unit, based on budgeted 10,000 units pa	0.80

1 What is the company's breakeven point?

A 8,333 units
B 9,091 units
C 10,000 units
D 10,909 units

Circle your answer

A   B   C   D

2 It is now expected that the variable production cost per unit and the selling price per unit will each increase by 10%, and fixed production costs will rise by 25%.

What will the breakeven point now be, to the nearest whole unit?

A 9,470 units
B 11,885 units
C 12,295 units
D 12,397 units

Circle your answer

A   B   C   D

123

7: MARGINAL COSTING AND BREAKEVEN ANALYSIS

3 The following is a graph of cost against volume of output:

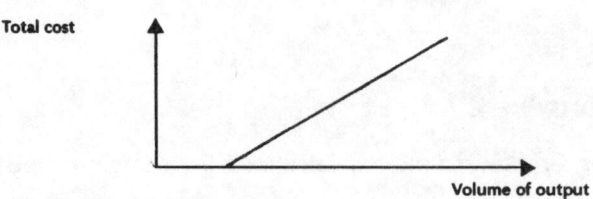

To which of the following costs does the graph correspond?

A Electricity bills made up of a standing charge and a variable charge

B Bonus payments to employees when production reaches a certain level

C Salesmen's commissions payable per unit up to a maximum amount of commission

D Bulk discounts on purchases, the discount being given on all units purchased

Circle your answer

A   B   C   D

4

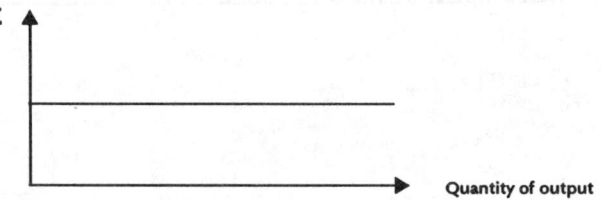

Which of the following does the graph illustrate?

A Fixed cost per unit
B Variable cost per unit
C Full cost of production per unit
D Full cost of sales per unit

Circle your answer

A   B   C   D

5 Ian Tyrol Hats Limited has recorded the following data in the two most recent periods:

Total costs of production (£)	Volume of production (units)
13,500	700
18,300	1,100

What is the best estimate of the company's fixed costs per period?

7: MARGINAL COSTING AND BREAKEVEN ANALYSIS

A £4,800
B £5,100
C £9,900
D £13,500

Circle your answer

A B C D

Data for questions 6 - 9

Danzig plc sells one product for which data is given below:

	£
Selling price per unit	10
Variable cost per unit	6
Fixed cost per unit	2

The fixed costs are based on a budgeted level of activity of 5,000 units for the period.

6 What is Danzig plc's breakeven point in £ of sales revenue?

A 2,500
B 5,000
C 25,000
D 50,000

Circle your answer

A B C D

7 How many units must be sold if Danzig wishes to earn a profit of £6,000 for the period?

A 2,000
B 4,000
C 6,000
D 8,000

Circle your answer

A B C D

8 What is Danzig's margin of safety for the budget period if fixed costs prove to be 20% higher than budgeted?

A 60%
B 40%
C 33⅓%
D 20%

Circle your answer

A B C D

125

7: MARGINAL COSTING AND BREAKEVEN ANALYSIS

9 If the selling price and variable cost increase by 20% and 12% respectively by how much must sales volume change compared with the original budgeted level in order to achieve the original budgeted profit for the period?

    A   24.2% decrease
    B   24.2% increase
    C   37.9% decrease
    D   37.9% increase

Circle your answer

A   B   C   D

10 Hans Bratch Ltd is a manufacturing company that employs a marginal batch costing system in its cost accounts. Which of the following cost items will be included in the company's marginal production costs of finished output?

Item
1   Marginal cost of products scrapped at routine final inspection
2   Carriage inwards
3   Set-up costs (variable with each batch produced)
4   Salesmen's travelling expenses

    A   Items 1, 2, 3 and 4
    B   Items 1, 2 and 3 only
    C   Items 1 and 2 only
    D   Items 2 and 3 only

Circle your answer

A   B   C   D

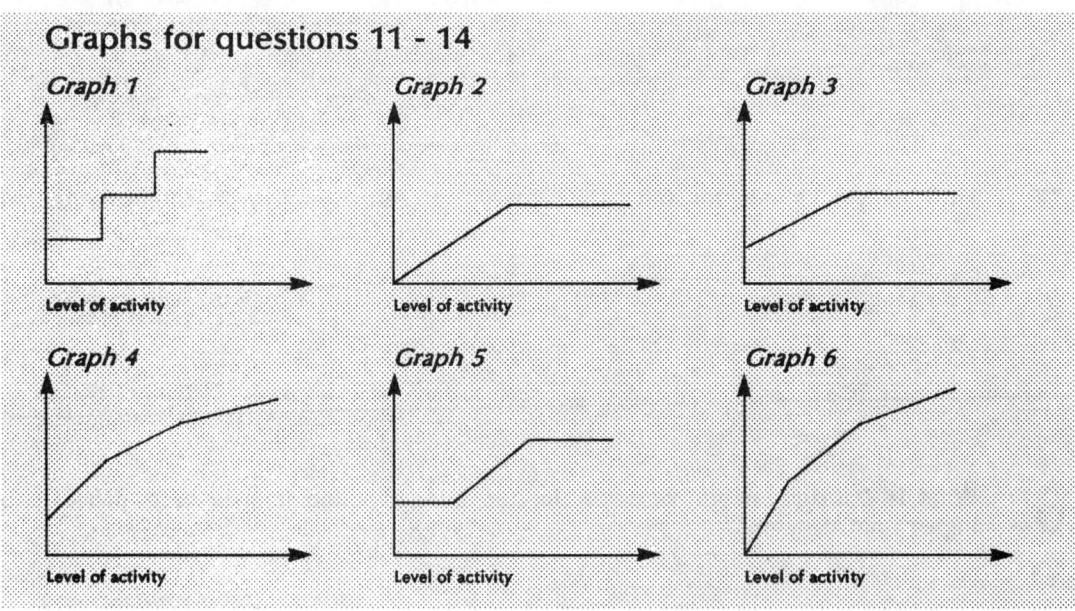

Graphs for questions 11 - 14

7: MARGINAL COSTING AND BREAKEVEN ANALYSIS

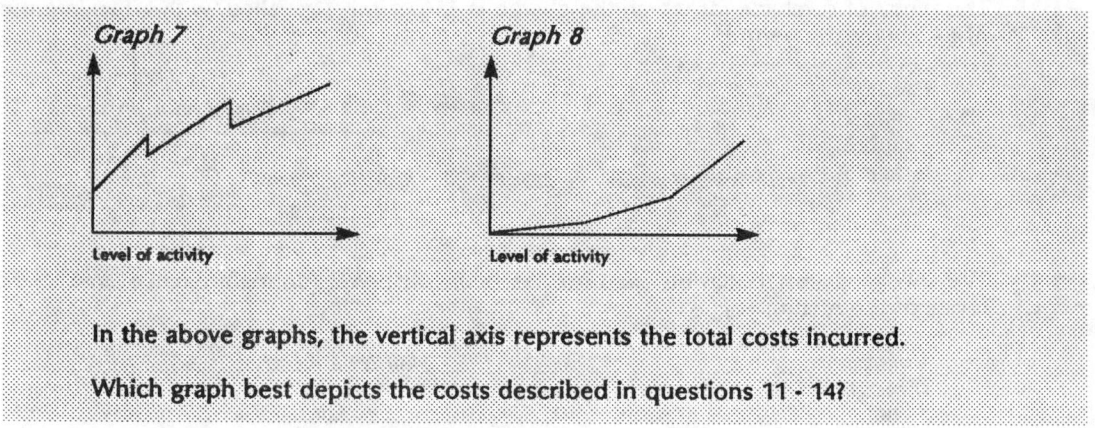

In the above graphs, the vertical axis represents the total costs incurred.

Which graph best depicts the costs described in questions 11 - 14?

11 The rental of a machine for which the charges are £50 per hour, subject to a minimum charge of £1,000 and a maximum charge of £5,000.

A Graph 1
B Graph 2
C Graph 3
D Graph 5

Circle your answer

A   B   C   D

12 The cost of electricity, where there is a basic charge of £2,000, plus an amount based on the units consumed:

1 to 99 units	£16 per unit
next 100 units	£8 per unit
thereafter	£4 per unit

A Graph 4
B Graph 6
C Graph 7
D Graph 8

Circle your answer

A   B   C   D

13 Supervisors' salaries at £1,000 each per month.

One supervisor is required for the first 100 units.
For production volumes between 101-300 units, two supervisors are required.
For production volumes above 300 units, three supervisors are required.

A Graph 1
B Graph 4
C Graph 5
D Graph 6

Circle your answer

A   B   C   D

127

7: MARGINAL COSTING AND BREAKEVEN ANALYSIS

14 The rental of a vehicle for which the charge is £5 per mile travelled, with a maximum charge of £4,000 for the period.

A   Graph 1
B   Graph 2
C   Graph 3
D   Graph 5

Circle your answer

A   B   C   D

15 The following cost behaviour pattern has been observed for maintenance costs at various levels of production

Volume (hours)	Maintenance cost £
14,000	26,800
9,800	21,760
10,560	22,672
15,400	28,480

What will be the likely maintenance cost for a volume of 12,000 hours?

A   £22,192
B   £22,971
C   £24,400
D   £26,645

Circle your answer

A   B   C   D

Data for questions 16 - 19

Eagle plc manufactures a single product, the costs and selling price of which are:

	£ per unit
Direct materials	7
Direct labour	3
Variable overheads	2
Fixed overheads	2
Selling price	18

These figures are based on an expected volume of production of 15,000 units.

16 The company's breakeven point is:

A   7,500 units
B   £135,000 revenue
C   15,000 units
D   £90,000 revenue

Circle your answer

A   B   C   D

7: MARGINAL COSTING AND BREAKEVEN ANALYSIS

17 The company's expected margin of safety is:

A   5,000 units
B   33%
C   £90,000 revenue
D   67%

Circle your answer

A   B   C   D

18 If the company wants to make profit of £9,000, how many units must be sold?

A   5,000
B   6,500
C   9,750
D   15,000

Circle your answer

A   B   C   D

19 If all costs increase by 10% but selling prices remain unchanged, by how much must sales change from the original expected volume (15,000) to achieve profit of £9,000?

A   41.7% decrease
B   45.8% decrease
C   54.2% decrease
D   58.3% decrease

Circle your answer

A   B   C   D

Data for questions 20 - 21

Square Wheels Ltd, a small transport company, operates with just two vehicles, and has produced the following forecast for next year.

Operating kilometres	60,000
	£
Total wages cost	40,000
Total vehicle running costs	48,000
Other costs (all fixed)	24,000
Revenue	120,000

Revenue and vehicle running costs vary with operating kilometres.

7: MARGINAL COSTING AND BREAKEVEN ANALYSIS

20 The breakeven point for the year, in operating kilometres, is

A 45,000
B 50,000
C 53,333
D 54,000

Circle your answer

A   B   C   D

21 If the forecast were to be only 55,000 kilometres, and wages were reduced to £32,000, the breakeven point in operating kilometres would be

A 41,250
B 42,778
C 44,000
D 46,667

Circle your answer

A   B   C   D

Data for questions 22 - 23

Stan Dalone Limited manufactures a single product, for which the costs and selling price are:

Variable production costs	£50 per unit
Selling price	£125 per unit
Fixed production overhead	£200,000 per quarter
Fixed selling and administration overhead	£80,000 per quarter

Normal capacity is 20,000 units per quarter.

Production in quarter 1 was 19,000 units, and sales volume was 16,000 units. There was no opening stock in the quarter.

22 The absorption costing profit for Stan Dalone Limited for quarter 1 was

A £920
B £950
C £960
D £970

Circle your answer

A   B   C   D

7: MARGINAL COSTING AND BREAKEVEN ANALYSIS

23 The marginal costing profit for Stan Dalone Limited for quarter 1 was

    A   £920
    B   £950
    C   £960
    D   £970

Circle your answer

    A   B   C   D

24 The cost accountant of Rhia Gunner Ltd has obtained the following data for April 19X1.

		£
Opening stock:	Direct costs	2,500
	Production overhead	5,000
		7,500
Costs in April 19X1	Direct materials consumed	£4,600
	Direct labour	£3,200
	Depreciation	£500
	Other production overhead	£14,000
Production overhead absorption rate:		200% of direct costs
Closing stock: Direct costs		£3,000
Sales in April 19X1		£38,000

The cost accountant wants to know how much different the reported gross profit would have been if marginal costing had been used instead of absorption costing. What would the difference have been?

    A   Marginal costing profit £2,500 higher
    B   Marginal costing profit £1,000 higher
    C   Absorption costing profit £1,000 higher
    D   Absorption costing profit £6,000 higher

Circle your answer

    A   B   C   D

25 Soups Inn Limited produced the following units (with associated total cost) for a recent five month period:

	Units	Total cost £
August	5,400	38,020
September	5,000	37,500
October	8,400	45,660
November	8,300	45,050
December	5,900	39,420

7: MARGINAL COSTING AND BREAKEVEN ANALYSIS

If x = the number of units produced, an equation which can be used for forecast total cost based upon units produced is:

A £22,900 + £2.8x
B £24,300 + £2.55x
C £25,000 + £2.5x
D £25,500 + £2.4x

Circle your answer

A   B   C   D

26 Viennese Walls Ltd wishes to analyse the fixed and variable components of a semi-variable cost. The following information is available:

Month	Output (units)	Costs £
1	1,000	12,000
2	700	10,000
3	1,100	14,000
4	600	9,000
5	1,400	19,000
6	1,200	15,000

Using the high-low method, which one of the following is correct?

A variable costs are £15 per unit
B variable costs are £10 per unit
C fixed costs are £1,500 per month
D fixed costs are £1,000 per month

Circle your answer

A   B   C   D

27 Rumbletum's Restaurant achieves a weekly trading profit as follows:

	£	£
Sales (average price per meal £7)		5,600
Operating costs		
Materials	3,080	
Power (80% variable cost, 20% fixed cost)	600	
Staff	680	
Building occupancy costs	880	
		5,240
Profit		360

The restaurant owner, Dai O'Rhea, has estimated that if the restaurant started to sell take away meals as well as restaurant meals:

(a) take away sales would be 720 meals per week, at an average selling price of £3.20 and an average variable cost of £1.70;

(b) additional fixed costs would be £1,200 per week;

(c) take away sales would attract more custom into the restaurant, and for every 10 take away sales there would be 1 extra sale of a restaurant meal;

(d) total staff costs would remain the same each week.

If the take-away service is introduced, by how much would the weekly profit figure for the business change?

A £63.6 increase
B £45.6 increase
C £8 decrease
D £120 decrease

Circle your answer

A   B   C   D

28 Arbiter Limited budgets to make 70,000 units of its standard product each month. Budgeted fixed costs are £175,000 per month. The company uses an absorption costing system for measuring profits.

During March 19X1, sales were 69,000 units at £5 each. Production of 72,000 units cost £270,000, and the closing stock was valued at £11,250. There was no opening stock at the beginning of March.

If marginal costing had been used instead of absorption costing, the profit that the company would have made in March 19X1 is

A £78,750
B £83,250
C £86,250
D £93,750

Circle your answer

A   B   C   D

29 Bonzo Ltd manufactures and sells a single product, with the following estimated costs for next year.

	Unit cost 100,000 units of output £	150,000 units of output £
Direct materials	20.0	20.0
Direct labour	5.0	5.0
Production overheads	10.0	7.5
Marketing costs	7.5	5.0
Administration costs	5.0	4.0
	47.5	41.5

Fixed costs are unaffected by the volume of output.

133

7: MARGINAL COSTING AND BREAKEVEN ANALYSIS

Bonzo's management think they can sell 150,000 units per annum if the sales price is £49.50.

The breakeven point, in units, at this price is

A   95,400 units
B   90,000 units
C   75,000 units
D   60,000 units

Circle your answer

A   B   C   D

Data for questions 30 - 32

Mardigras Manufacturing Ltd's budget for the next year, when it expects to be operating at 75% capacity, is as follows:

			£	£
Sales	18,000 units at £48			864,000
Less	Direct materials		216,000	
	Direct wages		162,000	
	Production overhead:	fixed	126,000	
		variable	54,000	
				558,000
Gross profit				306,000
Other costs:	fixed		108,000	
	varying with sales volume		81,000	
				189,000
Net profit				117,000

30 The company's breakeven point in sales revenue is

A   £414,700
B   £448,000
C   £576,000
D   £630,000

Circle your answer

A   B   C   D

31 It has been estimated that if the selling price were reduced to £42, sales demand would rise to 90% of the firm's output capacity. The profit at this price and sales volume would be

A   £16,000
B   £32,400
C   £36,000
D   £57,600

Circle your answer

A   B   C   D

7: MARGINAL COSTING AND BREAKEVEN ANALYSIS

32 It has also been estimated that in order for sales to reach 100% of the company's output capacity, the sales price must be reduced by 15% below budget and an advertising campaign costing £25,000 would be needed.

If the company decided to take this option, its breakeven point in sales revenue terms, to the nearest £000, would now be

A £859,000
B £843,000
C £831,000
D £816,000

Circle your answer

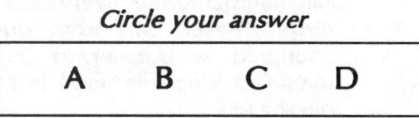

33

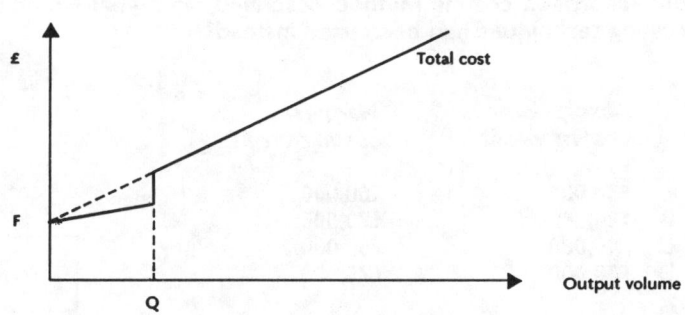

What causes the change in the total cost line at output Q?

A The supply price of raw materials changes, and all quantities of raw materials must be paid for at a higher price

B There is an increase in fixed costs, due to greater supervision and testing requirements at the higher volumes of output

C There is an increase in labour costs, because the work force must be paid an overtime premium at output volumes in excess of Q

D The company reaches capacity in its ability to produce components itself for assembly. Additional components must be purchased externally from subcontractors

Circle your answer

A   B   C   D

135

7: MARGINAL COSTING AND BREAKEVEN ANALYSIS

34 Hump Ltd manufactures a single product, which had the following sales and production results over two operating periods.

	Period 1	Period 2
Sales (units)	50,000	60,000
Production (units)	70,000	50,000

The sales price is £10 per unit. Direct materials and direct labour costs are £5 per unit. All manufacturing overheads are absorbed into product costs at a predetermined rate of output, based on normal output of 60,000 units per period. Any under- or over-absorbed overhead is transferred to the P&L account at the end of each period. Budgeted manufacturing overhead is £180,000 per period for fixed costs and £1 per unit of variable overhead.

Assuming that actual costs were as expected, what was the profit reported in period 2 using the absorption costing method described, and what would the profit have been if marginal costing techniques had been used instead?

	Absorption costing profit	Marginal costing profit
A	£30,000	£60,000
B	£30,000	£70,000
C	£40,000	£60,000
D	£50,000	£70,000

Circle your answer

A   B   C   D

35 Perry Striker Ltd manufactures and sells a single product. Monthly fixed costs are £80,000. At a selling price of £5, the company breaks even at 40,000 units of sale per month. Actual sales at this price are 50,000 units per month.

The company's management estimate that if they reduced the selling price to £4.50 per unit, monthly sales would rise to 60,000 units. If they raised the selling price to £5.50, monthly sales would fall to 46,000 units.

Given just the three options for a selling price, £4.50, £5 or £5.50 per unit, the maximum monthly profit that Perry Striker could achieve is

A   £10,000
B   £20,000
C   £35,000
D   £50,000

Circle your answer

A   B   C   D

7: MARGINAL COSTING AND BREAKEVEN ANALYSIS

Data for questions 36 - 37

A hotel company operates a small hotel, but only during the summer season of 20 weeks a year. The following budget data has been prepared.

(1) *Accommodation*
80 single rooms let on a daily basis
40 double rooms let on a daily basis, at 175% of the single room rate.

(2) *Expected demand*
Double rooms to be fully booked every day of the season
Single rooms to be operated at only 75% capacity throughout the season.

(3) *Costs*
Fixed costs per year   £206,200
Variable costs per day of use   Single room   £7
                                 Double room   £12

36 What are the charges that should be made for double rooms if the hotel wishes to make a £50,000 profit each year?

A £18.20 per day
B £21.00 per day
C £31.85 per day
D £36.75 per day

Circle your answer

A   B   C   D

37 There is a proposal to keep the hotel open for a further 10 weeks a year, to increase profits to £60,000. Fixed costs would now be £246,600.

What should the price be per double room for the season if the hotel were to stay open for a further 10 weeks a year, as proposed, operating at 50% capacity for both double and single rooms during these extra 10 weeks?

A £20
B £27
C £35
D £45

Circle your answer

A   B   C   D

7: MARGINAL COSTING AND BREAKEVEN ANALYSIS

38 Which one of the following statements is correct?

A If a company reduces its selling price by 10%, and sales volume increases by 11% as a result, then the profit earned by the company would not change.

B Fixed costs are items of cost which remain the same regardless of the volume of output

C All direct costs are variable costs

D Sunk costs are irrelevant when providing decision-making information

Circle your answer

A   B   C   D

CHAPTER 8

COSTS FOR DECISION-MAKING

> This chapter covers the following topics:
> - Relevant costs and management decisions
> - Recognising decision problems
> - Limiting factor decisions. Make-or-buy decisions
> - Capital expenditure decisions and DCF

1. Relevant costs and management decisions

1.1 Much of cost accounting deals with either

- recording and reporting costs and profits or
- budgetary control, and comparing actual results against a budget, standard or target.

Even a budget, in accounting terms, is largely the formulation of what a business expects its reported profits to be at the end of the budget period.

Unfortunately, 'traditional' accounting data doesn't help managers to make decisions about what to do in the future in order to improve profits.

1.2 Decisions affect the future, and never the past. It follows that the costs and revenues to take into consideration with decision-making are only those that will arise in the future as a result of the decision that is taken. Accounting for decision-making should therefore only use future revenues and relevant costs.

1.3 | A relevant cost is a future cash flow arising as a direct consequence of a decision.

- A relevant cost is a *future* cost. Costs that have been incurred in the past should never influence a decision that is taken now (eg development costs already incurred, when deciding whether or not to continue with a product development project).

- A relevant cost is a *cash flow*. Notional costs such as depreciation are never relevant to a decision, although the cash paid or received for buying or selling a fixed asset will be. Absorption of overhead is never relevant, although cash overhead expenditure incurred will be.

- A relevant cost is one arising as a *direct consequence of the decision*. Any costs that will be incurred anyway - eg committed costs or fixed costs, cannot be relevant to a decision that a manager is making now to improve or maximise profits.

8: COSTS FOR DECISION-MAKING

> 1.4 In general terms, in order to improve or maximise profits a decision should be taken if the future benefits that will flow from the decision exceed the relevant costs.

1.5 Relevant costs are given a variety of different names. Check that you know them.

> - *Incremental cost*
>
>   An extra cost that will be incurred
>
> - *Opportunity cost*
>
>   The benefit forgone by taking one course of action, expressed in terms of the net cash flows lost by not being able to do the next most profitable alternative thing. Opportunity costs imply a shortage of available resources
>
> - *Differential cost*
>
>   The difference in relevant costs between choice 1 and choice 2, two alternative decision options.
>
> - *Out-of-pocket expense*
>
> - *Minimum price*
>
>   The selling price for an item that will only just cover the *relevant* costs of making/supplying/selling it to the customer.

1.6 *Variable costs* are often, but not always, relevant costs in a decision. There is a close connection between marginal costing, CVP analysis and relevant costs.

2. Recognising decision problems

2.1 For anyone taking an examination in cost accounting, it obviously helps to be able to spot a relevant costing problem from the wording of the question. Key words that often (but not always) appear in these questions, and which can be a valuable pointer, are as follows.

> - Decide/decision
> - Advise/advice
> - Recommend
> - Whether
> - Minimum price
> - Anything suggesting restricted production capacity or a limited amount of labour/machine time/materials/cash.

2.2 Decisions can be about anything, and vary widely in character. The more 'usual' sort of matters for which a decision by management could be needed and which should involve relevant costs include:

> - Limiting factor decisions (described later)
> - Pricing decisions
> - Decisions about whether to carry out some work internally or to get an external supplier to do it ('make or buy' decisions)
> - Decisions about whether or not to continue with a project or operation ('shutdown' decisions)
> - Choosing between two alternative courses of action ('mutually exclusive options')
> - Decisions about whether to launch a new project or activity
> - Capital expenditure decisions (described later)

3. Limiting factor decisions. Make or buy decisions

3.1 On occasions, a business will have a shortage of resources - labour, machine time, materials etc - which prevents it from achieving the output and sales volume that it would otherwise be able to. The scarce resource is called a *limiting factor*, *key budget factor* or *principal budget factor*.

3.2 When there is a limiting factor, profits will be maximised by concentrating on the production and sale of items that *maximise the amount of contribution earned per unit of scarce resource*.

- If direct labour is in short supply, seek to maximise total contribution by producing items that earn the highest contribution per direct labour hour (up to the sales budget quantity for the item).
- Similarly, if machine time is in short supply, seek to maximise total contribution by producing items that earn the highest contribution per machine hour (up to sales budget limits).

3.3 Limiting factors can be overcome by purchasing items from outside suppliers (eg sub-contracting work). When this option exists, we have a *make-or-buy decision* to make. Which items should be made 'in house' and which (if any) should be purchased externally?

3.4
> The general rule is to compare the cost of purchasing externally with the relevant costs of making the item in-house.
>
> - External purchase will usually cost more than in-house production, but some external purchases are necessary
> - By purchasing externally, the demand for the limiting factor item is reduced
> - The extra cost of external purchase should be expressed as an extra cost per unit of limiting factor (for which demand will be reduced)
> - Items to be purchased externally are those for which this extra cost per unit of limiting factor *is least*.

4. Capital expenditure decisions and DCF

4.1 When you are learning cost accounting, you may be expected to know something about capital expenditure decisions (investment decisions) and discounted cash flow (DCF).

4.2 The differentiating features of capital expenditure decisions are that

- a cash outlay is made 'now' to acquire a fixed asset
- the benefits from the asset will be earned over a period of time, typically a number of years
- the relevant costs and benefits from the project might vary from year to year over the life of the project.

4.3 With capital expenditure decisions, the principles of relevant costing apply, just as for any other type of management decisions, and only future *cash flows* should be taken into account. However, some recognition is given to the timescale of a project involving capital expenditure, and to the time value of money.

Two ways of recognising the time value of money

Payback
How long will it take, in years, before the initial cash outlay (the capital expenditure) is 'paid back' from the net cash inflows of the project?

Discounted cash flow
Recognising that £1 now is worth more than £1 in a year's time, which is worth more than £1 in 2 years' time etc, because money can be invested to earn a return over time. Put another way, £1 in the future isn't worth as much as £1 now

4.4 Discounted cash flow takes the relevant net cash flows from a capital expenditure project, usually assuming that the cash flows for each year of the project occur at the *end* of the year. (Year 1 = end of 1st year. Year 0 = 'now').

4.5 Since £1 now is worth more than £1 in a future year, *the expected cash flows in future years are discounted to a present value equivalent*. The interest rate used for discounting is the company's cost of capital = required rate of return.

4.6 The rates of discount to apply to future cash flows, to convert them into present values, are obtainable from discount tables.

4.7 If the present value of expected revenues/savings exceeds the present value of incremental cash expenditures on the project, the *net present value (NPV)* will be positive, and from a basic financial or accounting point of view, the capital expenditure project should go ahead.

8: COSTS FOR DECISION-MAKING

QUESTIONS

1 What is the name given to a costing technique or method of preparing ad hoc information, whereby, for a range of stepped changes in the nature or level or activity, the additional costs and revenues that are likely to result from each stepped change are estimated?

A Zero base budgeting
B Flexible budgeting
C Opportunity costing
D Incremental costing

Circle your answer

A   B   C   D

Data for questions 2 - 4

Saber Fencing has already incurred research and development costs of £100,000 on a contract, and expects to incur £150,000 more in costs before the R & D project is completed in one year's time. The estimated future costs are as follows.

	Expected future costs £
Materials	60,000
Staff costs	50,000
Overheads	40,000
	150,000

The expected sales value of the completed research is just £60,000.

Materials. Contracts have already been exchanged for the purchase of the remaining £60,000 of materials needed. If not used, the materials must be disposed of at a cost of £2,500.

Staff costs. The expected future staff costs represent the annual salaries of Ray Peer and Chris Swords, who each earn £20,000 per annum, and an allocation of £10,000 of the salary of their supervisor A Pay, who is in overall charge of several research projects. If this project is abandoned, Ray and Chris will be made redundant, each receiving £9,000 in compensation.

Overheads. Future overhead costs represent depreciation of £20,000 on plant and machinery and an allocation of the general fixed overheads incurred by the business. The plant and equipment was bought for the project and has no other use. Its current disposal value is £18,000 and in one year's time will be £11,000.

The company is considering whether or not to continue with the research project.

8: COSTS FOR DECISION-MAKING

2 What are the materials costs that are relevant to the decision about whether to continue with the project or not?

A Nil
B £2,500
C £60,000
D £62,500

Circle your answer

A B C D

3 What are the staff costs that are relevant to the decision about whether to continue with the project or not?

A £18,000
B £22,000
C £28,000
D £40,000

Circle your answer

A B C D

4 Ignoring interest costs, what are the costs of the plant and machinery, plus the costs of general overheads, that are relevant to the decision about whether to continue with the project or not?

A £7,000
B £18,000
C £27,000
D £38,000

Circle your answer

A B C D

5 Cox L'Espair Ltd is a specialist components manufacturer working below full capacity. Its chief executive, Rowan Attstroke, would like to fill up capacity by taking on extra work at low prices. A potential customer has offered to buy 1,000 units of component FGH. Each unit of FGH requires 2 units of Material M111 and 5 units of Material M222.

The stock position of Cox L'Espair is as follows:

Material	Units in stock	Original purchase price per unit £	Current replacement price per unit £	Disposal value per unit £
M111	1,500	3.00	3.50	2.40
M222	4,000	2.00	2.50	1.80

Notes
1. Material M111 is in continuous use by the company.
2. Material M222 is no longer used by the company, and existing stocks are now surplus to requirements.

8: COSTS FOR DECISION-MAKING

For Rowan Attstroke to calculate a minimum price for the customer's order, what would be the relevant cost of the materials?

A £15,050
B £16,700
C £16,750
D £19,500

Circle your answer

A   B   C   D

6 Scorsatz Okker Ltd has a machine which it purchased two years ago for £15,000, and which now has a net book value of £5,000. Perry Striker, the company's chief executive, is wondering whether to use the machine for a one year project. If not used, it would have no other use, and although it could be sold, there would be a loss on disposal of £2,000. If used for the project, the machine would have a one-year life, after which it would have no resale value, but would cost £1,500 to dispose of. The variable operating costs of the machine would be £6,000 for the year.

In deciding whether to go ahead with the one year project, and ignoring interest costs, the relevant costs of the machine would be

A £9,000
B £9,500
C £10,500
D £12,500

Circle your answer

A   B   C   D

7 Eddie Ball runs a jobbing business and is trying to decide whether or not to take on an extra job for a customer, to produce 20 units of a component. Each component would require 2 hours of skilled labour and 3 hours of unskilled labour to make. Eddie has sufficient skilled labour to do the work, but he would have to take them off another job, which would then have to be done by unskilled labour. He has a shortage of unskilled labour and would need to recruit temporary agency staff for any unskilled work that needs doing. Rates of pay are

Skilled workers	£5 per hour
Unskilled workers	£3 per hour
Agency workers	£4 per hour

What would be the incremental labour costs for the business if the extra job were to be carried out?

A £360
B £380
C £400
D £440

Circle your answer

A   B   C   D

145

8: COSTS FOR DECISION-MAKING

8 Which of the following statements is/are correct?

Statement

1. The incremental cost of buying a larger quantity of materials might be a negative cost, which is a cost reduction.

2. If a company reduces its selling price by 20% so that sales volume increases by 25%, total profit will remain unchanged.

3. A direct cost need not be a variable cost, but might be a fixed cost.

A   Statement 1 only is correct
B   Statements 1 and 2 only are correct
C   Statements 2 and 3 only are correct
D   Statements 1 and 3 only are correct

Circle your answer

A   B   C   D

Data for questions 9 - 10

Roll and Maul Ltd is having serious problems in obtaining supplies of raw material M, which is used in the four products that it makes. The company has current stocks of M amounting to 15,000 kilos, which cost £60,000. Expected demand, selling prices and costs for each of the four products are as follows.

Product	Kilos of material M per unit of product	Labour and variable overhead costs per unit	Sales price per unit	Budgeted sales demand in the period
	Kg	£	£	units
W	0.7	15	22	8,000
X	0.5	8	14	7,200
Y	1.0	12	23	12,000
Z	1.5	10	22	10,000

9 If Roll and Maul Ltd cannot obtain any further supplies of material M in the period, what quantities of the products should be produced in order to maximise the period profits?

	Units of W	Units of X	Units of Y	Units of Z
A	4,000	6,400	0	6,000
B	8,000	0	9,400	0
C	0	0	12,000	2,000
D	0	7,200	11,400	0

Circle your answer

A   B   C   D

8: COSTS FOR DECISION-MAKING

10 If Roll and Maul Ltd can obtain supplies of material M, but at a price of £9.50 per kilo, how many kilos should the company purchase in the period in order to maximise profits? (It can be assumed that the price of the materials will subsequently fall to £4 per kilo in future periods).

A None
B 600 kilos
C 6,200 kilos
D 21,200 kilos

Circle your answer

A B C D

11 Finnish Inline Ltd manufactures component Q and end-product T. One unit of Q goes into the manufacture of one unit of T. Budgeted manufacturing costs are as follows.

	Component Q £	Product T £
Component Q	-	10
Raw materials	2	2
Direct labour	4	8
Variable overhead	1	2
Fixed overhead	_3_	_6_
	10	28
Sales price		35
Profit		_7_

Direct labour is a variable cost. The company is working at full capacity, and can only just produce enough units of component Q to meet the demand for product T.

An outside customer asks Finnish Inline Ltd to sell it 3,000 units of component Q. If the company agrees, it will incur additional inspection and testing costs of £3,000.

What is the minimum price per unit of Q that Finnish Inline would have to charge if it agreed to supply the customer, so as not to suffer any drop in profits?

A £17
B £21
C £24
D £31

Circle your answer

A B C D

147

8: COSTS FOR DECISION-MAKING

Data for questions 12 - 13

Battenball Ltd manufactures three products using the same direct labour force. Budgeted data is as follows.

	Product X £	Product Y £	Product Z £
Sales price per unit	8.0	18.0	22.0
Variable cost per unit	6.5	12.0	15.0
Fixed cost per unit	0.5	4.5	4.0
Total cost per unit	7.0	16.5	19.0
Profit per unit	1.0	1.5	3.0
Direct labour hours per unit	½ hr	1½ hrs	2 hrs
Budgeted monthly sales	500 units	300 units	400 units

There are 1,200 direct labour hours available in normal working hours each month. Direct labour employees are paid £4 per hour in normal time and £6 per hour in overtime. Direct labour is regarded as a variable cost.

12 On the basis of the data provided, if no overtime hours are worked, what monthly production budget should be planned, in order to maximise profits?

	Units of X	Units of Y	Units of Z
A	500	100	400
B	0	300	375
C	0	400	300
D	50	250	400

Circle your answer

A   B   C   D

13 Suppose extra direct labour hours a month up to a maximum of 250 hours a month can be made available in overtime. What *additional* production should be planned to use up the extra hours available (if required) in order to maximise profits, and by how much would profits increase? (Assume no change in fixed costs.)

	Units of X	Units of Y	Units of Z	Extra profit per month
A	None	None	None	£0
B	100	0	100	£350
C	350	50	0	£325
D	400	0	25	£275

Circle your answer

A   B   C   D

148

8: COSTS FOR DECISION-MAKING

Data for questions 14 - 16

Annette Cord has developed a new design of short-handled tennis racket. She has done this in her spare time, and must now decide whether or not to set up in business to market this new product. The potential sales volume is difficult to predict, but the following estimates have been made.

Sales price per racket	Sales volume per year
£14	17,500 rackets
£15	15,000 rackets
£21	10,000 rackets
£23	9,000 rackets

She plans to have the rackets manufactured for her by an external supplier and to organise selling and distribution through her own company. Production and selling costs would be as follows.

	Variable cost per racket	Fixed costs
For up to 10,000 rackets per year	£9	£110,000
For over 10,000 rackets per year	£6	£120,000

The costs above exclude the following considerations.

(1) Annette has already spent £5,000 on market research and she intends to spend a further £2,000.

(2) Annette will pay herself a monthly salary of £1,000. If she decides to go ahead with the product development, she will have to give up her job with a sports goods manufacturer, which pays her a salary of £800 per month.

In deciding whether or not to set up the business, Annette Cord should consider the relevant costs and benefits of each decision option.

14 In the assessment of the relevant costs of the decision to set up in business, market research costs are

A a sunk cost of of £7,000

B a sunk cost of £5,000 and an incremental cost of £2,000

C a sunk cost of £2,000 and an incremental cost of £5,000

D an opportunity cost of £7,000

Circle your answer

A   B   C   D

8: COSTS FOR DECISION-MAKING

15 In the assessment of the relevant costs of the decision to set up in business, Annette Cord's salary cost should be treated as

A an incremental benefit of £200 per month net

B an opportunity cost of £200 per month net

C an opportunity cost of £800 per month

D an opportunity cost of £1,000 per month

Circle your answer

A   B   C   D

16 If Annette Cord *does* decide to set up in business, which of the four selling prices per racket should she charge, on the basis of the estimates provided, in order to maximise profits?

A £14 per racket
B £15 per racket
C £21 per racket
D £23 per racket

Circle your answer

A   B   C   D

17 Trackie Vents Ltd manufactures two components in its machining division, in which capacity per month is limited to 3,500 machine hours.

Production costs are as follows.

	Component X £	Component Y £
Variable costs	15	20
Fixed overhead	<u>10</u>	<u>15</u>
	<u>25</u>	<u>35</u>
Monthly requirements	1,000 units	1,000 units

Fixed overhead rate = £5 per machine hour
Component X can be bought from an external supplier for £31 per unit and component Y can similarly be bought for £47 per unit.

What are the minimum total costs per month of the machining division and external purchases, given that all the monthly requirements for units of each component must be either manufactured or purchased?

A £53,250
B £56,000
C £64,500
D £67,000

Circle your answer

A   B   C   D

8: COSTS FOR DECISION-MAKING

18 Forte Verty manufactures a single product which it sells for £100 per unit. Budgeted costs are as follows.

Production/sales volume units	Total cost £
25,000	2,600,000
35,000	3,600,000
45,000	4,425,000

(1) Fixed costs increase by £200,000 if output is 35,000 units or more in the period.

(2) Variable costs per unit increase by £10 per unit for each additional produced when output exceeds 42,500 units.

What is or are the breakeven selling points for the product?

A 30,000 units and 40,000 units
B 30,000 units and 41,250 units
C 37,500 units
D 41,250 units

Circle your answer

A   B   C   D

19 Kortinder Slipps Ltd manufactures and sells two products X and Y, and operates at full capacity. Its annual budget is as follows.

	Product X	Product Y
Production and sales	40,000 units	60,000 units
Total cost per unit	£20	£15
Sales price per unit	£25	£18
Machining time per unit (hours)	3	2

Fixed costs are budgeted at £720,000 for the year and are absorbed into product costs on a machine hour basis. Saleem Iddon, the chief executive, wishes to reconsider the sales price of X. He believes that increasing the sales price of product X will reduce demand as follows:

Price of X	Sales demand
£26	37,000 units
£27	34,000 units
£28	31,000 units

At output and sales of less than 35,000 units of X, fixed costs will fall to £705,000.

Which price for product X will maximise the company's profits per period?

A £25
B £26
C £27
D £28

Circle your answer

A   B   C   D

8: COSTS FOR DECISION-MAKING

20 Steeple Chairs Ltd manufactures a range of components and products. Budgeted data for three of these are shown below.

	Product PQ	Product RS	Component Z
	£	£	£
Variable cost	15	32	21
Fixed overhead	8	9	10
	23	41	31
Production requirement	-	-	7,000 units
Machine hours per unit	3	6	4
Sales budget	5,000 units	4,000 units	-
Sales price per unit	£24	£44	

All three items are made on the same type of machine, for which production capacity is 40,000 hours for the budget period.

Component Z can be purchased from an external supplier for £30 per unit. The 7,000 units of Z must be either produced or purchased externally.

What is the profit-maximising production budget?

	Product PQ	Product RS	Component Z
A	None	2,000 units	7,000 units
B	None	4,000 units	4,000 units
C	5,000 units	4,000 units	250 units
D	5,000 units	None	6,250 units

Circle your answer

A   B   C   D

21 Homard Vantage Ltd manufactures four components, W, X, Y and Z, using the same machines for each. Unit production costs, for components produced in-house, are as follows.

	W	X	Y	Z
	£	£	£	£
Direct materials	5	2	6	3
Direct labour	15	6	9	8
Variable overhead	8	6	9	4
Production overhead	16	12	18	8
	44	26	42	23
Budgeted production requirements (units)	4,500	6,000	4,000	9,000

Variable overheads are incurred at the rate of £2 per machine hour. Direct labour is a fixed cost, and the unit costs above represent an apportionment of this cost.

Only 54,000 hours of machine time will be available during the year, and a sub-contractor who has short term excess capacity has quoted the following unit prices for supplying components in the next budget period.

    W £41
    X £23
    Y £42
    Z £20

152

8: COSTS FOR DECISION-MAKING

Which component should be purchased externally so as to minimise total costs in the budget period?

A   Component W
B   Component X
C   Component Y
D   Component Z

Circle your answer

A   B   C   D

Data for questions 22 - 23

Ken Dough Ltd is considering whether to purchase a new machine to make product Z. The machine would cost £100,000, and have a 4 year life and no scrap value at the end of this time. 5,000 units of sales are expected in each of years 1 and 4 of the project and 60,000 units of sales are expected in each of years 2 and 3. Unit costs are as follows.

	Sales of 50,000 units pa £	Sales of 60,000 units pa £
Direct materials	0.5	0.5
Direct labour	0.5	0.5
Overheads	1.4	1.2
	2.4	2.2
Sales price	3.0	3.0
Profit	0.6	0.8

All overheads are cash expenditure items, with the exception of depreciation of £25,000 pa and allocated general fixed overheads of £5,000 pa. The company's cost of capital is 20% pa.

	Discount factor at 20%
Year 1	0.833
Year 2	0.694
Year 3	0.579
Year 4	0.482

22 Assuming even cash flows throughout each year, what is the payback period for the machine, in years, to one decimal place?

A   1.0 years
B   1.5 years
C   2.5 years
D   3.3 years

Circle your answer

A   B   C   D

153

8: COSTS FOR DECISION-MAKING

23 What is the NPV of the project, to the nearest £1,000?

A £1,000
B £31,000
C £65,000
D £78,000

Circle your answer

A   B   C   D

Data for questions 24 - 25

Marta Door Ltd is considering a proposed project involving the purchase of a new machine, that would cost £30,000. Estimated profits and losses are as follows.

Year	Profit/(loss) £
1	(3,000)
2	15,000
3	20,000
4	20,000
5	10,000

These figures allow for a straight-line depreciation charge based on the assumption that the machine will be disposed of for £5,000 in 5 years' time, at the end of the project.

Discount factors at 10%: Year 1 0.909; Year 2 0.826; Year 3 0.751; Year 4 0.683; Year 5 0.621

24 What is the payback period for the project in years to 1 decimal place, assuming even cash flows throughout each year?

A 2.1 years
B 2.3 years
C 2.7 years
D 2.9 years

Circle your answer

A   B   C   D

25 What is the net present value of the project, to the nearest £1,000, if Marta Door's cost of capital is 10%?

A £18,000
B £34,000
C £37,000
D £45,000

Circle your answer

A   B   C   D

CHAPTER 9

JOINT PRODUCTS AND BY-PRODUCTS

> This chapter covers the following topics:
>
> - Definitions
> - Costing for by-products
> - Costing for joint products
> - Decision problems with joint products and by products

1. Definitions

1.1 In some processes, two or more products are produced as output from the same process. When this happens, there are joint products and/or by products.

1.2 *Joint products* are two or more products that are separated in the course of processing. Each has sufficient sales value to merit recognition as a main product.

1.3 A *by-product* is a product that emerges in the course of processing and that can be sold (perhaps after some further processing or packaging operation). However, it has a low net realisable value in comparison with the sales value of the main product or products.

1.4 In costing for joint products and by-products, we are dealing with process costing techniques. In addition, there are *joint costs* of processing, which must be apportioned between the products that are produced.

2. Costing for by-products

2.1 Because it has such a small sales value relative to the main product(s), a by-product is not charged with any of the joint processing costs.

There are two alternative ways for dealing with by-products in cost accounts. In each case, we take the sales value of the by-product that has been produced, minus any further processing costs needed to get it ready for sale (ie net sales value).

Method 1	Method 2
• Deduct the net sales value from the process costs, thus reducing the (net) costs of the main products.	• Credit the net sales value of the by-product to the P & L account, as extra revenue.
In double entry terms, we are crediting the process account with the net sales value of the by-product.	By this method, the process account is unaffected by the by-product's sales value.

3. Costing for joint products

3.1 Joint products are given a share of the joint processing costs. The appropriate share of cost for each joint product depends on the method of apportionment used. There are two main stages in costing for joint products.

3.2 *Stage 1.* Establish the joint costs of the finished output of all the joint products together, as a total cost. This could involve process costing techniques, with equivalent units of output (and costs) being attributed to finished output, unfinished closing stocks and abnormal loss/gain.

3.3 *Stage 2.* Apportion the total costs of finished output (established in Stage 1) between the joint products, with the basis of apportionment being one of the following.

- *Physical units produced.* Units of each joint product need to be comparable, eg all in kilos of weight or all in litres etc.

- *Sales value at the point of separation.* After the process where the joint products emerge, the products might have a sales value. Costs can then be apportioned on the basis of their relative sales value at this 'split-off' point.

- *Sales value less further processing costs after separation.* Where joint products need further individual processing to get them into a condition for sale, and do not have a market value at the point of separation, joint costs can be apportioned on the basis of the relative final sales value of the joint products produced, minus their further processing costs after the point of separation.

- *Weighted physical units.* Units of each joint product can be given a weighting, perhaps to make solid products comparable with liquids or gases. Apportionment of joint costs is then on the relative weighted units output of each product.

4. Decision problems with joint products and by-products

4.1 As with any decision problems, decisions affecting joint products or by-products should consider only relevant costs and benefits.

There are three fairly common types of decision involving joint products.

9: JOINT PRODUCTS AND BY-PRODUCTS

- The *further processing decision*

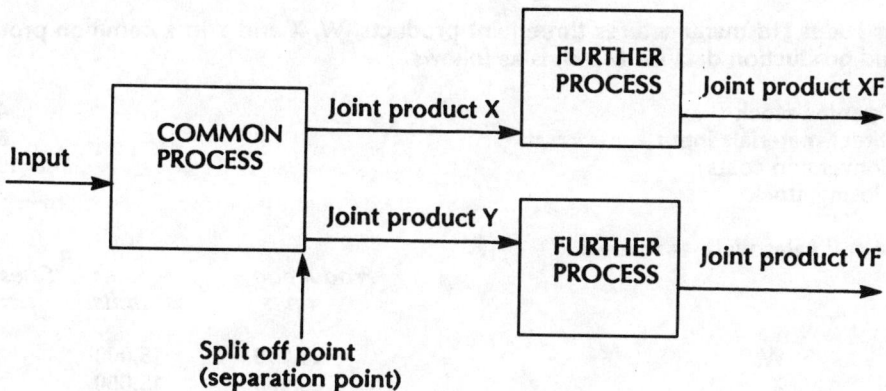

Should a joint product be sold at the split off point, or further processed before selling? The relevant items are (1) the additional sales revenue from further processing and (2) the incremental costs of further processing.

- The *additional processing decision*. How much extra would it cost to produce a given extra quantity of one joint product? Marginal costing principles generally apply. It is important to recognise that joint products/by-products are usually output in fixed proportions, so that making more of a joint product involves making (at least up to split-off point) extra quantities of other joint products/by-products.

- The *sales price decision*. A selling price to be measured might be a price based on full cost plus a fixed profit margin, or a minimum price based on relevant costs.

9: JOINT PRODUCTS AND BY-PRODUCTS

QUESTIONS

1 Rhodes Hides Ltd manufactures three joint products, W, X and Y in a common process. The cost and production data for March is as follows.

	£
Opening stock	40,000
Direct materials input	80,000
Conversion costs	100,000
Closing stock	20,000

Output and sales were as follows.

	Production units	Sales units	Sales price per unit £
W	20,000	15,000	4
X	20,000	15,000	6
Y	40,000	50,000	3

If costs are apportioned between joint products on a market value basis, what was the cost per unit of product X in March?

A £2.50
B £3.00
C £3.75
D £4.00

Circle your answer

A   B   C   D

2 Sieff Herry Ltd manufactures three joint products and one by-product from a single process. Data for May are as follows.

Opening and closing stocks	Nil
Raw materials input	£90,000
Conversion costs	£70,000

		Units	Sales price £
Output	Joint product J	2,500	36
	Joint product K	3,500	40
	Joint product L	2,000	35
	By-product M	4,000	1

By-product sales revenue is credited to the process account. Joint costs are apportioned on a physical units basis.

What were the full production costs of product K in May?

A £68,250
B £70,000
C £71,750
D £72,800

Circle your answer

A   B   C   D

9: JOINT PRODUCTS AND BY PRODUCTS

3 Ellie Copters Ltd manufactures three joint products, JP1, JP2, and JP3 and a by-product BP, all in a single process. Results for July were as follows.

Opening and closing stocks	Nil
Input raw materials	10,000 kg, cost £24,000
Conversion costs	£28,000
Output	4,000 kg of JP1, sales value £11 per kg
	3,000 kg of JP2, sales value £10 per kg
	1,000 kg of JP3, sales value £26 per kg
	2,000 kg of BP, sales value £1 per kg

By-product revenue is credited to the sales account. Process costs are apportioned on a sales value basis.

What was the cost per kilogram of JP1 in July?

A £5.20
B £5.50
C £5.61
D £5.72

Circle your answer

A B C D

Data for questions 4 - 6

Orson Cart Ltd manufactures two products XX and YY, as follows.

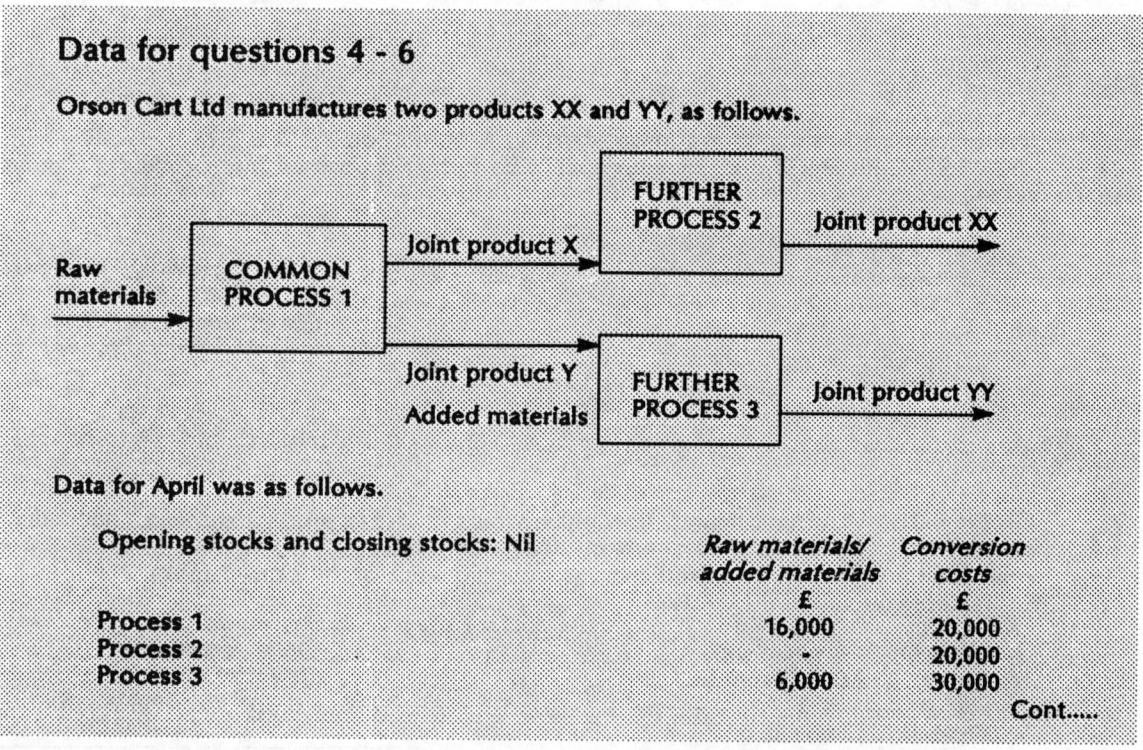

Data for April was as follows.

Opening stocks and closing stocks: Nil

	Raw materials/ added materials £	Conversion costs £
Process 1	16,000	20,000
Process 2	-	20,000
Process 3	6,000	30,000

Cont.....

9: JOINT PRODUCTS AND BY-PRODUCTS

> 25% of conversion costs in each of the three processes are variable costs, with the remainder being fixed costs. If either process 2 or process 3 were shut down, two-thirds of fixed costs would be saved.
>
> Product XX sells for £14 per unit and product YY sells for £12.5 per unit. Product X and product Y have a market value (at the split-off point) of £8 and £4 respectively.
>
> In April, 3,750 units of joint product X and 4,500 units of joint product Y were produced. After further processing, because of normal process losses, only 3,000 units of XX and 4,000 units of YY were completed.

4 What was the full production cost per unit of Product YY in April, if joint processing costs are apportioned on the basis of sales value at the split-off point?

A £10.875
B £11.7
C £12.375
D £12.6

Circle your answer

A   B   C   D

5 If the company wishes to maximise short term profits, on the basis of the April figures, should joint product X and joint product Y be further processed into product XX and YY respectively?

	Further process X into XX?	Further process Y into YY?
A	No	Yes
B	Yes	No
C	No	No
D	Yes	Yes

Circle your answer

A   B   C   D

6 On the basis of the April figures, how much would it cost to produce an *extra* 1,000 units of product YY, if the extra units of any product X or product XX that are made could not be sold? (Assume no change in fixed costs as a consequence of the extra output.)

A £11,500
B £8,625
C £6,975
D £6,500

Circle your answer

A   B   C   D

9: JOINT PRODUCTS AND BY-PRODUCTS

Data for questions 7 - 8

Dibble Decker Ltd operates a plant which works continuously, processing raw material M to produce joint products X, Y and Z. 20% of the input material by weight is lost in processing. Of the output, 50% by weight consists of X, 20% is Y and 30% is Z, in fixed proportions.

Cost data for January (actual costs = budgeted costs):

Opening and closing work in process	Nil
Raw materials input	30,000 kg, cost £60,000
Direct labour (2,000 hrs)	£8,000

Production overhead, which includes £1 per direct labour hour for variable overhead, is absorbed at the rate of £5 per direct labour hour.
A profit margin of 20% added to full production cost.

Joint costs are apportioned on a physical units basis. The plant has some spare capacity, and only enough output is produced to meet known sales demand.

7 What is the selling price per kilogram of joint product X?

A £3.12
B £3.25
C £3.90
D £4.00

Circle your answer

A   B   C   D

8 Suppose that a new customer asks for a special delivery of 3,000 kilograms of joint product X, but does not want to purchase any Y or Z. What is the *minimum* price that Dibble Decker Ltd would need to charge (so as to leave profits unchanged as a result of making and selling the extra quantities of X)?

A £700
B £840
C £1,400
D £1,750

Circle your answer

A   B   C   D

161

9: JOINT PRODUCTS AND BY-PRODUCTS

9 Will Klampps Ltd manufactures joint products S and T in a joint process. Data for February are as follows.

Opening stock	1,000 units, 60% complete: cost £8,400
Added materials	5,000 units, cost £31,800
Conversion costs	£20,000
Closing stock	2,000 units, 30% complete
Transfer to finished goods	S 1,800 units:
	T 1,200 units:
Sales prices:	Product S £30 per unit: Product T £15 per unit.

Normal loss, which is 10% of input in a period, is not costed. Abnormal loss, which is written off to the P & L account, is assumed to occur at the end of the process.

Process costs are apportioned between products on a sales revenue basis. Stock is valued on a FIFO basis.

What is the cost per unit in February of product T?

A £8.75
B £9.15
C £9.25
D £14.80

Circle your answer

A B C D

10 Pardell Steamers Ltd produces two joint products L and M and a by-product N in a joint process. Product L is then further processed to manufacture product LA and a waste material Z.

The budget for the next period has been drafted, as follows.

Joint process costs		Production and sales			
Variable	£6,000	L	400 units:	sales value at split-off point, per unit	£12.5
Fixed	£5,000	M	500 units:	sales price per unit	£30
		N	100 units:	sales price per unit	
Further process costs, excluding disposal cost of Z		LA	200 units:	sales price per unit	£160
		Z	200 units:	disposal cost per unit	£10
Variable	£12,000				
Fixed	£10,000				

Rowan Bote, the company's chief executive, believes that it would be possible to produce and sell an extra 50 units of product LA in the period at the budgeted sales price of £160 without any increase in fixed costs. The extra by-product N could be sold at its budgeted price although to sell any extra quantities of product M, the sales price would need to be reduced to £25 *for all units* of M produced in the period. Any unsold quantities of M must be disposed of at a cost of £4 per unit.

9: JOINT PRODUCTS AND BY-PRODUCTS

If all sales and distribution costs are fixed, by how much could the company's profits be increased if the extra 50 units of LA are made and sold in the period?

A £3,175
B £3,675
C £4,175
D £4,925

Circle your answer

A   B   C   D

11 Harrop Lane Ltd manufactures two products by passing materials through two consecutive processes. Results for June were as follows.

Process 1   Input materials at £1.5 per kilo: £9,000
Conversion costs: £5,850
Output to Process 2: 5,500 kilos
Defective production (scrapped on completion): 500 kilos

Process 2   Conversion costs: £14,675
Output: Joint Product X: 2,500 kilos, sales price £16 per kilo
Joint Product Y: 2,500 kilos, sales price £8 per kilo
By product Z: 500 kilos, sales price £2 per kilo

There were no opening or closing stocks in either process. Normal loss is 10% in Process 1 and nil in Process 2. Joint product costs are apportioned on a sales value basis. By-product income is credited to the process account. All output of Z was sold in June.

Taking profit as the difference between sales and full production costs, what was the profit per kilo of Joint Product X in June, to two decimal places?

A £8.05
B £8.32
C £8.39
D £8.72

Circle your answer

A   B   C   D

CHAPTER 10

RATIOS AND PERFORMANCE MEASUREMENT

> This chapter covers the following topics:
> - Comparing costs
> - Output, capacity and efficiency ratios
> - Marginal costing ratios
> - Working capital ratios

1. Comparing costs

1.1 Ratios can be used to measure the performance of a company, a department, a group or an individual. Actual performance ratios are compared with

- ratios achieved in previous months or years
- a target or standard
- ratios achieved by other individuals, groups, departments or companies.

1.2 Ratios of performance measurement vary widely, but include

- return on capital employed
- profit/sales ratio
- costs per activity unit or item (eg cost per employee, cost per tonne/mile)
- turnover per activity unit or item (eg sales turnover per employee)

2. Output, capacity and efficiency ratios

2.1 Employee efficiency can be measured by a *productivity index*, with changes in the index showing changes in employee efficiency over time.

2.2 Efficiency, capacity and output ratios might also be used within a budgeting/standard costing system.

10: RATIOS AND PERFORMANCE MEASUREMENT

```
                    ┌─────────────────────────┐
                    │ Production volume ratio │
                    └─────────────────────────┘
                    Standard hours of output achieved
                    Budgeted standard hours of output
```

Efficiency ratio	Capacity usage ratio
$= \dfrac{\text{Standard hours of output achieved}}{\text{Actual hours taken/worked}}$	$= \dfrac{\text{Actual hours worked}}{\text{Budgeted hours of output}}$

2.3 Idle capacity or non-productive capacity might also be measured (as a percentage in each case) as follows.

- *Idle capacity ratio* = $\dfrac{\text{Practical capacity minus budgeted output (both in standard hours)}}{\text{Practical capacity (in standard hours)}}$

- *Diverted hours ratio* = $\dfrac{\text{Hours that direct workers are diverted from direct labour work}}{\text{Available hours of direct workers}}$

3. Marginal costing ratios

3.1 Marginal costing was the subject of an earlier chapter, but you must be able to apply marginal costing techniques in use of the contribution/sales ratio (C/S ratio) and the net profit/sales ratio.

4. Working capital ratios

4.1 Working capital ratios (stock turnover, average debtors' payment period, average credit period taken from suppliers, current ratio etc) are probably familiar to you already. In cost accounting, they might be used for

- cash budgeting/funds flow forecasting
- monitoring cash flows and exercising control over cash flows.

10: RATIOS AND PERFORMANCE MEASUREMENT

QUESTIONS

1 What is the name given to a unit or a function of an organisation that is headed by a manager who has direct responsibility for its performance?

  A Responsibility centre
  B Cost unit
  C Business entity
  D Budget centre

Circle your answer

A   B   C   D

2 Gordon Bench Ltd measures the performance of its raw materials stores departments by means of two indicators.

	Indicator	*Method of calculation*
(1)	Operating efficiency %	Holding costs/value of issues
(2)	Activity efficiency %	Average stock value/sales turnover

Data for stores departments 1 and 2 in the years 19X1 and 19X2 are as follows.

	Department 1		Department 2	
	19X1	*19X2*	*19X1*	*19X2*
	£000	£000	£000	£000
Average stock value	525	525	406	488
Value of issues in the year	2,700	2,845	999	1,008
Holding costs	146	142	58	67
Sales turnover	8,100	8,800	5,800	6,090

In comparing departmental performance between the current year (19X2) and the previous year (19X1) which one of the following analyses is correct?

		Operating efficiency	*Activity efficiency*
A	Department 1:	Improved	Improved
	Department 2:	Worsened	Worsened
B	Department 1:	Improved	Worsened
	Department 2:	Worsened	Improved
C	Department 1:	Worsened	Improved
	Department 2:	Improved	Worsened
D	Department 1:	Worsened	Worsened
	Department 2:	Improved	Improved

Circle your answer

A   B   C   D

10: RATIOS AND PERFORMANCE MEASUREMENT

3 The management of Mowin and Growin Garden Stores have been comparing the operating costs of the store in the year just ended (19X2) with those in the previous year (19X1). Operating costs had risen from £240,000 to £280,000 per year, possibly due to the increase in shelf space, which at 4,400 cubic feet in 19X2 was 10% higher than in the previous year. However, sales turnover rose from £5 million in 19X1 to £6 million in 19X2, and the management were pleased with the fall in the ratio of operating costs to sales turnover.

What were the contributory factors to the reduction in this ratio?

A A faster shelf turnover rate and lower costs per cubic foot of shelf space

B A faster shelf turnover rate and higher costs per cubic foot of shelf space

C A slower shelf turnover rate and lower costs per cubic foot of shelf space

D A slower shelf turnover rate and higher costs per cubic foot of shelf space

Circle your answer

A   B   C   D

4 Flice Prey Ltd manufactures and sells a single product, product T, for which the following data applied last year.

Sales price per unit of T	£20
C/S ratio	60%
Direct labour cost (a variable cost)	2 hrs x £3 per hour

Negotiations are taking place with the work force about an improvement in productivity that would alter the productivity index of the work force from 100 to 120 next year. It has been agreed that the increase in unit profitability arising from this change should be divided equally between the company (as profits) and the work force (in the form of a higher hourly rate of pay). Given no change in other costs, and the same budgeted output and sales as last year, what would the new hourly rate be if the productivity agreement is made?

A £3.15
B £3.18
C £3.25
D £3.30

Circle your answer

A   B   C   D

10: RATIOS AND PERFORMANCE MEASUREMENT

5 Lorn Mower Ltd uses an absorption costing system, with fixed production overheads being absorbed into product costs on a direct labour hour basis. In the year just ended, the amount of under-absorbed overhead was $37\frac{1}{2}$% of the amount of overhead actually absorbed.

The reasons for this were that actual fixed overhead spending exceeded budget by 10% and the budgeted absorption rate of £8 per direct labour hour was also too low in view of the fact that actual direct labour hours worked were 20% below the budget of 200,000 hours.

What was the amount of absorbed fixed overhead in the year?

A £1,280,000
B £1,420,000
C £1,760,000
D £2,240,000

Circle your answer

A   B   C   D

6 Paddy Linpool Ltd manufactures three products, X, Y and Z. Production and sales data for the year just ended were as follows.

	X	Y	Y
Budgeted production (units)	3,000	2,000	5,000
Budgeted sales (units)	2,000	3,000	4,000
Standard direct labour hours per unit	6	4	2
Actual production (units)	4,000	2,000	6,000
Actual sales (units)	3,000	2,000	8,000

The direct labour force were paid for 45,000 hours, and were engaged on direct production work for 42,000 of these.

What was the efficiency ratio for the year as a percentage, to one decimal place?

A 95.5%
B 97.8%
C 104.8%
D 122.2%

Circle your answer

A   B   C   D

Data for questions 7 - 9

Walter Lilley Ltd uses a standard costing system, and its budgeted and actual production data for the year that has just ended are as follows.

Product	Budgeted production		Actual production
	Units	Standard machine hours	Units
W	15,000	3,000	12,000
X	20,000	8,000	25,000
Y	14,000	7,000	16,000
Z	6,000	9,000	5,000

Total machine hours worked in the period amounted to 29,000 hours.

10: RATIOS AND PERFORMANCE MEASUREMENT

7 What was the capacity usage ratio in the year, as a percentage to one decimal place?

A 87.3%
B 93.1%
C 103.3%
D 107.4%

Circle your answer

A   B   C   D

8 What was the production volume (activity) ratio in the year, as a percentage to one decimal place?

A 93.1%
B 96.8%
C 103.3%
D 107.4%

Circle your answer

A   B   C   D

9 What was the efficiency ratio in the year, as a percentage to one decimal place?

A 96.2%
B 96.8%
C 103.3%
D 103.9%

Circle your answer

A   B   C   D

Data for questions 10 - 11

Jos Pipe Ltd produces garden furniture. The available hours of its direct labour workforce in August were as follows.

	Hours
Contractual hours	1,470
Annual holidays	(280)
Absence though sickness	(35)
Available hours	1,155

During the period, the direct labour force spent 325 hours cleaning and repairing machines, leaving 830 hours for working on furniture production.

Production in August was as follows.

Opening work in progress	Nil
Finished output	1,000 standard hours
Closing work in progress	50 standard hours

169

10: RATIOS AND PERFORMANCE MEASUREMENT

10 What was the efficiency ratio of the workforce in August, as a percentage to one decimal place?

    A   71.4%
    B   90.9%
    C   120.5%
    D   126.5%

Circle your answer

A   B   C   D

11 What was the diverted hours ratio in August, as a percentage to one decimal place?

    A   28.1%
    B   30.5%
    C   39.2%
    D   43.5%

Circle your answer

A   B   C   D

Data for questions 12 - 13

The production plant of Rhoda Dendrons Ltd, a manufacturing company, has a practical capacity of 120,000 standard hours of output per year. For the year just ended, the following data is available.

Budgeted capacity (hours)	100,000
Efficiency performance expected	90%
Budgeted standard hours	90,000
Standard hours actually produced	80,000
Actual direct labour hours worked	84,000

12 For the year just ended, what was the production volume ratio, as a percentage to one decimal place?

    A   80.0%
    B   88.9%
    C   93.3%
    D   95.2%

Circle your answer

A   B   C   D

10: RATIOS AND PERFORMANCE MEASUREMENT

13 For the year just ended, what was the idle capacity ratio?

A   6.7%
B   10.0%
C   16.0%
D   25.0%

Circle your answer

A   B   C   D

14 Barbara Kew Ltd uses an absorption costing system, and its results in the year that has just ended have been summarised as follows.

Actual direct labour cost (all variable costs)	£400,000
Direct labour cost	20% of sales
Direct materials cost	25% of sales
Fixed production overhead absorption rate	150% of direct labour
Other overhead costs (all fixed)	15% of budgeted sales
Actual production and sales	125% of budgeted production and sales

What was the actual profit in the year, if there were no opening or closing stocks of finished goods or work in progress, and if actual fixed production overhead expenditure was as budgeted?

A   £200,000
B   £260,000
C   £380,000
D   £475,000

Circle your answer

A   B   C   D

15 In the year just ended, Will Barrow Ltd budgeted to achieve a net profit equal to 15% of sales and a C/S ratio of 35%. Budgeted sales were 10% higher than actual sales of £3,000,000 but in all other respects, actual results were as budgeted.

What was the actual profit for the year using marginal costing principles?

A   £390,000
B   £450,000
C   £495,000
D   £555,000

Circle your answer

A   B   C   D

16 Rose Ltd and Ivy Ltd each manufacture and sell a single product. Rose Ltd achieves a C/S ratio of 60% for its product (product X) and Ivy Ltd achieves a C/S ratio of 80% for its product (product Y). Their profits, measured by marginal costing techniques, would be exactly the same at an output and sales level of 150,000 units of product each per year. Rose Ltd has fixed costs that are twice as high as those of Ivy Ltd. Ivy Ltd's fixed costs are £120,000 per year. Product X has a selling price that is twice as high as the price of Product Y.

10: RATIOS AND PERFORMANCE MEASUREMENT

What is the selling price of product X?

A £2
B £3
C £4
D £5

Circle your answer

A   B   C   D

17 Grove Edge Ltd is a company that manufactures a single product. Ron Urbean, the cost accountant, has estimated that the margin of safety in the company's budget next year is 20%, measured as a percentage of budgeted sales. The company's contribution/sales ratio is 25%, the unit variable cost of sales is £6 per unit, and budgeted sales are 100,000 units for the year.

What are the budgeted fixed costs for the year?

A £120,000
B £160,000
C £240,000
D £320,000

Circle your answer

A   B   C   D

18 The following budgeted data relates to Compass Teape Ltd, a manufacturing company.

	£	£
Sales		1,200,000
Cost of sales		
Direct materials	360,000	
Direct labour	300,000	
Overheads (including depreciation £60,000)	240,000	
		900,000
Profit		300,000

The company's stock turnover in direct materials is 6 times per year, and its debtors' turnover is 4 times per year. The company takes 1½ months' credit from suppliers of 1 month's direct materials and an average of 1 month's credit for all overhead cost items (with the exception of depreciation). Accrued direct wages at the year end will be ½ month's direct labour costs. All sales and costs arise at an even rate throughout the year.

At the beginning of the year, the company expects to have the following items in its balance sheet: stocks £32,000, debtors £225,000, cash £20,000, direct materials creditors £46,000, accrued direct wages £10,000 and other creditors £12,000.

Required

Ignoring any other cash inflows and outflows in the year, by how much will the company's cash holdings be expected to increase by the end of the year?

10: RATIOS AND PERFORMANCE MEASUREMENT

A £201,500
B £261,500
C £266,500
D £281,500

Circle your answer

A   B   C   D

19 A company's management is concerned about its large bank overdraft, which it wishes to reduce over the budget period of one year. Which one of the four items below will not necessarily result in a lower bank overdraft?

A Reducing bad debts

B Taking longer credit from suppliers, without any loss of discounts

C Reducing wastage and loss through damage of regularly-used stock items

D Reducing unit costs of production

Circle your answer

A   B   C   D

SECTION 2

MARKING SCHEDULES
AND COMMENTS

1: MATERIALS AND LABOUR COSTS. COST CLASSIFICATION

1: MARKING SCHEDULE

Question	Correct answer	Marks for the correct answer	Question	Correct answer	Marks for the correct answer
1	A	1	15	B	1
2	C	1	16	A	1
3	C	1	17	C	1
4	B	1	18	C	1
5	D	1	19	C	1
6	B	1	20	A	1
7	D	2	21	C	1
8	A	2	22	C	1
9	A	1	23	D	1
10	A	1	24	D	1
11	B	1	25	D	2
12	D	1	26	D	1
13	A	1	27	D	1
14	A	1			

YOUR MARKS

Total marks available **30** Your total mark ☐

GUIDELINES - If your mark was:

0 - 9 You are struggling on these basic costing topics. Study this subject area again.

10 - 15 Quite good. There might be one or two important gaps in your knowledge to sort out, though.

16 - 24 Good. Check your errors carefully, to make sure that you can see what you did wrong.

25 - 30 Excellent mark. Well done.

COMMENTS

Question

1-2

The unit price of parts received was

3 August	£3.00
7 August	£3.30
11 August	£4.00
24 August	£3.50

Value of parts issued, using FIFO

		£	£
16 August	1,000 at £2.80 each (o/stock)	2,800	
	2,000 at £3 each	6,000	
	1,000 at £3.30 each	3,300	
			12,100
30 August	2,000 at £3.30 each	6,600	
	2,000 at £4 each	8,000	
	1,000 at £3.50 each	3,500	
			18,100
Total value of parts issued			30,200

Value of parts issued, using LIFO

		£	£
16 August	2,000 at £4	8,000	
	2,000 at £3.30	6,600	
			14,600
30 August	3,000 at £3.50	10,500	
	1,000 at £3.30	3,300	
	1,000 at £3	3,000	
			16,800
Total value of parts issued			31,400

3

The main problem here is whether the cost of the units of commodity X is taken before or after the discounts. (1) The bulk purchase discount *should* be deducted, to arrive at a net purchase price of £(5,000 - 250) = £4,750, or £19 per unit. (2) The discount for early payment is a financial transaction, which will be recorded as 'discounts received' (£150) in the P&L account. This discount will therefore *not* be used to reduce the purchase price of the stocks, and is not a trading account item.

	£
Cost of sales	
50 units (opening stock)	900
150 units x £19	2,850
	3,750
Sales value	6,600
Gross profit	2,850

1: MATERIALS AND LABOUR COSTS. COST CLASSIFICATION

Question

4-5

A new weighted average price is calculated every time there are receipts into stock.

		Units	Price per unit £	Value £
1 June	Opening stock	100	5.00	500
3 June	Receipts	300	4.80	1,440
		400	4.85 ◄------	1,940
5 June	Issues	220	4.85	1,067
		180		873
12 June	Receipts	170	5.2	884
		350	5.02 ◄------	1,757
24 June	Issues	300	5.02	1,506
30 June	Closing stock	50	5.02	251

6

Use of the last in, first out stock valuation method results in closing stocks being valued at the oldest prices. Since prices are rising, the oldest prices will be the lowest prices. Next in, first out uses the next price to be paid for materials, which in this case is likely to be the highest price of all, for both materials issued and for closing stock valuations.

7

	£
Sales (1,250 x £4)	5,000
Gross profit	2,500
Material cost of sales	2,500

Cost of units sold:	£
1st 400 units (x £1.80)	720
Next 600 units (x £2.10)	1,260
	1,980
Total cost of 1,250 units sold	2,500
Balance: cost of last 250 units sold	520

Cost per unit (£520 ÷ 250) = £2.08

8

Cost of sales

Date	LIFO Units sold	LIFO Unit cost £	LIFO Total cost £	FIFO Units sold	FIFO Unit cost £	FIFO Total cost £
12 May	600	32	19,200	300	30	9,000
	100	30	3,000	400	32	12,800
c/f	700		22,200	700		21,800

COMMENTS

Question

8

Date	Units sold	LIFO Unit cost £	Total cost £	Units sold	FIFO Unit cost £	Total cost £
b/f	700		22,200	700		21,800
29 May	200	35	7,000	200	32	6,400
	200	34	6,800	200	34	6,800
	400		13,800	400		13,200
Total cost of sales			36,000			35,000

The cost of sales is lower with FIFO, and so profit must be £1,000 higher.

9

With LIFO, if newer stocks cost more to buy from suppliers than older stocks, the costs of materials issued and used will be higher. It follows that the cost of sales will be higher and the profit lower.

Closing stocks with LIFO will be priced at the purchase price of earlier items that were received into stock. In a period of rising prices, this means that closing stocks will be valued at old, out-of-date and low prices.

10

Stock item		Quanity units	Lower of cost and NRV £	Value £
206		30		
	plus issues	20		
		50	12	600
357		70		
	minus receipts	40		
		30	6	180
429		50	8	400
				1,180

11

Stock control is 'the systematic regulation of stock levels with respect to quantity, cost and lead time' (CIMA Official Terminology). Items A, C and D are all aspects of this. The protection of stocks against fire, theft and damage is an aspect of storekeeping, rather than stock control.

1: MATERIALS AND LABOUR COSTS. COST CLASSIFICATION

Question

12 An excess in the quantity delivered or ordered could explain an excessive level of the item in stock. Similarly, a reduction in the usage rate, without any change in the re-order level, could result in excessive stocks when a new supply order is delivered. A *reduction* in the lead time, with new supplies arriving sooner than expected, could also explain a high stock level, but a longer lead time (item D) would have the effect of reducing stock levels below their minimum 'safe' level, rather than increasing them.

13 Economic order quantity

$$= \sqrt{\frac{2cd}{h}}$$

$$= \sqrt{\frac{2 \times 400 \times (250 \times 48)}{10\% \text{ of } £20}}$$

$$= \sqrt{4,800,000}$$

$$= 2,191 \text{ units}$$

14 Continuous stocktaking is defined in the question. Perpetual inventory is a stock recording system whereby each movement in or out of stock is recorded as it occurs, and so stock records for *every* item are always up-to-date. ABC inventory analysis is a stock control system which categorises stock items into three categories, according to the proportion and value of total stock usage of the item. The stock items in category A which represent the largest proportion of stock usage by value (but the smallest number of items) merit the greatest amount of stock control effort. Low-value or small-usage items in Category C merit the least amount of stock control.

15 £25,185 + £5,440 = £30,625. The only direct costs are the wages paid to direct workers for ordinary time, plus the basic pay for overtime. Overtime premium and shift allowances are usually treated as overheads. However, if and when overtime and shiftwork are incurred specifically for a particular cost unit, they are classified as direct costs of that cost unit. Sick pay is treated as an overhead and is therefore classified as an indirect cost.

16

	£	£
Cost of normal hours actively worked		
(38 hours - 10 hours + 8 hours) x £5		180
Group bonus		12
Direct cost		192
Idle time: 10 hours x £5	50	
Overtime premium: 8 hours x £2.5	20	
Indirect cost		70
Total cost		262

COMMENTS

Question

If the overtime had been worked for a specific job, the overtime premium could have been charged as a direct cost to the job. However, there is no indication in the question that this situation arises here, and so the indirect cost of Grant's labour is £70 rather than £20. The group bonus will have been earned because the work group has achieved a certain output/productivity target, and so the cost of the bonus will be included in direct labour costs.

17

	Units		Time hrs	Rate	Cost £
Shoe Type A	4,800	(x 24 mins)	1,920	£3.6 per unit	17,280
Shoe Type B	3,000	(x 36 mins)	1,800	£6 per hour	10,800
			3,720		28,080
Non-productive time (20%)			744	£4 per hour	2,976
Total cost					31,056

18

The direct labour cost will include the premium bonus, which is a form of productivity bonus.

Standard time for 340 units (x 2 minutes)	680 minutes
Actual time (8 hours per day)	480 minutes
Time saved	200 minutes

	£
Bonus = 75% x 200 minutes x £6 per hour =	15
Basic pay: 8 hours x £6	48
Total direct labour cost	63

19

Item B describes *costs* of an activity or cost centre. Item A describes *cost units*. Item D describes *budget centres*. A cost centre is defined in the CIMA Official Terminology as 'a location, function or items of equipment in respect of which costs may be ascertained and related to cost units for control purposes'.

20

The costs of the computer department as a whole will be analysed and attributed first of all to cost centres. In this situation, the cost centres will be (1) software development, (2) data preparation and (3) mainframe operations. Item B is a job cost. Item C is the cost of a cost unit. Item D is a cost of the department as a whole, which will be apportioned between the three cost centres.

21

A cost per cost unit can be ascertained for each cost centre's activities. In this situation, the cost unit costs that will be established are (1) cost per hour of development work in the software development section, (2) cost per key depression (or per thousand key depressions) in data preparation and (3) cost per hour of mainframe operations.

Question

22

	Software development	Data preparation	Mainframe operations
Total budgeted costs	£161,000	£130,000	£178,000
Budgeted activity	14,000 hours	26 million key depressions	4,000 hours
Cost per cost unit	£11.50 per development hour	£0.005 per key depression	£44.50 per mainframe hour

Job 678
   Development work (36 hrs x £11.5)   £
   Development work (36 hrs x £11.5)   414
   Data preparation (120,000 x £0.005)   600
   Mainframe operations (4 x £44.5)   178
   Cost   1,192
Profit mark-up (25%)   298
Charge   1,490

23

The coding system is

    Digits 1 and 2   Location code
    Digits 3 and 4   Function code
    Digits 5, 6 and 7   Type of expense

Thus for (1) Cardiff (2) production and (3) factory depreciation we have

                  12   22   432

24

The accountant is an expense of the Manchester office, and hotel costs will be classified as subsistence costs (rather than travel or entertainment).

Thus for (1) Manchester (2) finance and (3) subsistence we have

                  17   24   512

COMMENTS

Question

25

	Hours	Hours		Cost £
Contractual hours		144	(x 5)	720
Overtime		24	(x 6.25)	150
		168		870
Absences				
Bank holidays	15			
Annual holidays	36			
Certified sickness	14			
Other	22			
		87		
Available hours		81		

Total cost per available hour $\frac{870}{81}$ = £10.74

In this period, Rhonda's availability has been reduced by holidays and sickness etc, and so the total cost of her available time in the month (direct plus indirect cost) is relatively high.

26

The direct cost or variable cost per mile travelled will be

(1) Fuel and oil, because their consumption varies with vehicle usage
(2) Replacement parts, because the question states that they vary with mileage.

Tyre replacements might sometimes be considered as variable with mileage, but the question states that tyres are replaced every 3 months, regardless of mileage. Drivers' wages do not vary with mileage, nor does vehicle depreciation: these are direct costs per *vehicle,* but not direct costs *per mile travelled.*

27

The direct *standing* costs per vehicle per year are the direct costs of keeping a vehicle, even if it isn't used. This means that running cost items (4, 5 and 10) are excluded. Indirect costs are the costs shared by more than one vehicle, and these are rent etc, management salaries, security costs and the wages of the single mechanic (who works on all the vehicles, not just one of them). This leaves the seven items listed in answer D as direct standing costs per vehicle per year. (*Note.* If you were tempted to think of tyre replacement costs as a cost that ought to vary with miles travelled, the question states specifically that this is not the case with this particular company.)

2: MARKING SCHEDULE

Question	Correct answer	Marks for correct answer	Question	Correct answer	Marks for correct answer	Question	Correct answer	Marks for correct answer
1	D	1	12	B	1	23	B	2
2	C	1	13	A	1	24	B	1
3	A	1	14	D	1	25	B	1
4	D	1	15	C	1	26	D	1
5	A	1	16	B	1	27	C	1
6	A	1	17	B	1	28	B	1
7	A	2	18	D	1	29	D	1
8	C	1	19	A	1	30	A	1
9	A	1	20	A	1	31	D	1
10	C	1	21	C	1	32	A	1
11	C	1	22	D	1	33	C	1

YOUR MARKS

Total marks available: 35   Your total mark: ☐

Absorption costing has always been a difficult topic to learn, and several of the questions were quite difficult.

GUIDELINES - If your mark was:

0 - 11 Go back to your study notes on absorption costing, and try to re-learn the subject carefully.

12 - 17 Fair, but you are probably making some mistakes fairly consistently. Can you identify what these are?

18 - 27 Good. You have probably got to grips with the essentials of overhead costing, but there may be a few useful lessons to be learned from your incorrect answers.

28 - 35 An extremely good mark, in view of the difficulty of this topic.

COMMENTS

Question

1 All of the suggested overhead absorption rates could be acceptable. However, a time-based method should be used whenever possible because most items of overhead expenditure tend to increase with time. A direct labour cost percentage is to an extent time based, but if differential wage rates exist this can lead to inequitable overhead absorption. Since Department 1 appears to be primarily for machine work, a machine hour rate should be used.

2 For the same reasons as for question 1, a time-based method should be used. Since Department 1 appears to be labour intensive, a direct labour hour rate is the most appropriate.

3 The overhead absorption rates from questions 1 and 2 are (£27,000 ÷ 45,000 =) £0.6 per machine hour in department 1 and (£18,000 ÷ 25,000 =) £0.72 per direct labour in department 2. The total production cost can be calculated as follows:

	£
Direct material	40.00
Direct labour	
- department 1 4 hours x £5	20.00
- department 2 9 hours x £4	36.00
Overhead	
- department 1 65 machine hours x £0.60	39.00
- department 2 9 labour hours x £0.72	6.48
	141.48

The machine hour in department 2 is not relevant to the calculation, because the overhead absorption is based on labour hours. If you included one machine hour at £60 in your calculation, you would have answered D, which is incorrect.

4 Definitions A, B and D are all taken from the CIMA Official Terminology.

A is the definition of cost allocation, which is part of cost attribution.
B is the definition of cost ascertainment.
Cost apportionment is also part of cost attribution.

2: ABSORPTION COSTING

Question

5

Overhead absorbed = 48,000 x £5.60 =	£268,800
Overhead incurred =	£275,000
Overhead under-absorbed	£6,200

Overhead was under-absorbed because absorbed overhead is less than actual costs incurred.

6

	£
Budgeted absorption rate per hour	
Fixed (£36,000 ÷ 18,000 hrs)	2.0
Variable (£9,000 ÷ 18,000 hrs)	0.5
Total	2.5

	£
Overheads absorbed 20,000 hrs x £2.50 per hr	50,000
Overheads incurred (£39,000 fixed + £12,000 variable)	51,000
Under-absorbed overhead	1,000

7

	Production	Overheads Admin	Sales & dist'n	Total
	£000	£000	£000	£000
Energy and water (6:3:1)	6	3	1	10
Electricity for machines	5			5
Building rental (6:3:1)	54	27	9	90
Building repairs (6:3:1)	6	3	1	10
Machine repairs	8			8
Machinery depreciation	52			52
Security (6:3:1)	18	9	3	30
Carriage outwards			70	70
Indirect production wages	50			50
Salesmen's costs			76	76
General admin		38		38
Advertising			30	30
	199	80	190	469

Notes The costs relating to the building must be apportioned between production, administration and sales. Carriage inwards costs are added to the cost of the materials, and are not an overhead. Carriage outwards is a distribution cost.

Total budgeted production overhead costs = £199,000

8

Budgeted sales and distribution overheads	£190,000
Budgeted sales	£4,000,000

Absorption rate = 4.75% of sales value

COMMENTS

Question

9

	£000
Budgeted full production	
Direct materials	350
Direct labour	171
Carriage inwards	30
Production overheads	<u>199</u>
	750
Budgeted administration overheads	£80,000
Absorption rate for admin overheads (80 ÷ 750) =	10.7% of full production cost

10

When expenditures are as budgeted, but actual and budgeted production activity levels are different, only *fixed* overhead can be under- or over-absorbed.

Under-absorbed overhead = 1,000 hrs x £4 = £4,000

Variable overhead absorbed would be (1,000 x £2.50) £2,500 less than budgeted in the fixed budget, but variable overhead incurred would be £2,500 less as well, leaving neither under- nor over-absorbed variable overheads.

11 Apportionment of service department costs.

	Ratio	
Dept Z	3	42,000 (given)
Dept X	5	70,000
Dept Y	2	<u>28,000</u>
		140,000

Absorption rate, Dept Y:	£
Allocated overheads	44,000
Apportioned service dept costs	<u>28,000</u>
	<u>£72,000</u>
Normal capacity	6,000 hrs
Absorption rate	£12 per machine hour

12

Under-absorbed overhead, Dept Y	6,720
Absorption rate per hour	£12 per hr
Difference between actual hours and normal hours	560 hrs

Under-absorbed overhead, given actual expenditure equal to budget, means actual hours less than normal hours.

Cont...

Question

Normal machine capacity, Dept Y	6,000 hrs
Difference	560 hrs
Actual machine hours	5,440 hrs

13

Department X budgeted and actual overheads	£
Allocated	74,000
Apportioned service dept costs	70,000
	144,000

Absorption rate per hr (given) £7.2

Normal capacity (machine hours)(144,000 ÷ 7.2)   20,000 hrs

	£
Absorbed overheads (21,200 hrs x £7.20)	152,640
Actual overheads	144,000
Over-absorbed overhead	£ 8,640

14 Department Z

	£
Actual overhead expenditure (same as budget, £61,500 + £42,000)	103,500
Under-absorbed overhead	(11,500)
Overhead actually absorbed into production costs	92,000

Actual machine hours	10,000 hrs
Absorption rate per hour	£9.20

Normal capacity = $\dfrac{\text{Budgeted overheads}}{\text{Absorption rate}}$ = $\dfrac{£103,500}{£9.20 \text{ per hr}}$

= 11,250 hrs

15 Statement C would be correct *EXCEPT* that the profit in each year depends partly on opening and closing stock values of finished goods and WIP. Opening stock + Costs of production - Closing stock = Cost of sales. Since unit overhead costs will differ if 'actual' overhead costs are used, rather than pre-determined overhead absorption rates, opening and closing stock values will differ.

Statement D is correct because 'actual' overhead costs, based on actual overhead expenditure and actual activity for the period, cannot be determined until after the end of the period (the month, or the year).

COMMENTS

Question

16

	Dept 1	Dept 2
Budgeted fixed overheads	£360,000	£90,000
Budgeted hrs	30,000 hrs	15,000 hrs
Absorption rate	£12 per hr	£6 per hr

Product P

	£	£
Dept 1 overheads		
Fixed 2 hrs x £12	24.0	
Variable 2 hrs x £0.5	<u>1.0</u>	
		25.0
Dept 2 overheads		
Fixed 1.2 hrs x £6	7.2	
Variable 1.2 hrs x £1	<u>1.2</u>	
		<u>8.4</u>
Total overhead cost per unit		<u>33.4</u>

17

Sales budget	6,000 units
Finished goods closing stock budget	<u>1,000 units</u>
	7,000 units
Finished goods opening stock budget	<u>500 units</u>
Completed units of product needed	<u>6,500 units</u>

	Units		Hours to complete
Opening stock of WIP	500	(x 60% x 2 hrs)	600
Further completed production units	<u>6,000</u>	(x 2 hrs)	<u>12,000</u>
	6,500		12,600
Closing stock of WIP	1,000	(x 60% x 2 hrs)	<u>1,200</u>
Production hours budgeted			<u>13,800</u>

(* Only 40% complete to start. 60% more work per unit needed to complete)

Overhead absorption rate $\frac{£187,680}{13,800 \text{ hrs}}$ = £13.60   per direct labour hour

18

	Product M	Product R
Budgeted direct labour costs, Dept 2	£180,000	£600,000
Labour cost per unit, Dept 2	£6	£15
Production budget (units)	30,000 units	40,000 units

		£000	£000
Budgeted overheads			
Product M Dept 1 (30,000 x 16)		480	
Dept 2 (30,000 x 12)		<u>360</u>	
			840
Product R Dept 1 (40,000 x 10)		400	
Dept 2 (40,000 x 30)		<u>1,200</u>	
			<u>1,600</u>
Total production overheads			<u>2,440</u>

Question

19

Production overhead per unit of M (fixed and variable) in Department 1	£16
Overhead absorption rate per machine hour	£2
Machine hours per unit of M in Dept 1	8 hours
Excess production of M over budget	3,000 units
Over-absorbed overhead in Dept 1	£42,000
Fixed overhead absorption rate per unit of M (42,000 ÷ 3,000)	£14

Note: There would be no over-absorption of variable overhead due to an excess production volume of M, since variable overheads incurred, as well as variable overheads absorbed, increase with extra output.

Variable overhead rate per unit of M (£16 - £14) =	£2
Rate per hour (£2 ÷ 8 hrs)	£0.25 per hr

20

	Product S	Product T
Sales	6,000 units	8,000 units
Closing stock	<u>1,000 units</u>	<u>5,000 units</u>
	7,000 units	13,000 units
Opening stock	<u>2,000 units</u>	<u>3,000 units</u>
Production (budget)	5,000 units	10,000 units
Hours per unit	2 hrs	3 hrs
Budgeted hours	10,000 hrs	30,000 hrs
	(Total	40,000 hrs)

Overhead absorption rate £180,000 ÷ 40,000 hrs = £4.5 per hour

	Product S		Product T
	£ per unit		£
Direct materials cost	10		10
Direct labour cost	10		15
Fixed production overhead (2 hrs x £4.5)	<u>9</u>	(3 hrs x £4.5)	<u>13.5</u>
Production cost per unit	<u>29</u>		<u>38.5</u>

Cost of sales (FIFO basis)

			£	£
S Opening stock sold	2,000 units		56,000	
Further sales	4,000 units x £29		<u>116,000</u>	
				172,000
T Opening stock sold	3,000 units		107,000	
Further sales	5,000 units x £38.5		<u>192,500</u>	
				<u>299,500</u>
Total				<u>471,500</u>

COMMENTS

Question

21

	£	£
Actual overheads absorbed		
S 5,000 units produced x £9	45,000	
T 12,000 units produced x £13.5	162,000	
		207,000
Overheads incurred (as budgeted)		180,000
Over-absorbed overhead = profit increase over budget		27,000

(The extra 2,000 units of T produced will have a closing stock value of (x £38.5) £77,000, which includes (x £13.5) £27,000 of fixed overheads. The answer could have been calculated more quickly as 2,000 units produced in excess of budget x £13.5 fixed overhead per unit = £27,000 (over-absorbed overhead).

22

Hours for job 34679 =	400 hrs
Production overhead cost	£4,000
Overhead absorption rate (4,000 ÷ 400)	£10 per direct labour hour
Budgeted direct labour hours	45,000
Budgeted production overheads in total (45,000 x £10)	£450,000
Budgeted direct wages cost	£180,000
Absorption rate on a % of direct wages cost basis	
(450 ÷ 180)	250%

Cost of job 34679	£
Direct materials	2,000
Direct labour, including overtime premium	2,500
Overhead (250% x £2,500)	6,250
Total production cost	10,750

23

The apportionment of service department costs can be accomplished using either repeated distribution or an algebraic method. Algebra is the quickest method.

Let S be the total overhead apportioned from the stores department
Let M be the total overhead apportioned from the maintenance department

$$S = 5,000 + 0.1M \quad \text{(i)}$$
$$M = 4,000 + 0.2S \quad \text{(ii)}$$

From (i)	S - 0.1M	=	5,000	(iii)
From (ii)	-0.2S + M	=	4,000	(iv)
Multiply (iii) by 10	10S - M	=	50,000	(v)
Add (iv) and (v)	9.8S	=	54,000	
	S	=	5,510	

Substituting in (ii)	M	=	4,000 + (0.2 x 5,510)
		=	5,102

Question

The final apportionment can now be calculated:

	Dept X £
Initial allocation	5,015
Apportion S (30% x £5,510)	1,653
Apportion M (80% x £5,102)	4,082
Total cost centre overhead	10,750

24 Closing stocks are valued at full production cost

	£
Direct costs	10
Factory overhead:	
variable	2
fixed (£240,000 ÷ 80,000)	3
Value per unit of closing stock	15

25

	£000	£000
Sales 60,000 x £30		1,800
Cost of production 80,000 units x £15	1,200	
less closing stock 20,000 x £15	300	
		900
		900
Selling costs		
Variable 60,000 x 5	300	
Fixed	120	
		420
Profit		480

Note:

	£
Production overhead absorbed (80,000 x £3)	240,000
Production overhead incurred	240,000
Under/over-absorbed overhead	0

26

	Department P	Department Q
Budgeted overhead expenditure	£78,000	£114,000
Budgeted activity	2,500 machine hrs	8,000 direct labour hrs
Absorption rate	£31.20 per machine hr	£14.25 per direct labour hr

	£
Overhead absorbed:	
Department P 2,000 machine hrs x £31.2	62,400
Department Q 10,000 labour hours x £14.25	142,500
Total overhead absorbed	204,900

Question

27

	£
Overhead absorbed (see 26 above)	204,900
Overhead incurred (81,000 + 112,000)	193,000
Over-absorbed overhead	11,900

28 Budgeted idle time should be ignored for the purposes of calculating the absorption rate, and overheads are not absorbed into any idle time costs that are actually incurred.

(1)
	Budget	Actual
X	2,000 × 3 hrs = 6,000 hrs	1,500 × 4 hrs = 6,000 hrs
Y	3,000 × 3 hrs = 9,000 hrs	4,000 × 2½ hrs = 10,000 hrs
	15,000 hrs	16,000 hrs

(2) Absorption rate (direct labour hour basis) = $\frac{£144,000}{15,000 \text{ hrs}}$ = £9.6 per direct labour hour

(3) Overheads absorbed: 16,000 hrs × £9.6 = £153,600

(Note: if overheads had been absorbed on a *unit* basis, the overhead rate per unit would have been £28.8 per unit for each of X and Y. Total absorbed overhead would then have been 5,500 units × £28.8 = £158,400.)

29 Budgeted absorption rate for *fixed* overhead = $\frac{£360,000}{8,000 \text{ units}}$ = £45 per unit

Actual production: 9,000 units

	£
Fixed overhead absorbed (9,000 × 45)	405,000
Variable overhead absorbed (9,000 × 3)	27,000
Total production overhead absorbed	432,000

30

	£
Production overhead incurred (actual)	
Variable (9,000 × 3)	27,000
Fixed	432,000
	459,000
Overhead absorbed	432,000
Under-absorbed overhead	27,000

31 Budgeted absorption rate (£150,000 ÷ 30,000) = £5 per unit

	£
Overheads absorbed (actual production × absorption rate = 29,000 × £5)	145,000
Overheads actually incurred	148,000
Under-absorbed overhead (actual overhead not fully absorbed into production costs)	3,000

2: ABSORPTION COSTING

Question

The reason for this under-absorbed overhead can be analysed.

	£		
Budgeted fixed expenditure	150,000	Budgeted production	30,000 units
Actual fixed expenditure	148,000	Actual production	29,000 units
Expenditure difference	(Fav) 2,000	Production volume difference	(Adv) 1,000 units
		x £5 per unit	(Adv) £5,000

32

You need to spot here that the overhead costs are a mixture of fixed and variable items. We can separate fixed from variable costs as follows.

	£
Fixed + variable costs of 30,000 units	114,000
Fixed + variable costs of 20,000 units	100,000
Difference = variable costs of 10,000 units	14,000

Variable overhead cost per unit (14,000 ÷ 10,000) £1.40

	£
Fixed + variable costs of 20,000 units	100,000
Variable costs of 20,000 units (20,000 x £1.4)	28,000
Difference = fixed costs	72,000

Normal output	25,000 units
Absorption rate for fixed costs (72,000 ÷ 25,000)	£2.88 per unit

33

	£ per unit
Fixed overhead absorption rate	2.88
Variable overhead absorption rate	1.40
Total overhead absorption rate	4.28

	£
Overheads absorbed (28,000 x £4.20)	119,840
Overheads incurred	102,000
Over-absorbed overhead	17,840

3: MARKING SCHEDULE

Question	Correct answer	Marks for the correct answer	Question	Correct answer	Marks for the correct answer
1	D	1	12	D	1
2	D	1	13	A	1
3	C	1	14	B	1
4	A	1	15	A	2
5	B	1	16	C	1
6	A	1	17	C	1
7	D	1	18	B	2
8	D	2	19	D	1
9	B	1	20	D	1
10	A	1	21	D	2
11	C	1			

YOUR MARKS

Total marks available: 25   Your total mark: ☐

GUIDELINES - If your mark was:

0 - 7 — Obviously, this is a difficult topic area for you. If you need to, revise it carefully.

8 - 12 — You are possibly beginning to understand this topic, but there are still some important gaps in your knowledge.

13 - 19 — Good, but you still might be struggling with one or two aspects of this subject. Can you spot what they are?

20 - 25 — Very good. You seem to know the essential features of cost book-keeping very well indeed.

3: COST CONTROL ACCOUNTS

COMMENTS

Question

1

Stores ledger control account

	£		£
Opening stock b/fwd	18,500	Creditors (returns)	2,300
Creditors/cash (deliveries)	142,000	Overhead accounts (indirect matls)	25,200
		WIP (balancing figure)	116,900
		Closing stock c/fwd	16,100
	160,500		160,500

2

Wages control account

	£		£
Cost ledger control account (or income tax a/c, cash a/c, employees' Nat Ins, employer's Nat Ins) (65,500 + 7,800)	73,300	Work in progress (direct wages)	70,800
		Production overhead (indirect wages)	2,500
	73,300		73,300

3

Rent account

	£		£
Cash	40,000	Production overhead	28,000
		Admin overhead	8,000
		Marketing overhead	4,000
	40,000		40,000

Answer C is therefore correct.

4 & 5

Production overhead control account

	£		£
Cost ledger control account*	195,000	Work in progress (see below)	205,000
Over-absorbed overhead a/c	10,000		
	205,000		205,000

Absorption rate		*Absorbed overhead*	£
Dept X (£90,000 ÷ 30,000) = £3 per hr		35,000 hrs x £3 =	105,000
Dept Y (£80,000 ÷ 20,000) = £4 per hr		25,000 hrs x £4 =	100,000
		Total	£205,000

* Interlocking accounts are used and so answer B is incorrect and answer A is the correct answer to Question 4.

COMMENTS

Question

6 & 7

Extracts from the control accounts, shown below, might show you how the double entry accounting operates.

Production overhead account

Expenses incurred	67,000	Work in progress (absorbed)	60,000
		Under-absorbed overhead a/c	7,000
	67,000		67,000

Work in progress account

Direct costs	131,000	Finished goods a/c	191,000
Production overhead a/c	60,000		
	191,000		191,000

Finished goods account

WIP a/c	191,000	Cost of sales a/c	191,000

Under/over absorbed overhead

Production overhead account	7,000	P&L account	7,000

P&L account

Cost of sale	?
Under absorbed overhead	7,000

Note in particular:

Debit	Finished goods	191,000
Credit	WIP	191,000
Debit	P&L account	7,000
Credit	Under absorbed overhead account	7,000

8

Work in progress

	£		£
Direct materials	120,000	Finished goods	360,000
Direct labour	80,000		
Production overhead	160,000		
	360,000		360,000

Production overhead

	£		£
CLC (Cost ledger control)	140,000	WIP	160,000
Over-absorbed overhead	20,000	(200% of 80,000)	
	160,000		160,000

Finished goods

O/Stock	30,000	P&L (or cost of sales)	355,000
WIP	360,000	C/Stock	35,000
	390,000		390,000

3: COST CONTROL ACCOUNTS

Question

Under/over absorbed overhead

	£		£
P&L	20,000	Production overhead	20,000

P&L account

	£		£
Finished goods	355,000	Over absorbed overhead	20,000
Other overheads	60,000	Sales	500,000
*Profit (CLC)	105,000		
	520,000		520,000

9

Stores ledger control account

	£		£
Opening balance b/f	8,000	Work in progress a/c	34,000
Cash/creditors	75,000	Production overhead a/c	4,000
		Closing balance b/f	45,000
	83,000		83,000

The transfer of materials between jobs does not affect any control account, only individual job accounts.

10

Work in progress control account

	£		£
Opening balance b/f	15,000	Finished goods control a/c	
Stores ledger control a/c	34,000	(balancing figure)	77,500
Wages control account	15,500		
(23,000 - 2,500 - 5,000)			
Production overhead account	31,000		
(200% of £15,500)		Closing balance c/f	18,000
	95,500		95,500

11

Production overhead control account

	£		£
Prepayments b/f	1,000	Capital equipment	
Stores ledger control a/c	4,000	(Fixed asset a/c, 5,000 x 200%)	10,000
Wages control a/c		Work in progress control a/c	
Direct workers	2,500	(see above, solution to Q10)	31,000
Indirect workers	11,000		
Cash/creditors	16,000		
Over-absorbed overhead a/c			
(balancing figure)	6,500		
	41,000		41,000

199

COMMENTS

Question

12

Finished goods control account

	£		£
Opening stock b/f	22,000	Cost of goods sold a/c	65,000
Work in progress control a/c	77,500	Scrap - P&L a/c	2,000
(see solution to Q10)		Closing stock c/f	32,500
	99,500		99,500

13

Profit and loss account

	£		£
Cost of goods sold a/c	65,000	Sales	110,000
Selling and dist'n o'hd	12,000		
Finished goods a/c - scrap	2,000		
Under-absorbed o'hd a/c	9,000		
Profit (c/fwd)	22,000		
	110,000		110,000

14

In a system of interlocking accounts, all items which would otherwise be credited or debited to an account in the financial accounting system are credited or debited instead to the Cost Ledger Control account (CLC). Thus, instead of *Credit* Sales a/c, *Debit* Debtors a/c or Cash a/c, we have *Credit* Sales a/c, *Debit* Cost Ledger Control a/c. And we also record profits by debiting the Cost Ledger Control a/c and crediting the Costing P&L account. These accounting entries would have been made *before* arriving at the closing balance on the CLC account, and so the trial balances at 31.3.X2 would be

	£	£
Stores ledger control account	25,000	-
Work in progress control account	15,000	-
Finished goods control	80,000	-
Cost ledger control account	-	120,000
	120,000	120,000

These would be the opening balances carried forward in the cost accounts at the start of the next year (1 April 19X2).

15

Production overhead control account

	£		£
Prepayment b/fwd	8,000	Accruals b/fwd	20,000
Creditors/Cost ledger control a/c	60,000	Work in progress control a/c	
Wages control a/c	40,000	(Absorbed 30,000 hrs x £5)	150,000
Stores ledger control a/c	15,000	Prepayment c/fwd	5,000
Provision for depreciation a/c	25,000	Under-absorbed o'hd a/c	
Accruals c/fwd	30,000	(balancing item)	3,000
	178,000		178,000
Prepayments b/fwd	5,000	Accruals b/fwd	30,000

200

Question

16

Notional rent account

	£		£
Cost ledger control	30,000	Production overhead a/c	30,000

Items A and D have debit and credit items mixed up. Item C is correct.

17

Stores account

	£		£
Creditors (400 x 2.5)	1,000	WIP (300 x 2)	600
		Price variance a/c (balance, or 400 x 0.5)	200
		Closing stock c/fwd (100 x 2)	200
	1,000		1,000

Price variance

	£
Stores a/c	200

If closing stocks were valued at their 'actual' cost of £250, rather than at standard cost of £200, the accounting entry would have been *Credit* Stores a/c £150, *Debit* Price variance a/c £150.

18

Remember that a higher opening stock value adds to the cost of sale (and reduces profit) whereas a higher closing stock value reduces the cost of sale (and adds to profit).

	£
Profit in the cost accounts	95,000
Stock differences:	
Opening stock of raw materials: cost a/cs higher by	2,400
Closing stock of raw materials: cost a/cs lower by	2,000
Opening stock of finished goods: cost a/cs lower by	(4,900)
Closing stock of finished goods: cost a/cs higher by	(1,700)
Profit in the financial accounts	92,800

19

	£
Profit in the financial accounts	40,000
Stock valuation differences:	
Cost accounts opening stock lower in value by	5,000
Cost accounts closing stock lower in value by	(4,000)
	41,000
Items in the financial accounts and not in the cost a/cs	
Dividends received	(2,500)
Loss on sale of machine	4,000
Cost accounting profit	42,500

COMMENTS

Question

20 The notional interest charge in the cost accounts is a self-cancelling item, since the extra cost of £5,000 in the production overheads (compared with the financial accounts) is matched by extra 'revenue' of £5,000 in the costing P&L account.

	£
Financial accounting profit	80,000
Cost accounts opening stock higher by	(4,000)
Cost accounts closing stock higher by	<u>6,000</u>
	82,000
Items in the financial accounts but not in the cost accounts (none itemised)	<u>0</u>
Cost accounting profit	<u>82,000</u>

21

Cost accounts: Cost ledger control account

	£		£
Under-absorbed overhead		Unadjusted balance b/d	105,000
(profit reduction-see note below)	8,000	Factory overhead a/c	18,000
Adjusted balance c/d	<u>115,000</u>	(depreciation now recorded)	
	<u>123,000</u>		<u>123,000</u>

Note:
	£
Factory overhead over-absorbed	10,000
less Depreciation expense not recorded yet	<u>18,000</u>
Under absorbed overhead - profit reduction	<u>8,000</u>

4: JOB COSTING. CONTRACT COSTING. PROCESS COSTING

4: MARKING SCHEDULE

Question	Correct answer	Marks for correct answer	Question	Correct answer	Marks for correct answer	Question	Correct answer	Marks for correct answer
1	D	1	16	D	1	31	D	1
2	C	1	17	C	1	32	A	2
3	A	1	18	B	1	33	A	2
4	B	1	19	C	1	34	C	1
5	B	1	20	D	1	35	B	1
6	D	1	21	C	1	36	B	1
7	D	1	22	A	1	37	C	1
8	A	1	23	A	1	38	C	2
9	A	2	24	B	1	39	A	1
10	D	1	25	D	1	40	C	1
11	D	1	26	A	1	41	B	2
12	D	1	27	A	1	42	B	1
13	D	1	28	A	1	43	B	1
14	C	1	29	C	1	44	D	1
15	D	1	30	A	1			

YOUR MARKS

Total marks available 50   Your total mark ☐

GUIDELINES - If your mark was:

0 - 15 You haven't got to grips yet with this difficult subject area.

16 - 29 Quite good. You may have understood many of the basic principles of this topic, but there will be a few important issues that you probably need to learn still.

30 - 39 Good. There are a lot of mistakes that are easily made in this subject. Can you identify any errors you have been making and why your approach was incorrect?

40 - 50 Very good mark. You have understood most, if not all, of the principles of job costing, contract costing and process costing.

COMMENTS

Question

1

	Dept A £	Dept B £	Total £
Direct materials	5,000	3,000	8,000
Direct labour	1,600	1,000	2,600
Production overhead	1,600	800	2,400
Full production cost			13,000
Other overheads (20%)			2,600
Cost of the job			15,600
Profit (25% of sales = 33⅓ % of cost)			5,200
Sales price			20,800

2

	£
Materials issued less transfers	4,600
Grade x labour (200 hours x £3)	600
Overtime premium (direct cost of job 3579)	100
Supervisor (direct labour) (20 hrs x £5)	100
Production overhead 220 hrs x £5	1,100
Job cost	6,500

3-5

	£
Direct material Y 400 kilos x £5	2,000
Direct material Z (800 - 60 - 20) kilos x £6	4,320
Total direct material cost	6,320

The £120 abnormal loss on the damaged 20 kilos of Z will be charged direct to the profit and loss account.

	£
Department P 320 hours x £4	1,280
Department Q 200 hours x £5	1,000
Total direct labour cost	2,280

Rectification work, being normal and expected, is included in the direct labour cost of Department P. Overtime premium will be charged to overhead in the case of Department P, and to the job of the customer who asked for overtime to be worked in the case of Department Q.

	£
Direct material cost	6,320
Direct labour cost	2,280
Production overhead (520 hours x £3)	1,560
	10,160

Question

6

Statement A is correct.
Job costs are identified with a particular job, whereas process costs (of units produced and work in process) are averages, based on equivalent units of production.

Statement B is also correct. The direct cost of a job to date, excluding any direct expenses, can be ascertained from materials requisition notes and job tickets or time sheets.

Statement C is correct, because without data about units completed and units still in process, losses and equivalent units of production cannot be calculated.

Statement D is incorrect, because the cost of normal loss will usually be incorporated into job costs as well as into process costs. In process costing, this is commonly done by giving normal loss no cost, leaving costs to be shared between output, closing stocks and abnormal loss/gain. In job costing, it can be done by adjusting direct materials costs to allow for normal wastage, and direct labour costs for normal reworking of items or normal spoilage.

7

This is a problem which calls for sorting out accruals and prepayments - a task that will often be included in examination questions on contract costing.

	Site wages £	Contract expenses £	Total £
Cash paid in 19X2	400,000	200,000	
less accruals at 31.12.X1	(15,000)	-	
add prepayments at 31.12.X1	-	8,000	
	385,000	208,000	
add accruals at 31.12.X1	22,000	5,000	
Chargeable to the contract for 19X2	407,000	213,000	620,000

8

Contract 1

	£		£
Cumulative turnover	270,000	Cumulative costs incurred	200,000
Cumulative payments on account	220,000	Transferred to cost of sales	200,000
Amount recoverable	50,000	Closing WIP	0

Note. The cumulative gross profit on the contract to date is £(270,000 - 200,000) = £70,000.

COMMENTS

Question

9

Contract 2

	£
Cumulative turnover	150,000
Cumulative payments on account	175,000
Excess payments on account	25,000

This should be offset against any debit balance on the contract in respect of stocks (work in progress).

	£
Costs incurred to date	120,000
Recorded as cost of sales to date	110,000
Debit balance on contract	10,000
Excess payments on account	25,000
Payment received on account	15,000 — to be shown as a creditor in the balance sheet

Note The cumulative gross profit on the contract to date is £(150,000 - 110) = £40,000.

10

Contract 3

	£
Cumulative turnover	300,000
Cumulative payments on account	330,000
Excess payments on account	30,000

As with Contract 2, this should be offset against any debit balance on the contract in respect of stocks.

	£
Costs incurred to date	260,000
Costs charged to cost of sales to date	210,000
Debit balance on contract	50,000
less Excess payments on contract	30,000
Closing stocks, Contract 3	20,000

11

Contract 4

(1) Debtors = Cumulative turnover minus cumulative payments received on account

(2) Loss on the contract

	£
Turnover to date	120,000
Cost of sales to date	140,000
Loss to date	(20,000)
Provision for foreseeable loss	(15,000)
Gross loss	(35,000)

The loss on the contract should be accounted for as soon as it becomes foreseeable.

4: JOB COSTING. CONTRACT COSTING. PROCESS COSTING

Question

12

Contract account

	£'000		£'000
Cost of contract b/f	370		
Plant on site b/f	30		
Materials on site b/f	10		
Materials from stores	190		
Sub-contractors' costs	200	Plant on site c/f	15
Wages and salaries	200	Materials on site c/f	5
Overheads	100	Cost of contract c/f (balance)	1,080
	1,100		1,100

13

No profit had been taken on the contract prior to 19X2, and so profit is quite simply:

	£'000
Value of work certified to 31.12.X2	1,200
Cost of work certified to 31.12.X2	950
Gross profit to 31.12.X2	250

14

	£'000
Total contract costs incurred to date	1,080
Cumulative cost of sales to date	950
Contract WIP	130

Turnover exceeds payments on account, by the retention of 10%, or £120,000, which will be included in *debtors* in the balance sheet.

15

	Process 1	Process 2	Process 3
	£'000	£'000	£'000
Opening stock	8	13	2
Value of goods transferred	-	32	50
Added materials	20	4	5
Conversion costs	10	10	16
	38	59	73
less closing stock	(6)	(9)	4
Goods transferred	32	50	69

207

COMMENTS

Question

16

	Units
Input	6,000
Normal loss (5%)	300
Expected output	5,700
Actual output	5,800
Abnormal gain	100

Cost per unit Total costs   £(13,060 + 5,000 + 1,500) = £33,060
               Expected output   5,700 units
               Cost per unit   £5.8

Full cost of output = £5.8 x 5,800 = £33,640

17

Here is the process account in full.

	Units	£		Units	£
Opening WIP b/f	0	0	Finished goods	5,800	33,640
Direct materials	6,000	13,060	Normal loss	200	0
Direct labour		5,000			
Production overhead		15,000			
	6,000	33,060			
Abnormal gain	(100)	580	Closing WIP c/f	0	0
	5,900	33,640		6,000	33,640

Value of abnormal gain = £5.8 x 100 = £580.

18

Input	110%
Normal loss	10%
Output	100%

Input	3,300 units
Normal loss (10/110 of input)	300 units
Expected output	3,000 units
Actual output	2,750 units
Abnormal loss	250 units

Cost per expected unit of output = $\frac{£(59,100 + 30,000)}{3,000}$

= £29.7

Full cost of finished output (2,750 units x £29.7)   £81,675
Cost of abnormal loss   (250 units x £29.7)   £7,425

4: JOB COSTING. CONTRACT COSTING. PROCESS COSTING

Question

19 The process account will be as follows. The units column is for memorandum purposes only.

Process account

	Units	£		Units	£
Opening WIP	0	0	Normal loss	300	0
Direct materials	3,300	59,100	Abnormal loss	250	7,425
Direct labour/overhead		30,000	Finished goods	2,750	81,675
			Closing WIP	0	0
	3,300	89,100		3,300	89,100

20 *Process 1*

	Units
Input	2,200
Normal loss (10%)	220
Expected output	1,980
Actual output	2,000
Abnormal gain	20

Cost per unit £43,560 ÷ 1980 *expected* units of output = £22.

21 *Process 2*

	Total
Input from Process 1	2,000
Normal loss (10%)	200
Expected output	1,800
Actual output	1,700
Abnormal gain	100

Cost per unit £(44,000 + 6,760) ÷ 1,800 = £28.20

Value of output completed = 1,700 x £28.2 = £47,940.

22

Input	1,000 units
Normal loss (10%)	100 units
Expected output	900 units
Actual output	800 units
Abnormal loss	100 units

Cost per unit of expected output

	£
Materials	5,100
Labour and overhead	3,000
	8,100
less Scrap value of normal loss	180
	7,920

209

COMMENTS

Question

Expected output 900 units
Cost per unit £8.80

Full cost of finished output 800 × £8.8 = £7,040

23

	£
Cost of abnormal loss (100 × £8.8)	880
Less scrap value of abnormal loss (100 × £1.8)	180
Net value written off to P & L account	700

24

	£
Materials	5,100
Labour overhead	3,000
Total cost	8,100

Expected output 900 units
Cost per unit £9

Cost of finished goods 800 × £9 = £7,200

25

	Total units	Equivalent units Materials	Labour/ overhead
Finished units	400	400	400
Closing stock	100	100	80
	500	500	480
Cost		£9,000	£11,520 (£3,840 × 300%)
Cost per equivalent unit		£18	£24

Cost of completed units = 400 × £(18 + 24) = £16,800.

4: JOB COSTING. CONTRACT COSTING. PROCESS COSTING

Question

26-28

Average pricing is used by the company.

	Total units	Equivalent units Materials	Conversion costs
Finished output	36,000	36,000	36,000
Closing stock	5,000	5,000	2,000
Normal loss	2,000	0	0
	43,000	41,000	38,000

		£	£
Costs			
Opening WIP		2,920	2,800
Costs in December		42,180	37,100
		45,100	39,900
Cost per equivalent unit		£1.10	£1.05

Cost of output transferred to finished goods stock
= 36,000 × £(1.10 + 1.05) = £77,400

Value of closing work in process

	£
Direct material (5,000 × £1.10)	5,500
Conversion costs (2,000 × £1.05)	2,100
	7,600

28

All loss is costed as 'abnormal' loss.

Because it occurs halfway though the process, the loss should be attributed a full share of materials cost, but only a half-share of labour and overhead costs.

	Total units	Equivalent units Materials	Labour/ overhead
Finished items	3,800	3,800	3,800
Loss	200	200 (50%)	100
		4,000	3,900
Cost		£29,640	£74,100
Cost per equivalent unit		£7.41	£19

Cost of loss (200 × £7.41) + (100 × £19) = £3,382.

COMMENTS

Question

29-30

	Total units	Equivalent units Materials	Equivalent units Labour	Equivalent units Overhead
Finished output	20,000	20,000	20,000	20,000
Scrapped items	5,000	4,000	2,000	2,000
Closing stock	5,000	3,000	1,000	1,000
		27,000	23,000	23,000
				(£6 x 2,070)
Costs		£13,500	£6,210	£12,420
Cost per equivalent unit		£0.50	£0.27	£0.54

		Cost of scrap £		Value of closing WIP £
Direct materials	(4,000 x 0.5)	2,000	(3,000 x 0.5)	1,500
Direct labour	(2,000 x 0.27)	540	(1,000 x 0.27)	270
Overhead	(2,000 x 0.54)	1,080	(1,000 x 0.54)	540
		3,620		2,310

31

	Total units	Equivalent units Materials	Equivalent units Conversion costs
Opening stock			
Work already done	200	200	50
To complete in March		0	150
Other finished work	1,000	1,000	1,000
Closing stock	200	200	100
	1,400	1,200	1,250

Equivalent units of work done in March

Materials	1,200
Conversion costs	1,250

32

	Materials	Conversion cost	Total
Costs incurred in March	£168,000	£158,125	
Equivalent units of work in March	1,200	1,250	
Cost per equivalent unit	£140	£126.5	£266.5

Cost of finished goods produced

	£
Opening stock (200 units) value b/f	30,095
Cost to complete 150 x £126.5	18,975
	49,070
Cost of other units produced in March (1,000 units x £266.5)	266,500
Total cost of finished goods produced	315,570

(The closing stock value would be (200 x £140) plus (100 x £126.5) = £40,650)

4: JOB COSTING. CONTRACT COSTING. PROCESS COSTING

Question

33

Using weighted average costing, the equivalent units would be

	Materials	Conversion costs	
Finished goods	1,200	1,200	
Closing stock	200	100	(50%)
	1,400	1,300	
Cost	£25,200	£4,895	
	+£168,000	+£158,125	
	£193,200	£163,020	
Cost per equivalent unit	£138	£125.4	

Value of closing stock =
    200 units of materials x £138
    100 units of conversion cost x £125.4

£
27,600
12,540
40,140

(Note: the value of finished output would be 1,200 units @ £(138 + 125.4) = £316,080).

34 – 36

Obviously, if you didn't get this answer correct, your answers to the next two questions will be wrong.

Item	Total units	Equivalent units Materials	Labour/ overhead
Transferred to finished goods	7,600	7,600	7,600
Normal loss (10% of input)	1,000	0	0
Closing stock	1,000	1,000	700
	9,600		
Abnormal loss	400	400	400
	10,000	9,000	8,700

Normal loss, since it is given no cost, is 0 equivalent units. Abnormal loss is costed, and since units are fully worked before rejection, are 1 equivalent unit each.

Costs   £309,600   *£207,000

* Direct labour + 100% for overhead

Cost per equivalent unit: £
    Materials   (£309,600 ÷ 9,000)   34.40
    Labour overhead   (£207,000 ÷ 8,700)   23.79
    Total   58.19

Cost of abnormal loss   (400 x £58.19)   £23,276

COMMENTS

Question

Value of closing WIP

			£
Materials	(1,000 x £34.40)		34,400
Labour and overhead	(700 x £23.79)		16,653
			51,053

37

Did you spot that normal loss units are 10% of finished units, not input units?

	Units	Units
Opening stock		2,000
Added materials		5,000
		7,000
Output to Process 2	6,000	
Normal loss (10% of output)	600	
		6,600
Abnormal loss		400

	Total units	Equivalent units Materials	Labour/ overhead
Opening stock	2,000	0 (60%)	1,200
Other finished units	4,000	4,000	4,000
	6,000	4,000	5,200
Abnormal loss	400	400	400
	6,400	4,400	5,600

38

		£189,200	£160,160
Cost		£189,200	£160,160
less scrap value of normal loss (600 x £4.4)		2,640	-
		186,560	
Cost per equivalent unit		£42.40	£28.60

Costs	Materials	Labour/ overhead	Total
	£	£	£
Opening stock: cost b/f	80,000	20,000	100,000
cost to complete	0	34,320	34,320
	80,000	54,320	134,320
Further 4,000 units completed	169,600	114,400	284,000
Costs of units transferred to Process 2	249,600	168,720	418,320
Closing stock	0	0	0
Abnormal loss	16,960	11,440	28,400
	266,560	180,160	446,720

Question

39

Cost of abnormal loss	£28,400
less scrap value of abnormal loss (400 x 4.4)	1,760
Written off to P & L account	£26,640

You might like to see these figures set out in T accounts.

40 - 41

	Total units	Equivalent units Materials	Labour/overhead
Normal loss (10% of 10,000)	1,000	1,000	1,000
Finished output	7,900	7,900	7,900
Closing stock	1,500	1,500	900
	10,400		
Input	10,000		
Abnormal gain	400	(400)	(400)
Equivalent units		10,000	9,400
Costs		£38,880	£50,337
Cost per equivalent unit		£3.888	£5.355

Cost of normal loss = 1,000 x £(3.888 + 5.355) = £9,243

Abnormal gain = 400 x £(3.888 + 5.355) = £3,697

Closing stock:		£
Materials	(1,500 x £3.888)	5,832
Labour/overhead	(900 x £5.355)	4,819
Total		10,651

The process 2 account will be:

	Units	£		Units	£
Opening WIP		0	Finished goods*		
Materials	10,000	38,880	and normal loss	8,900	82,263
Labour/overhead		50,337			
		89,217			
Abnormal gain	400	3,697	Closing WIP	1,500	10,651
	10,400	92,914		10,400	92,914

* 7,900 x £(3.888 + 5.355) plus normal loss cost of £9,243 = £82,263.

COMMENTS

Question

42-44

There are 2 special problems here. (1) There are two sorts of loss, toxic waste and loss through evaporation. (2) Toxic waste has a disposal cost, rather than a scrap value, and the disposal cost of normal toxic waste should be treated similarly to scrap value, except that it should be *added* to the process costs (debited to the process account).

For 10,000 kilos of input	Toxic waste units	Evaporation loss units	
Normal loss	600	400	
Actual loss	900	300	(10,000 - 8,800 - 900)
Abnormal gain/(loss)	(300)	100	

Costs of the process

	£
Direct materials	50,000
Conversion cost	31,000
Disposal cost of normal toxic waste (600 x £3)	1,800
	82,800

Expected good output from 10,000 kilos of input = 9,000 kilos
Cost per kilo of output = £9.20

Abnormal gain on evaporation 100 units x £9.20 = £920

Value of completed units = 8,800 x £9.20 = £80,960

	£
Cost of abnormal toxic waste 300 x £9.2	2,760
add extra disposal costs incurred 300 x £3	900
Net loss written off to profit and loss account	3,660

5: MARKING SCHEDULE

Question	Correct answer	Marks for correct answer	Question	Correct answer	Marks for correct answer	Question	Correct answer	Marks for correct answer
1	C	1	17	B	1	33	B	1
2	A	1	18	B	1	34	D	1
3	B	1	19	B	1	35	A	1
4	D	1	20	C	1	36	A	1
5	D	1	21	D	1	37	D	2
6	A	1	22	A	1	38	D	1
7	D	1	23	D	1	39	A	1
8	C	1	24	B	1	40	B	1
9	C	2	25	C	2	41	B	1
10	B	1	26	C	1	42	B	1
11	D	1	27	A	1	43	A	1
12	B	1	28	C	1	44	C	1
13	C	1	29	C	1	45	D	1
14	B	1	30	B	1	46	A	1
15	D	1	31	D	1	47	A	1
16	D	1	32	B	1			

YOUR MARKS

Total marks available 30   Your total mark ☐

GUIDELINES - If your mark was:

0 - 15 Disappointing. There is a lot for you to sort out about budgeting

16 - 25 Fair, but quite a lot of mistakes. Can you see what you are doing wrong? There are probably a few key mistakes that you are making regularly.

26 - 39 Good. You have got to grips with the essential elements of budgeting. Check your errors carefully though to see what kind of mistakes you are making.

40 - 50 Very good. You are sorting out the involved computational work in budgeting.

COMMENTS

Question

1 A functional budget (or department budget) is a budget applicable to a particular function or department. Items A, C and D are examples, but a cash budget is not.

2 A sales budget and budgeted changes in finished goods stocks are needed to prepare a production budget. The production budget and budgeted changes in raw materials stocks are needed to prepare a purchases budget for raw materials. A purchases budget is needed to prepare a cash budget.

3

Increase in finished goods stock required	1,000 units
Budgeted sales of product Alpha	60,000 units
Production required	61,000 units
Raw materials usage budget (x 3kg)	183,000 kg
Decrease in raw materials stock budgeted	8,000 kg
Raw materials purchase budget	175,000 kg

4

Reduction in finished goods stock budgeted	(3,600) units
Budgeted sales	18,000 units
Budgeted production of completed units	14,400 units
Allowance for defective units	
(10% of input = 1/9 of output)	1,600 units
Production budget	16,000 units
Raw materials usage budget (16,000 x 6kg)	96,000 kg
Budgeted increase in raw materials stock	3,400 kg
Raw materials purchase budget	99,400 kg

5

	units
Planned closing stock, product Charlie	5,000
Opening stock	3,000
Stock increase	2,000
Budgeted sales	40,000
Budgeted production	42,000
Materials usage budget (x 5 kilos per unit)	210,000 kilos

Question

6

		Units
Budgeted sales		80,000
Finished goods: opening stock	4,000	
closing stock	1,000	
Planned stock reduction		(3,000)
Finished production required, product Delta		77,000

	Total units		Equivalent units
To complete opening WIP	2,000	(25%)	500
Other finished production required	75,000		75,000
	77,000		
To manufacture closing WIP	3,000	(25%)	750
Production budget			76,250

	Kgs
Materials usage budget (x 6 kgs)	457,500
Planned reduction in raw materials stock (16,000 - 12,000)	4,000
Materials purchases budget	453,500

7

Planned increase in stocks of finished goods	4,600 units
Budgeted sales	36,800 units
Budgeted production (to pass quality control check)	41,400 units

This is 92% of total production, allowing for an 8% rejection rate.

Budgeted production = $\frac{100}{92}$ x 41,400 = 45,000 units

Budgeted direct labour hours = (x 5 hrs per unit) 225,000 hrs.

8

	Units
Budgeted increase in finished good stocks	1,950
Budgeted sales	90,675
Budgeted production (to pass the quality control checks)	92,625

This represents $97\frac{1}{2}$% of units produced, allowing for rejections at the first quality control check (5%) and re-working of units ($2\frac{1}{2}$%).

Budgeted production   92,625 x $\frac{100}{97.5}$ = 95,000 units

	hours
Direct labour hours to produce 95,000 units (x 4 hrs)	380,000
Re-working of units ($2\frac{1}{2}$% of 95,000 x 2 hrs)	4,750
Direct labour hours budget	384,750

COMMENTS

Question

9

Note: Of the 95,000 units produced, 5% of 4,750 will get rejected. Of these rejected units, 2,375 (one half) will be re-worked, so that completed production will be 95,000 - 4,750 + 2,375 = 92,625 units.

	£	£
Raw materials opening stock		23,200
Purchases		140,000
Raw materials closing stock		(17,300)
Raw materials usage budget		145,900
Direct labour budget		120,000
Production overhead (30,000 hrs x £5)		150,000
Production budget		415,900
WIP Opening stock	4,700	
Closing stock	8,200	
		(3,500)
Budgeted output to finished goods (completed production)		412,400
Finished goods opening stock		16,600
Finished goods closing stock		(18,800)
Production cost of goods sold		410,200
Administration overhead		80,000
Sales and distribution overhead		120,000
Total cost of sales		610,200
Sales		620,000
Budgeted profit		9,800

10

Production budget (= sales budget)	125,000 units
Raw materials usage (x 1.1 kg)	137,500 units

	£
Cost of raw materials (before discount) x £2.2	302,500
less bulk purchase discount (5%)	15,125
Purchase budget	287,375

11

	units
Increase in closing stocks	1,800
Sales budget	9,000
Budgeted production (units that pass quality control check)	10,800
Items rejected	
(20% of inspected items = 25% of items completed and passed)	2,700
Budgeted production, including rejects	13,500

Standard hours per unit = 10 hours, but efficiency is only 90% of standard

Budgeted hours per unit 10 hrs x $\dfrac{100}{90}$ = 11.111 hrs

Direct labour hours budget = 150,000 hrs.

Question

12 Improved productivity (Measure 1) results in more units produced per hour, at the same total labour cost, and so the labour cost per unit is less. Reducing the rate of rejections (Measure 3) has the same result, with more units produced per hour which pass the inspection test. Measure 2 will increase output but will also increase total labour costs, leaving direct labour costs per unit unchanged.

13 This question deals with the link between budgeted production, budgeted overhead expenditure and absorption costing. You need to work back from the actual results and the under-absorption of overhead to calculate what the original budget was.

Only *fixed overhead* is under or over-absorbed when there is a difference between the budgeted and actual level of activity, and so the £2,100 refers to fixed overhead only.

	£
Actual fixed production overhead	52,500
Under-absorbed overhead	2,100
Absorbed fixed production overhead	50,400
Direct labour hours worked	7,200 hrs
Absorption rate per hour, fixed overhead	£7

Variable production overhead rate per hour £7,200 ÷ 7,200 hrs = £1 per hour.

Total absorption rate £7 + £1 = £8 per hour
Budgeted hours = 7,200 + 300 = 7,500 hours

	£
Budgeted fixed production overheads (same as actual costs)	52,500
Budgeted variable production overheads (7,500 x £1)	7,500
Total budgeted production overhead	60,000

14

	Kg of Z
Planned increase in stocks of finished goods	6,000
Budgeted sales	90,000
Budgeted production of Z	96,000

Plant hours needed (÷ 600)	160 hrs
Plant hours available, normal time 36 hrs x 4 weeks	144 hrs
Overtime hours needed for the plant	16 hrs
Overtime hours - direct labour (x 100 operatives)	1,600 hrs

Direct labour cost	£
100 men x 160 hours x £4 per hour	64,000
Overtime 1,600 hours x £2 per hour	3,200
	67,200

COMMENTS

Question

15

		Material P		Material Q
Materials usage budget (for 96,000 of Z)	(× 0.6)	57,600 kg	(× 0.5)	48,000 kg
Increase in stocks		10,000 kg		30,000 kg
Materials purchases budget		67,600 kg		78,000 kg
Cost per kg		£1		£2
Purchases in £		£67,600	+	£156,000
	=	£223,600		

16

	£	£
Production costs		
Material P 57,600 kg × £1		57,600
Material Q 48,000 kg × £2		96,000
Total material cost		153,600
Direct labour, including overtime		67,200
Production indirect expenses		63,000
		283,800
Finished goods: closing stock (64,000 × £3)	192,000	
opening stock	174,000	
		(18,000)
Production cost of goods sold		265,800
Administration and marketing costs		80,000
		345,800
Sales (90,000 × £4)		360,000
Profit		14,200

17–19

	Unit cost of production £
Direct material	4.00
Direct labour	8.00
Variable production overhead (28,080 ÷ 36,000)	0.78
Fixed production overhead (140,400 ÷ 36,000)	3.90
	16.68

Month 1

	£	£
Sales (5,000 × £20)		100,000
Production cost of sales		
Opening stock	64,000	
Production costs (3,000 units × £16.68)	50,040	
	114,040	
Closing stock (2,000 units × £16.68)	33,360	
Gross profit		80,680
		19,320
Other overheads (120,000 ÷ 12)		10,000
Net profit		9,320

Question

19 If actual production is 50 units higher than budgeted, but sales remain 5,000 units, there will be over-absorbed *fixed* overhead in the month of 50 x £3.90 = £195, which will add to profit.

(Variable costs *per unit*, including variable overhead, will be as in the budget for the year as a whole and so the only effect on profit would be the over-absorbed fixed overhead).

20 Incremental budgeting is a term used to describe budgets prepared on the basis of last year's costs plus an extra percentage, for inflation etc. Rolling budgets describe the continuous preparation of budgets, such as annual budgets prepared monthly, with one extra month added at the end and the 'old' first month, now ended, taken off the beginning, each time a budget is prepared. Rolling budgets (or continuous budgets) are likely to be more accurate than 'traditional' annual budgets, especially in a period of high inflation.

21

	Material X Units	Material Y Units
Raw materials usage budget	15,000	20,000
less Raw materials opening stock	(8,000)	(10,000)
	7,000	10,000
plus Raw materials closing stock	9,000	12,000
Raw materials purchase budget	16,000	22,000
Price per unit (add 10% for inflation)	£2.20	£0.55
Purchases budget	£35,200 +	£12,100
		= £47,300

22

	£
Opening debtors	80,000
Sales (5,000 x £25)	125,000
	205,000
Receipts from debtors	86,000
Closing debtors	119,000

23

	£
Opening trade creditors	29,000
Purchases	47,300
	76,300
Payments to creditors	26,000
Closing trade creditors	50,300

COMMENTS

Question

24

	£
50% of sales in February (cash sales)	30,000
25% of sales in January	20,000
25% of sales in December	52,500
	102,500

25

The quickest method of calculation is to take opening debtors plus sales minus closing debtors.

	£000
Debtors at 1 January 19X1 (25% of 160 + 25% of 210)	92.5
Sales in January - June (80 + 60 + 100 + 90 + 120 + 150)	600.0
	692.5
Debtors at 30 June 19X2 (25% of 120 + 25% of 150)	67.5
Cash receipts in January - June	625.0

26

There are no stocks, and so purchases in any period will relate to sales in the same period. Since 1½ months' credit is taken, the payments in the January - June period will be for the following purchases:

½ of November 19X0 purchases
Purchases in December - April
½ of May 19X1 purchases

This is (in £000) 75% (80 + 210 + 80 + 60 + 100 + 90 + 60) = 510

27

	£
Closing stock required (½ x £24,000)	12,000
Cost of goods sold in the year (12 months x £24,000)	288,000
	300,000
Opening stock	24,000
Purchases in the year	276,000

	£
Opening creditors	24,000
Purchases	276,000
	300,000
Closing creditors (2 x £24,000)	48,000
Payments to creditors	252,000

Question

28

	£	£
Opening debtors		60,000
Sales in 19X2 (12 x £30,000)		<u>360,000</u>
		420,000
less Cash discounts (25% of £360,000 x 5%)		<u>4,500</u>
		415,500
less Closing debtors		
$37\frac{1}{2}$% of November 19X2 sales	11,250	
75% of December 19X2 sales	<u>22,500</u>	
		<u>33,750</u>
Cash receipts in 19X2		<u>381,750</u>

29

	With changes £		Without changes £
Receipts	381,750	12 x £30,000)	360,000
Payments	<u>252,000</u>	(12 x £24,000)	<u>288,000</u>
Net cash inflow	<u>129,750</u>		<u>72,000</u>
Difference		<u>£57,750</u>	

30-33

	January £000	Receipts in February £000	March £000
December sales	80,000 ⁽¹⁾		
January sales	42,750 ⁽²⁾	45,000	
February sales		71,250 ⁽³⁾	75,000
March sales			114,000 ⁽³⁾
	<u>122,750</u>	<u>116,250</u>	<u>189,000</u>

Notes:
(1) Opening debtors must all be credit customers from December.
(2) 95% of 50% of £90,000
(3) 95% of 50% of £150,000
(4) 95% of 50% of £240,000

Cash budget	January £	February £	March £
Receipts from sales	<u>122,750</u>	<u>116,250</u>	<u>189,000</u>
Payments to suppliers	54,000	108,000	180,000
Payments for expenses			
(= expenses minus depreciation)	18,000	23,000	23,000
Dividend	20,000	-	-
Loan interest	-	-	<u>5,000</u>
Total payments	<u>92,000</u>	<u>131,000</u>	<u>208,000</u>
Receipts less payments	30,750	(14,750)	(19,000)
Opening cash balance	<u>(17,000)</u>	<u>13,750</u>	<u>(1,000)</u>
Closing cash balance	<u>13,750</u>	<u>(1,000)</u>	<u>(20,000)</u>

COMMENTS

Question

	£	£
Sales		480,000
less discounts (5% of 50% of £480,000)		12,000
		468,000
Purchases	380,000	
less discounts	38,000	
	342,000	
Stock change	0	
		342,000
		126,000
Expenses, including depreciation		(70,000)
Interest (3 months x £5,000 pa)		(1,250)
Profits for the 3 months		54,750

34

This question calls for the use of a source and application of funds statement.

	£	£
Budgeted profit before tax		100,000
Items not involving the movement of funds		
Depreciation		22,000
		122,000
Tax to be paid	25,000	
Dividends to be paid	20,000	
Fixed asset purchases	70,000	
		115,000
		7,000
Increase in stocks	(3,000)	
Reduction in debtors	13,000	
Increase in creditors	15,000	
		25,000
Change in cash position		32,000
Opening cash		24,000
Closing cash		56,000

35

		£
Receipts from	October sales (25% of 90% of £40,000)	9,000
	November sales (50% of 90% of £80,000)	36,000
	December sales (20% of 90% of £140,000)	25,200
	January sales (Cash: 10% of £60,000)	6,000
		76,200

36

	£
Cash receipts from	
November sales (25% of £50,000)	12,500
December sales (50% of £55,000)	27,500
January sales (15% of £60,000)	9,000
Total receipts in January	49,000

Question 37

	£	£
Opening debtors		
November sales (35% of £50,000)	17,500	
December sales (85% of £55,000)	46,750	
		64,250
Sales in the year		
January - June (6 x £60,000)	360,000	
July - December (6 x £70,000)	420,000	
		780,000
		844,250
Less bad debts written off in the year		
In £000: 10% of (50 + 55 + (60 x 6) + (70 x 4))		74,500
		769,750
Closing debtors		
November sales (35% of £70,000)	24,500	
December sales (85% of £70,000)	59,500	
		84,000
Cash receipts		685,750

The change in the *provision* for bad debts will affect profits for the year, reducing profits by £6,000, but this has no effect on cash receipts.

The bad debts written off in the year must be allowed for; otherwise it will be assumed that opening debtors plus sales minus closing debtors will be the amount of cash received, which is not the case because of bad debts.

Questions 38-40

	December £000	January £000	February £000	March £000
Finished goods: closing stock[1] (at sales value)	120	90	110	160
Sales in the month	70	80	40	50
	190	170	150	210
Finished goods: opening stock[1] (at sales value)	150	120	90	110
Production in month, at sales value	40	50	60	100
Raw materials usage in production (30% of sales value of goods produced)	12	15	18	30
Raw materials: closing stock[2]	51	45	63	84
	63	60	81	114
Raw materials: opening stock	57	51	45	63
Raw material purchases	6	9	36	51

Notes
(1) Closing stock at sales value = next 2 months' sales. Opening stock in any month is the closing stock from the previous month.
(2) Closing stock - next 3 months' sales multiplied by 30% (raw materials content)

The cost of purchases for January - March is, in £000, (9 + 36 + 51) = £96,000.
The payment to suppliers in January is the amount of purchases in December, which is £6,000.
The payments in January - March are, in £000, (6 + 9 + 36) = £51,000

COMMENTS

Question

41

	£
Net book value (£24,000 - 14,400)	9,600
Profit on sale	2,300
Cash value of sale	11,900

42

Fixed production overheads

	£	£
Total expenditure budget		693,000
Depreciation		
On fixed asset disposed of (9 months x 20% pa x £24,000)	3,600	
On other fixed assets held on 31.12.X1		
(20% x £(360,000 - 24,000))	67,200	
On fixed asset purchased (9 months x 20% pa x £108,000)	16,200	
		87,000
Cash expenditure in fixed overheads (Solution).		606,000
less Rent	80,000	
Insurance	16,000	
		96,000
		510,000
Regular monthly cash payments, fixed overheads (÷ 12)		42,500

43

Cash payments for production overheads in April

	£
Regular cash payments, fixed overheads	42,500
Rent	80,000
Variable overheads (20,000 x £2)	40,000
	162,500

44

The learning effect applies to labour and labour-related costs only, not to materials costs.

Average cost for 1st two units   = 80% of cost of 1st unit
                                             = 800 hrs x £4
                                             = £3,200 each

	£
Materials costs (6,000 x 2)	12,000
Labour costs (3,200 x 2)	6,400
Total direct costs	18,400

5: BUDGETS

Question

45

The key item to look for is what happens to the average unit time when output doubles.

Cumulative output Units		Average time per unit Hours
2	(500 ÷ 2)	250
4	(750 ÷ 4)	187.5
8	(1,125 ÷ 8)	140.625

$$\frac{187.5}{250} = 0.75 \qquad \frac{140.625}{187.5} = 0.75$$

A 75% learning rate applies.

46

Average time per unit, 1st 4 units = 90% x 90% x 200 hrs
= 162 hrs
Total time for 1st 4 units = 162 x 4 = 648 hrs

	£
Labour cost, 1st 4 units (648 x £4)	2,592
Variable overhead cost, 1st 4 units (648 x £1)	648
	3,240
less Labour and variable overhead cost of 1st unit (800 + 200)	1,000
Labour and variable overhead cost of units 2 - 4	2,240
Materials cost of 3 units (3,000 x £3)	9,000
Total variable cost of units 2 - 4	11,240

47

Average time for 1st 8 units = 100 hrs x 80% x 80% x 80% = 51.2 hrs
Total time for 1st 8 units = 51.2 hrs x 8 = 409.6 hrs
Time for 1st unit   100.0 hrs
Time for units 2-8   309.6 hrs

	£
Materials cost of order (7 x £900)	6,300
Direct labour cost (309.6 hrs x £5)	1,548
Production overhead cost (309.6 hrs x £10)	3,096
Full production cost	10,944
Profit margin (25% of sales = $33\frac{1}{3}$% of cost)	3,648
Sales price	14,592

6: BUDGETARY CONTROL. STANDARD COSTING

6: MARKING SCHEDULE

Question	Correct answer	Marks for correct answer	Question	Correct answer	Marks for correct answer	Question	Correct answer	Marks for correct answer
1	D	1	13	C	1	25	D	1
2	A	1	14	D	2	26	C	1
3	A	1	15	B	1	27	B	1
4	A	1	16	B	1	28	A	1
5	C	1	17	A	2	29	C	1
6	A	1	18	B	1	30	B	1
7	A	1	19	D	1	31	B	1
8	A	1	20	A	1	32	C	1
9	D	2	21	C	1	33	B	1
10	D	1	22	B	1	34	D	2
11	B	1	23	A	1	35	D	1
12	C	1	24	C	1	36	B	1

YOUR MARKS

Total marks available   40   Your total mark   [ ]

GUIDELINES - If your mark was:

0 - 12 You haven't sorted out variance analysis and budgetary control yet. Go back to your study text.

13 - 20 Quite good, but there are likely to be some important mistakes that you are making. Check our solutions carefully.

21 - 32 Good. You have sorted out most of the problems with variance analysis.

33 - 40 Very good. You are getting well on top of this subject.

6: BUDGETARY CONTROL. STANDARD COSTING

COMMENTS

Question

1

	55% level of activity £
Direct materials	25,135
Direct labour	45,650
Production overhead (part fixed, part variable)	72,900
Other overhead	60,000
	203,685

2

The original selling and distribution overhead budget consists of £20,000 variable costs and £60,000 fixed costs. The budget should be flexed to £480,000 of sales = 24,000 labour hours.

	£	£
Sales		480,000
Direct materials	72,000	
Direct labour	84,000	
Variable production overhead	6,000	
Fixed production overhead	90,000	
Administration overhead	60,000	
Selling and distribution overhead (5% of £480,000) + £60,000	84,000	
		396,000
Profit		84,000

3

Since sales revenue is expected to vary with direct labour hours worked, 23,000 labour hours should produce revenue of £460,000.

	Materials £		Selling and distribution £
Expected costs	69,000	(5% of £460,000 + £60,000)	83,000
Actual costs	67,000		85,500
Cost variance	2,000 (F)		2,500 (A)

4

An attainable standard represents future performance and objectives that are reasonably attainable. It will be more 'demanding' than a current standard (which is a short-term standard reflecting current conditions, possibly developed from a longer term basic standard). It will be less demanding than an 'ideal' standard, which makes no allowance for spoilage, wastage and machine breakdowns, and assumes ideal operating conditions.

COMMENTS

Question

5

Closing stocks are valued at standard cost, and so the materials price variance is calculated on the quantities purchased in the month, and not on the quantities used.

		Per kilo £	Total £
28,300 kilos	should cost	5.00	141,500
	did cost	5.25	148,575
Price variance		0.25 (A)	7,075 (A)

6

	Kilos of R
8,500 units of product Z should use (x 3)	25,500
did use	26,200
Usage variance in kilos	700 (A)
Standard cost per kilo	£5
Usage variance in £	£3,500 (A)

7

Closing stocks are valued at actual cost, and so the materials price variance is calculated on the quantities used in the month, and not the quantities purchased.

Since FIFO is used to value 'actual' materials costs, the closing stock of 1,800 litres of L must be valued at £1.75 per litre. Actual usage is:

	Litres	Price per litre £	Total value £
Opening stock	2,000	1.40	2,800
Purchases on 15 May	4,500	1.55	6,975
All but 1,800 litres of purchases on 26 May	1,700	1.75	2,975
	8,200		12,750

	£
8,200 litres of L should have cost (x £1.50)	12,300
did cost	12,750
Materials price variance	450 (A)

8

1,400 units of M should use (x 6)	8,400 litres of L
did use	8,200 litres
Usage variance	200 litres (F)
Standard price per litre	£1.50
Usage variance in £	£300 (F)

6: BUDGETARY CONTROL. STANDARD COSTING

Question

9

Since stocks are valued at actual cost, the raw materials price variance is calculated on materials quantities used (rather than quantities purchased).

	£
21,600 kg of V did cost	128,304
Price variance	1,296 (F)
21,600 kg of V should cost	129,600

Standard cost per kg of V = £6.

Usage variance is £2,880 (A).

	Kg
Usage variance in kg (£2,880 ÷ £6)	480 (A)
4,800 units of T did use	21,600
4,800 units of T should use	21,120

Standard usage per unit of T   4.4kg

10

Early settlement discounts (item D) are a financial matter and do not affect the actual purchase price of materials. In a period of inflation, and with a mid-year standard price, reported price variances in the early part of the year (item A) ought to be favourable. Item B refers to the possibility of bulk purchase discounts. With item C, an alternative supplier might offer a lower price perhaps in order to win new business.

11

Variations in output volume (item B) should not affect usage of materials *per unit* produced. A high quality of material (item A) might reduce wastage or scrap levels (item D) which would in turn improve the materials usage rate. With lower quality control standards (item C), there should be fewer rejected items, a higher proportion of successfully-completed items, and so an improvement in materials usage.

12

	£
9,700 hours worked should cost (x £3.6)	34,920
did cost	36,400
Rate variance	1,480 (A)

5,000 units of W should take (x 2 hrs)	10,000 hrs
did take	9,700 hrs
Efficiency variance in hours	300 hrs (F)
Standard rate per hour	£3.6
Efficiency variance in £	£1,080 (F)

(Standard direct labour cost of 5,000 units of W = 5,000 x £7.20 = £36,000. Actual cost = £36,400. Total direct labour cost variance = £400 (A) which is the sum of the rate variance and the efficiency variance).

COMMENTS

Question

13

Hours spent actively working (160 - 4 - 15) = 141 hours.

2,340 units should take (x 4 minutes)	156 hours
did take	<u>141 hours</u>
Efficiency variance in hours	15 hours (F)
Standard rate per hour	£3.50
Efficiency variance in £	£52.50 (F)

Idle time variance = 19 hours x £3.50 per hour = £66.5 (A).

14

	£
4,840 hours did cost	14,520
Rate variance	<u>968</u> (A)
4,840 hours should cost	<u>13,552</u>
Standard rate per hour	£2.80
Efficiency variance in £	£1,232 (F)
Standard rate per hour	£2.80
	hours
Efficiency variance in hours	440 (F)
2,200 units did take	<u>4,840</u>
2,200 units should take	<u>5,280</u>
Standard hours per unit	2.4 hours

Note. Standard direct labour cost = 2.4 hrs x £2.80 = £6.72. The standard direct labour cost of 2,200 units of Q is £14,784, is £264 more than actual cost. This £264 (F) total variance is the sum of the rate and efficiency variances.

15

Standard performance for labour is described in the question. An item of production, or quantity of work achievable, at standard performance will be measured in terms of standard hours or standard minutes (item D), and this is the *standard time* (item A) for the work.

16

If the standard efficiency level is too *low*, efficiency variances will be favourable (item B). Poor work scheduling (item A), and machine breakdowns (item C) create abnormal amounts of idle time. Idle time is a form of efficiency (or inefficiency) variance. Less training (item D) will often make staff less efficient in doing their work.

6: BUDGETARY CONTROL. STANDARD COSTING

Question

17

The only cause of the rate variance was the back-dated pay rise of 10%, which must be 10/110 or 1/11 of the actual amount paid. The rate variance is therefore £51,700 ÷ 11 = £4,700 (A).

Actual pay at the 'old' pay rate was therefore £51,700 - £4,700 = £47,000.
At the old pay rate, 6,250 policies should cost

$$\frac{6,250}{8,000} \times £56,000 = £43,750$$

Since they did cost £47,000, there is an adverse variance of £3,250, which must be an efficiency variance, since the rate variance has already been taken out of the figures.

	£	£
Budgeted standard cost of 6,250 policies		43,750
Rate variance	4,700 (A)	
Efficiency variance	3,250 (A)	
		7,950 (A)
Actual cost		51,700

18-19

The first step is to calculate the number of equivalent units of production in the month.

	Total units	Direct materials Equivalent units of output		Direct labour Equivalent units of output
Opening stock completed (no more loss to be incurred)	400	0	75%	300
Other completed output	4,300	4,300		4,300
Total completed output	4,700	4,300		4,600
Closing stock	800	800	75%	600
		5,100		5,200

5,100 units of output should use (x 1.2)	6,120 litres of input
did use	6,000 litres
Materials usage variance	120 litres (F)
Standard price per litre	x £5
Materials usage variance in £	£600 (F)

5,200 units of output should take (x 0.25)	1,300 hrs
did take	1,350 hrs
Efficiency variance	50 hrs (A)
Standard direct labour rate	£4 per hour
Direct labour rate efficiency variance	£200 (A)

COMMENTS

Question

20

Budgeted sales in units	2,400
Actual sales in units	2,700
Sales volume variance in units	300 (F)
Sales volume variance, at standard profit	£1,200 (F)
Standard profit per unit (1,200 ÷ 300)	£4
Budgeted profit in the month (2,400 units x £4)	£9,600

21

	£
Standard profit per unit	4.0
Standard cost per unit	21.0
Standard selling price per unit	25.0

	£
2,700 units should sell for (x £25)	67,500
Sales price variance	300 (A)
2,700 units did sell for	67,200

22 - 24

The fixed overhead expenditure variance is the difference between budgeted and actual fixed overhead expenditure.

	£
Budgeted expenditure (4,800 x £24)	115,200
Actual expenditure	126,000
Expenditure variance	10,800 (A)

4,500 units should take (x 4 hrs)	18,000	hours
did take	18,800	hours
Efficiency variance in hours	800	hours (A)
Fixed overhead absorption rate per hour	£6	
Fixed overhead efficiency variance	£4,800 (A)	

Budgeted hours (4,800 x 4)	19,200	hours
Actual hours	18,800	hours
Volume/capacity variance	400	hours (A)
	x £6 per hour	
	£2,400 (A)	

Note. 4,500 units were produced, and the standard fixed overhead cost of these units is (x £24) £108,000.

Cont...

Question

	£
Standard fixed overhead cost of units produced (4,500 x £24)	108,000
Fixed overhead efficiency variance	4,800 (A)
Fixed overhead volume/capacity variance	2,400 (A)
Budgeted fixed overhead expenditure	115,200
Fixed overhead expenditure variance	10,800 (A)
Actual fixed overhead expenditure	126,000

The three variances together explain the total under-absorbed fixed overhead of (£126,000 - £108,000) £18,000.

25-27

	£
Standard overhead cost of 6,200 units (x £16.5)(= overheads absorbed)	102,300
Overheads incurred (£9,200 + £92,800)	102,000
Total overhead variance (over-absorption = favourable)	300 (F)

	Fixed overhead £		Variable overhead £	Total £
Budgeted fixed overhead (6,000 x £15)	90,000		-	90,000
Variable overhead: 17,700 hrs should cost	-	(x£0.5)	8,850	8,850
	90,000		8,850	98,850
Actual overhead	92,800		9,200	102,000
Overhead expenditure variance	2,800 (A)		350 (A)	3,150 (A)

6,200 units should take (x 3hrs)	18,600 hrs
did take	17,700 hrs
Efficiency variance in hours	900 hrs (F)

Overhead efficiency variance in £	£
Variable overhead (x £0.5)	450 (F)
Fixed overhead (x £5)	4,500 (F)
Total (x £5.5)	4,950 (F)

Budgeted hours of work (6,000 x 3)	18,000 hrs
Actual hours worked	17,700 hrs
Volume (capacity) variance	300 hrs (A)
Fixed overhead rate per hour	x £5
Volume (capacity) variance	£1,500 (A)

Note. Expenditure variance + Efficiency variance + Volume (capacity) variance = Total overhead variance.

COMMENTS

Question

28

Actual sales	16,000 units
Sales volume profit variance, in £ = £4,500 (F)	
Sales volume variance, in units (÷ £3)	1,500 units (F)
Budgeted sales	14,500 units
Budgeted profit per unit	£3
Budgeted profit in total	£43,500

29

	£	£
Budgeted profit		43,500
Sales price variance		2,700 (A)
Sales volume/profit variance		4,500 (F)
		45,300
Variances		
Direct materials cost	1,700 (A)	
Direct labour cost	1,200 (F)	
Variable overhead cost	600 (F)	
Fixed overhead cost	9,000 (F)	
		9,100 (F)
Actual profit		54,400

30

	£
Total fixed overhead variance	9,000 (F)
Fixed overhead expenditure variance	3,000 (A)
Difference = fixed overhead efficiency + volume/capacity variance	12,000 (F)

This represents the difference between budgeted and actual production in units, multiplied by the standard fixed overhead rate per unit, = 12,000 ÷ 6 = 2,000 units (F).

Budgeted production	14,500 units
Difference from budget	2,000 units (F)
Actual production	16,500 units

Since sales were 16,000 units, closing stocks must be 500 units, valued at (x £17) £8,500.

31

	£
16,000 units should sell for (x £20)	320,000
Sales price variance	2,700 (A)
Actual sales revenue	317,300

	£
14,500 units in the budget:	
Budgeted fixed overhead (x £6)	87,000
Fixed overhead expenditure variance	3,000 (A)
Actual fixed overhead expenditure	90,000

6: BUDGETARY CONTROL. STANDARD COSTING

Question

32-33

		£
Overheads absorbed = standard overhead cost		
Variable overhead	11,200 std hrs x £1.5	16,800
Fixed overhead	11,200 std hrs x £6	67,200
		84,000
Actual overhead cost		78,200
Total overhead variance		5,800 (F)

	£
10,900 hours worked should cost, in variable overhead (x £1.5)	16,350
Budgeted fixed overhead	60,000
Total expected overhead expenditure	76,350
Actual overhead expenditure	78,200
Expenditure variance	1,850 (A)

Note: there is an overhead efficiency variance of 11,200 hrs - 10,900 hrs = 300 hrs (F) x £7.50 per hr = £2,250 (F).

There is also a fixed overhead volume/capacity variance of 900 hrs (F), which is the difference between budgeted hours for the month (10,000) and actual hours. Priced at the standard fixed overhead rate per hour of £6, the volume/capacity variance is £5,400 (F).

	£
Expenditure variance	1,850 (A)
Efficiency variance	2,250 (F)
Volume/capacity variance	5,400 (F)
Total overhead variance	5,800 (F)

34

	£
Budgeted sales at new price (75% of £500,000)	375,000
Actual sales (at new price)	600,000
Increase in sales volume above budget = 60% of original budget	225,000

A sales volume variance is valued at *budgeted* or *standard* values. Thus, the sales volume variance at original budgeted values is 60% of £500,000 = £300,000 (F) in *sales revenue*.

The *contribution* in the budget is £500,000 - £200,000 = £300,000, or 60p per £1 of sales.

Sales volume variance (in contribution)	=	60% of £300,000 (F)
	=	£180,000 (F)
Actual sales in 19X1	=	£600,000
Sales price actually charged	=	75% of original budgeted sales price
Actual sales at original budget price	=	£800,000
Sales price variance (£800,000 - £600,000)	=	£200,000 (A)

COMMENTS

Question

35 Actual direct materials costs in 19X1 = £300,000. This is 80% of the original budgeted price. Actual purchase quantities at original budget price = £300,000 ÷ 0.80 = £375,000.

Materials price variance = £375,000 - £300,000
 = £75,000 (F)

36 Actual production and sales = 160% of original budgeted quantity.

160% of original budget quantity
 should use (x 1.6)   £320,000 of materials at budget price
 did use   £375,000 of materials at budget price
 Usage variance   £55,000 (A)

Note.
	£	£
Budgeted profit		50,000
Sales price variance	200,000 (A)	
Sales volume variance	180,000 (F)	
Materials price variance	75,000 (F)	
Materials usage variance	55,000 (A)	
Total variances		0
Actual profit (given in question)		50,000

7: MARKING SCHEDULE

Question	Correct answer	Marks for correct answer	Question	Correct answer	Marks for correct answer	Question	Correct answer	Marks for correct answer
1	D	1	14	B	1	27	A	1
2	B	1	15	C	1	28	A	2
3	B	1	16	D	1	29	B	1
4	B	1	17	D	1	30	C	2
5	B	1	18	B	1	31	D	2
6	C	1	19	A	1	32	A	1
7	B	1	20	C	1	33	A	2
8	B	1	21	D	1	34	A	1
9	A	1	22	B	1	35	C	1
10	B	1	23	A	1	36	D	2
11	D	1	24	C	1	37	C	2
12	A	1	25	D	1	38	D	1
13	A	1	26	C	2			

YOUR MARKS

Total marks available   45   Your total mark

GUIDELINES - If your mark was:

0 - 13 You need to learn more about breakeven analysis and marginal costing. Go back to your study text.

14 - 22 Still some weaknesses. You probably need to learn this topic more thoroughly.

23 - 34 You have reached a good intermediate standard. There are a few improvements that you could probably still make. Have you identified any regular mistakes you were making?

35 - 45 Very good. You are well on top of the essential principles of this topic.

COMMENTS

Question

1

Budgeted fixed costs (10,000 x £4) + (10,000 + £0.80)	£48,000
Unit contribution £(6 - 1.2 - 0.4)	£4.40
Breakeven point (£48,000 ÷ £4.4)	10,909 units

2

Selling costs are unchanged (both variable and fixed)

	£
New sales price (6 x 1.1)	6.60
New variable cost per unit (1.2 x 1.1) + 0.4	<u>1.72</u>
New unit contribution	<u>4.88</u>
New fixed costs (40,000 x 1.25) + 8,000	£58,000
New breakeven point (58,000 ÷ 4.88)	11,885 units

3

The graph shows a variable cost which only starts to be incurred *beyond* a certain volume of output. Only B fits this description of cost behaviour.

4

The cost *per unit* is the same for each additional unit produced. This is a variable cost. In contrast, although the *total* fixed cost is constant at all levels of output, the fixed cost *per unit* falls as output increases. Because the fixed costs per unit declines with increasing output, the full cost of production per unit and the full cost of sale per unit declines too.

5

The high-low method of estimating fixed and variable costs is used.

	£
Total cost of 1,100 units	18,300
Total cost of 700 units	<u>13,500</u>
Variable cost of 400 units	<u>4,800</u>
Variable cost per unit (÷ 400)	£12

	£
Total cost of 1,100 units	18,300
Variable cost of 1,100 units (x £12)	<u>13,200</u>
Fixed costs	<u>5,100</u>

Question

6
Budgeted fixed costs (5,000 x £2)	£10,000
Contribution per unit (£10 - 6)	£4
Units required to break even (£10,000 ÷ 4)	2,500 units
Sales revenue needed to break even (2,500 x £10)	£25,000

7
	£
Target profit	6,000
Fixed costs	<u>10,000</u>
Target contribution	<u>16,000</u>
Contribution per unit	£4
Units required to achieve target profit	4,000

8
Fixed costs (10,000 x 120%)	£12,000
Units required now to break even (÷ £4)	3,000
Budgeted units of sales	5,000
Margin of safety (5,000 - 3,000)	2,000

In % terms, MOS = $\frac{2,000}{5,000}$ x 100% = 40%

9
Original budgeted profit:

	£
Contribution (5,000 units x £4)	20,000
Fixed costs	<u>10,000</u>
Profit	<u>10,000</u>

	£
New sales price (£10 x 120%)	12.00
New variable cost (£6 x 1.12%)	<u>6.72</u>
New unit contribution	<u>5.28</u>
Contribution required	£20,000
Sales volume now needed (÷ £5.28)	3,788 units

This is 1,212 units or 24.24% less than the original budgeted level of 5,000 units of sales.

10 Item 4 is a selling cost, not a production cost. All the other three items are variable with the number of batches produced, and so would be included in the marginal production cost per batch of finished output.

COMMENTS

Question

11 The charge of £50 per hour between the minimum and maximum charges is indicated by the sloping 'variable cost' line which, if extended, would meet the origin of the graph. Up to 20 hours of use, however, the fixed minimum charge of £1,000 applies. 21 hours would cost £1,050, 22 hours £1,100 and so on. At 100 hours and above, the charge becomes a fixed cost of £5,000.

You might have been tempted to choose Graph 3, but this graph would indicate a minimum charge of £1,000 plus £50 per hour for *every* hour used, up to a maximum payment of £5,000. This isn't the nature of the cost described.

12 The fixed charge of £2,000 means that the cost line must start at a point on the y axis (£2,000) when x = 0. The variable cost per unit falls from £16 to £8 to £4, but only for subsequent units purchased, and so Graph 4 is appropriate rather than Graph 7.

13 This describes a 'step cost' pattern, in which cost items rise by a certain amount beyond a certain level of output. Within a certain range of output, the cost item could be regarded as fixed.

14 This is a variable cost item up to a certain level of activity (800 miles) and then becomes a fixed cost at higher activity levels.

15 Dividing each cost by the corresponding volume does not produce a constant figure, therefore this is not a linear variable cost. Using the high-low method to separate the fixed and variable costs:

	Hours	£
Low	9,800	21,760
High	15,400	28,480
Difference	5,600	6,720

Therefore, variable cost per hour = $\frac{£6,720}{5,600}$ = £1.20

Fixed cost = £21,760 - (9,800 × £1.20) = £10,000

Total maintenance cost for 12,000 hours = fixed cost   £10,000
            + variable cost (1.20 × 12,000)   £14,400
                £24,400

7: MARGINAL COSTING AND BREAKEVEN ANALYSIS

Question

16
Unit contribution = £(18 - 7 - 3 - 2) = £6
Budgeted fixed costs = (15,000 units x £2) = £30,000
Breakeven point = £30,000 ÷ £6 per unit
= 5,000 units
= 5,000 x £18
= £90,000 of sales revenue

17
Budgeted sales	15,000 units	
Breakeven volume	5,000 units	
Margin of safety	10,000 units	= 67% of budget

18
	£
Target profit	9,000
Fixed costs	30,000
Target contribution	39,000
Contribution per unit	£6
Units of sale needed to achieve target	6,500

19
	£
Unit selling price	18.00
Unit variable cost (7 + 3 + 2) x 110%	13.20
Unit contribution at new cost level	4.80

	£
Target profit	9,000
Fixed costs (30,000 x 110%)	33,000
Target contribution	42,000
Units of sale needed to achieve target = £42,000 ÷ £4.80 =	8,750

This is 6,250 units or 41.66% less than the original budget of 15,000 units.

20
The wording of the question indicates that only vehicle running costs are variable costs. Wages are fixed cost items.

	£
Revenue	120,000
Variable costs	48,000
Contribution	72,000
Contribution per kilometre	£1.20

Breakeven point = $\dfrac{\text{Fixed costs}}{\text{Cont'n per km}}$ = $\dfrac{£64,000}{£1.20 \text{ per km}}$ = 53,333 km

245

COMMENTS

Question

21

Fixed costs now reduced to (£32,000 + £24,000) £56,000

Breakeven point $\dfrac{£56,000}{£1.20 \text{ per km}}$ = 46,667 km

The change in the forecast operating distance has no relevance for the breakeven point.

22

SSAP 9 requires that the absorption of fixed production overhead is based on normal capacity, and so this is the basis we should expect cost accounts to use, as well as financial accounts.

Fixed production overhead absorption rate = $\dfrac{£200,000}{20,000}$

= £10 per unit

Therefore the full cost of production = £50 variable + £10 fixed = £60 per unit

Production in the quarter was 1,000 units lower than normal capacity, therefore fixed production overhead would be under-absorbed by 1,000 x £10 = £10,000.

The absorption costing profit can now be calculated:

		£000	£000
Sales	16,000 x £125		2,000
Less:			
full production cost of sales:			
opening stock		-	
production	19,000 x £60	1,140	
		1,140	
closing stock	3,000 x £60	180	960
			1,040
Adjust for under-absorbed overhead			10
Gross profit			1,030
Fixed selling and administration overhead			80
Absorption costing profit			950

23

With marginal costing, all units are valued at variable cost. Fixed overheads are treated as period costs and written off as they are incurred.

		£000	£000
Sales	16,000 x £125		2,000
Less: variable production cost of sales:			
opening stock		-	
production	19,000 x £50	950	
		950	
closing stock	3,000 x £50	150	800
Contribution			1,200
Fixed production overhead			(200)
Fixed selling and administration overhead			(80)
Marginal costing profit			920

Question

24

Quick method of calculation

	Absorption costing £	Marginal costing £
Opening stock	7,500	2,500
Closing stock	9,000	3,000
Increase in stock during month	+ 1,500	+ 500
Difference in profit		£1,000

Absorption costing profit is higher because the value of the net stock change is positive.

Alternative presentation

Absorption costing		£	£	Marginal costing		£	£
Opening stock			7,500	Opening stock			2,500
Direct costs:				Direct costs incurred			
Materials	4,600			Materials	4,600		
Labour	3,200			Labour	3,200		
	7,800				7,800		
Overheads absorbed	15,600			Overhead incurred	14,500		
(200%)			23,400				22,300
			30,900				24,800
Closing stock				Closing stock			
(3,000 + 200% of 3,000)			(9,000)	Cost of sales			(3,000)
			21,900				21,800
Overheads absorbed:	15,600						
Overheads incurred							
(500 + 14,000)	14,500						
Over-absorbed overhead			1,100				
Cost of sales (net)			20,800				

Difference £1,000
Lower cost of sales with absorption costing

25

The high-low method seems convenient and suitable here.

	£
Highest output 8,400 units, total cost	45,660
Lowest output 5,000 units, total cost	37,500
Difference in output 3,400 units, variable cost	8,160

Variable cost per unit £ $\frac{8,160}{3,400}$ =   £2.40

Substituting

	£
Total cost of 5,000 units	37,500
Variable cost of 5,000 units (x 2.4)	12,000
Fixed cost of 5,000 units	25,500

Thus y = £25,500 + £2.4X

COMMENTS

Question

26

		£
(Highest output) Total cost of	1,400 units	19,000
(Lowest output) total cost of	600 units	9,000
Variable cost of	800 units	10,000

Variable cost per unit £ 10,000 / 800 = £12.50

Substituting £
- Total cost of 600 units 9,000
- Variable cost of 600 units (x 12.5) 7,500
- Fixed costs 1,500

27

We are told (item (d)) that staff costs are fixed.

Restaurant meals £
- Sales 5,600
- Variable costs (3,080 + 80% of 600) 3,560
- Contribution 2,040

800 meals per week: contribution per restaurant meal £2.55

	£
Take away meals contribution (720 x £1.50)	1,080.0
Extra fixed costs	1,200.0
	(120.0)
Extra contribution from restaurant meals (10% of 720 x £2.55)	183.6
Increase in profits	63.6

28

	£	£
Opening stock		0
Production costs (72,000 units)		270,000
		270,000
Less closing stock (absorption costing)	(11,250)	
Remove fixed overheads (3,000 units x £2.50)	7,500	
Closing stock (marginal costing)		(3,750)
Cost of sales for 69,000 units (marginal costing)		266,250
Sales (69,000 x £5)		345,000
Profit (marginal costing)		78,750

Question

29

	£
Total cost of 150,000 units (x 41.5)	6,225,000
Total cost of 100,000 units (x 47.5)	2,750,000
Variable cost of 50,000 units	1,475,000
Variable cost per unit	£29.50
Substituting:	
Total cost of 100,000 units	4,750,000
Variable cost of 100,000 units (x £29.5)	2,950,000
Fixed costs	1,800,000

Breakeven point $\dfrac{£1,800,000}{£20}$ = 90,000 units

30

	£000
Sales	864
Less Variable costs (216 + 162 + 54 + 81)	513
Contribution	351

Contribution/sales ratio   0.40625

Fixed costs (126 + 108)	£234,000
Breakeven point (in sales revenue) ÷ 0.40625	£576,000

31

Variable cost per unit $\dfrac{£513,000}{18,000}$ = £28.5

At a sales price of £42, unit contribution = £13.5

90% capacity = 18,000 x $\dfrac{90}{75}$ = 21,600 units

	£
Contribution 21,600 x £13.5	291,600
Fixed costs	234,000
Profit	57,600

32

	£
New selling price (85% of £48)	40.8
Variable cost per unit	28.5
Contribution per unit	12.3

Contribution/sales ratio   0.3014705

Fixed costs (234 + 25)	£259,000
New breakeven point (÷ 0.3014705)	£859,122

Question

33 Beyond output Q, the variable cost per unit changes. This should be evident from the change in the slope of the total cost line. Answer B must therefore be wrong. The next clue is that the slope of the total cost line from output Q can be extended back to point F (fixed costs) at zero output, which indicates that once output exceeds Q the variable cost per unit is the *same for all units produced* including for the units up to output Q. At output Q, unit variable costs go up. Only answer A fits this change. Answers C and D involve changes in unit variable costs, but only for additional units beyond output Q.

34 *Absorption costing*

Fixed cost per unit = £180,000 ÷ 60,000 = £3
Total cost per unit = £5 + 3 + 1 = £9

		£
Opening stock 20,000 × £9		180,000
Costs of production 50,000 × £9		450,000
		630,000
Less Closing stock 10,000 × £9		(90,000)
Cost of sales		540,000
Sales (60,000 × £10)		600,000
Gross profit	£	60,000
Overhead absorbed 50,000 × £3	150,000	
Overhead incurred	180,000	
Under-absorbed overhead		(30,000)
Net profit		30,000

Marginal costing

	£
Sales (60,000 × £10)	600,000
Less variable costs of sales (60,000 × £(5 + 1) per unit)	360,000
Contribution	240,000
Fixed costs	180,000
Profit	60,000

Note. The difference in profit, £30,000, is the difference between the value of the reduction in stocks (by 10,000 units) during the period. In absorption costing, stock is reduced in value by £90,000 and in marginal costing (cost £6 per unit) the stock reduction would be only £60,000. Since these stock reductions become a cost of sales in the period, the marginal costing profit is higher by £30,000.

35 The key to this answer is to calculate the variable cost per unit.

The company's profit is £0 (nil) when the sales price is £5, fixed costs are £80,000 and monthly sales are 40,000 units.

Let the variable cost be £V.

$$P = (S - V)Q - F$$
$$0 = (S - V)\,40,000 - 80,000$$
$$40,000\,V = 200,000 - 80,000$$
$$= 120,000$$
$$V = 3$$

7: MARGINAL COSTING AND BREAKEVEN ANALYSIS

Question

	£	£	£
Sales price	4.5	5.0	5.5
Variable cost	<u>3.0</u>	<u>3.0</u>	<u>3.0</u>
Unit contribution	1.5	2.0	2.5
Unit sales	60,000	50,000	46,000
	£	£	£
Total contribution	90,000	100,000	115,000
Fixed costs	<u>80,000</u>	<u>80,000</u>	<u>80,000</u>
Profit	<u>10,000</u>	<u>20,000</u>	<u>*35,000</u>

* Maximum profit

36

Step 1

Estimated demand over 20 weeks = 140 days
Double rooms 40 x 140 = 5,600 days
Single rooms 80 x 140 @ 75% capacity = 8,400 days

Step 2

Revenue from double rooms is the equivalent of 5,600 x 175% = 9,800 days' revenue from single rooms.

Expected revenue, expressed in single room rates:

	days
Double rooms (5,600 x 175%)	9,800
Single rooms	<u>8,400</u>
Total	<u>18,200</u>

Step 3

Revenue needed to achieve profit of £50,000

	£
Variable costs	
Single rooms (8,400 x 7)	58,800
Double rooms (5,600 x 12)	67,200
Fixed costs	206,200
Profit target	<u>50,000</u>
Revenue needed	<u>382,200</u>
Single room rate per day (÷ 18,200)	£21
Double room rate (x 175%)	£36.75

COMMENTS

Question

37

Step 1

Estimated demand over 30 weeks, ie an extra 70 days

	days
Double rooms 5,600 + (50% x 70 x 40) =	7,000
Single rooms 8,400 + (50% x 70 x 80) =	11,200

Step 2

Revenue from double rooms is the equivalent of 7,000 x 175% = 12,250 days' revenue from single rooms.

Expected revenue in days' income, at single room rates:

	days
Double rooms	12,250
Single rooms	<u>11,200</u>
	<u>23,450</u>

Step 3

Revenue needed

	£
Variable costs	
Single rooms (11,200 x 7)	78,400
Double rooms (7,000 x 12)	84,000
Fixed costs	246,600
Profit target	<u>60,000</u>
Revenue needed	<u>469,000</u>
Single room rate per day (÷ 23,450)	£20
Double room rate per day (x 175%)	£35

38

Statement A is true for total *revenue* but not for profits.

Statement B is true only within a certain range of output levels. When output volume changes substantially, fixed costs can rise or fall a 'step' - ie fixed costs become step costs.

Statement C is incorrect because it ignores directly attributable fixed costs - ie fixed cost items which can be directly attributed to a particular activity or cost centre.

Statement D is a fundamental rule of accounting for decision making.

8: MARKING SCHEDULE

Question	Correct answer	Marks for the correct answer	Question	Correct answer	Marks for the correct answer
1	D	1	14	B	1
2	B	1	15	C	1
3	B	1	16	A	1
4	A	1	17	C	2
5	B	1	18	A	1
6	C	1	19	C	1
7	C	1	20	D	2
8	D	2	21	A	2
9	D	1	22	B	1
10	C	1	23	D	1
11	C	1	24	B	1
12	B	2	25	C	1
13	D	1			

YOUR MARKS

Total marks available: 30   Your total mark:

GUIDELINES - If your mark was:

0 - 9 You need to study this subject carefully, and try to improve your standard.

10 - 15 Fair, but there is still some work to do before you understand costing for decision-making properly

16 - 24 Good, although there are some mistakes that you could probably eliminate with a bit more practice.

25 - 30 Very good. You understand the concept of relevant costs very well indeed.

COMMENTS

Question

1 Budgeting is formal planning, not the preparation of ad hoc information, and so answers A and B cannot be correct. Incremental costing is defined in the wording of the question.

2 All past costs and committed costs are irrelevant to the decision. Relevant costs are just the disposal costs of £2,500 that would be incurred if the project were abandoned.

3 The full salary of A Pay is a cost that will be incurred whether or not the project goes ahead, and so the relevant cost of his allocated salary cost is nil. Relevant staff costs are

	£
Salaries of Ray Peer and Chris Swords (incurred if the project goes ahead)	40,000
less Redundancy payments (incurred if the project is abandoned)	18,000
Net relevant costs	<u>22,000</u>

4 The allocation of general fixed overheads is not a relevant cost for the decision. Depreciation is a notional (non-cash) cost and should be ignored. The only relevant cost is the loss of disposal value on the plant and machinery.

	£
Revenue if plant is sold now	18,000
Revenue if plant is sold in 1 year's time	11,000
Relevant cost of using plant for 1 year	<u>7,000</u>

5 Relevant costs can never be costs already incurred. Original purchase prices for M111 and M222 are irrelevant.

Relevant costs

		£
M111	(in continuous use, so quantities used will be replaced: 1,000 x 2 x £3.50)	7,000
M222	4,000 units in stock (which can be sold if not used) x £1.80	7,200
M222	Further 1,000 units to be purchased x £2.50	2,500
		<u>16,700</u>

Question

6

The company would lose the opportunity to sell the machine now, and would instead incur disposal costs in one year. These are both relevant costs.

	£	
Variable operating costs	6,000	
Current disposal value of machine (opportunity cost)	3,000	(5,000-2,000)
Disposal cost in one year's time	<u>1,500</u>	
	<u>10,500</u>	

7

Skilled labour for 20 x 2 = 40 hours' work must be replaced by unskilled labour, who in turn must be replaced by agency workers.

Incremental costs	£
Skilled labour for the job 40: hours x £4 (incremental cost of agency staff)	160
Unskilled labour for the job (agency staff): 60 hours x £4	<u>240</u>
	<u>400</u>

8

Statement 1. This can be true when there are bulk purchase discounts on larger quantities. For example, suppose that there is a bulk purchase discount of 10% on items costing £10 each, for orders above 100,000 units.

		£
Cost of 100,000	= 100,000 x £10	1,000,000
Cost of, say, 110,000	= 110,000 x £10 x 90%	<u>990,000</u>
Incremental cost of 10,000 units		<u>(10,000)</u>

Statement 2. This is true of *sales revenue*, but *not of profit*.

Statement 3. A direct cost is a cost that can be identified separately in a product cost, job cost or operation. Direct costs can often be fixed costs - eg many costs of a long term contract are direct fixed costs.

9

Production	Contribution per unit, ignoring materials costs £	Kilos of M per unit	Contribution per kilo of M £	Ranking for production	Kilos of M needed to meet sales demand
W	7	0.7	10	3rd	5,600
X	6	0.5	12	1st	3,600
Y	11	1.0	11	2nd	12,000
Z	12	1.5	8	4th	<u>15,000</u>
					<u>36,200</u>

		Quantity units	Kilos of M needed
The decision should be to make:	X	7,200	3,600
	Y (balance)	11,400	<u>11,400</u>
			<u>15,000</u>

255

COMMENTS

Question

10

Incremental production

	Contribution per kilo of materials ignoring material cost £	Subtract materials purchase cost per kilo £	Net contribution per per kilo £	Make/don't make
W	10	9.5	0.5	Make
Y	11	9.5	1.5	Make
Z	8	9.5	(0.5)	Don't make

Make

	Materials needed Kg
600 units of Y (to reach budget limit)	600
8,000 units of W (x 0.7)	5,600
	6,200

11

	£
Variable costs of making Q (3,000 x £7)	21,000
Contribution forgone from lost sales of T: 3,000 x £(35 - 2 - 8 - 2 - 7)	48,000
Incremental inspection and testing costs	3,000
	72,000

Minimum price (÷ 3,000 units) = £24

Note. Another way of expressing the relevant costs is to assume that the costs of making Q, which will be incurred anyway, are fixed, and so the contribution forgone from lost sales of T = 3,000 x £(35 - 2 - 8 - 2) = £69,000.

12

Hours required to meet sales budget

		Hours per month
Product X	500 units x ½ hr	250
Product Y	300 units x 1½ hrs	450
Product Z	400 units x 2 hrs	800
		1,500

Since there are only 1,200 hours available, direct labour is a limiting factor.

Contribution per direct labour hour

		Contribution per unit £	Hours per unit	Contribution per hour £	Priority
X	(8 - 6.5)	1.5	½	3.0	3rd
Y	(18 - 12)	6	1½	4.0	1st
Z	(22 - 15)	7	2	3.5	2nd

Cont...

8: COSTS FOR DECISION-MAKING

Question

The profit maximising budget is to make and sell 300 units of product Y (1st priority, with 450 hours needed to meet sales demand) and 375 units of Z (2nd priority, to use up the remaining 750 hours available per month).

Total contribution = (300 x £6) + (375 x £7)
= £4,425 per month.

Note. Making 400 units of Y (Option C) is not profit maximising, since the budgeted sales are only 300 units.

13

	Contribution per unit	
	X	Z
	£	£
In normal time working	1.5	7
Extra cost of overtime premium	1.0 (½ hr x £2 per hr)	4 (2hrs x £2 per hr)
Contribution per unit with overtime	0.5	3
Hours per unit	½	2
Contribution per hr in overtime	£1	£1.5
Priority for manufacture	2nd	1st

Conclusion: use up the remaining 250 hrs to make

	Hours needed/available	Extra contribution £
25 units of Z (up to sales budget of 400)	50	75
(Balance) 400 units of X (to use up hours available)	200	200
	250	275

14

£5,000 has been spent on market research already, and so is a sunk cost and irrelevant to the decision. The further £2,000 will only be spent if Annette Cord continues with the project, and so is an incremental (relevant) cost of the decision to go ahead.

15

Annette Cord will be giving up a salary of £800 per month if she sets up in business, and this is the relevant cost. The new business ought to be able to pay her at least this amount out of 'profits', otherwise Annette would be better off keeping her existing job. Whether or not the business can afford to pay her the incremental £200 per month that she wants is a separate matter, not addressed by the question.

COMMENTS

Question

16

Price per unit £	Variable cost per unit £	Contribution per unit £	Sales volume	Total contribution £000	Fixed costs £000	Profit £000
14	6	8	17,500	140	120	*20
15	6	9	15,000	135	120	15
21	9	12	10,000	120	110	10
23	9	14	9,000	126	110	16

Annette's salary cost and the incremental market research costs are common to all four price options, and so can be ignored.

17

	X	Y	Total
Machine hours per unit	2 hrs	3 hrs	
Total machine hours per month needed	2,000 hrs	3,000 hrs	5,000 hrs
Machine hours available			3,500 hrs
Shortfall			1,500 hrs

	£	£
Variable cost per unit	15	20
External purchase cost	31	47
Extra cost of purchase per unit	16	27
Hours saved by purchasing	2 hrs per unit	3 hrs per unit
Extra cost per hour saved	£8	£9

The company should therefore buy 750 units of X per month.

	£
In-house production costs	
Variable costs of X: (1,000 - 750) x £15	3,750
Y: 1,000 x £20	20,000
	23,750
Fixed costs 3,500 hrs x £5 per hr	17,500
	41,250
External purchase costs of X (750 x £31)	23,250
	64,500

18

	£
Cost of 35,000 units	3,600,000
Cost of 25,000 units	2,600,000
	1,000,000
Increase in fixed costs at 35,000 units	200,000
Variable cost of 10,000 units	800,000
Variable cost per unit	£80
Contribution per unit	£20

Cont...

Question

Fixed costs below 35,000 units = £2,600,000 − (25,000 × £80)
= £600,000

Breakeven = £600,000 ÷ 20 = 30,000 units

When fixed costs rise by £200,000 to £800,000, the company will start to incur losses again, and another breakeven point is reached at £800,000 ÷ £20 = 40,000 units.

The increase in variable costs at output above 42,500 units will not affect the breakeven point, since extra units sold then add £10 each to contribution and profit.

19

Note. This is another question intended to draw your attention to marginal costing principles and CVP analysis in a decision problem or budgeting problem.

Budgeted machine hours (original budget) (40,000 × 3) + (60,000 × 2) = 240,000 hours
Fixed overhead absorption rate = £720,000 ÷ 240,000 = £3 per hour
Variable cost per unit of X = £20 − £(3×3) = £11

Sales price for X £	Contribution per unit £	Sales units	Total contribution £000	Saving in fixed costs £000	Net contribution £000
25	14	40,000	560	0	560
26	15	37,000	555	0	555
27	16	34,000	544	+15	*559
28	17	31,000	527	+15	542

20

Total machine hours needed (5,000 × 3) + (4,000 × 6) + (7,000 × 4) =		67,000
Hours available		40,000
Shortfall		27,000

	PQ £	RS £	Z £
Variable cost per unit	15	32	21
Sales price/external purchase price	24	44	30
Contribution earned/saved	9	12	9
	÷ 3	÷ 6	÷ 4
Contribution earned/saved per hour	£3	£2	£2.25
Ranking for production	1st	3rd	2nd

Production budget   Hrs needed
       5,000 units of PQ (× 3)   15,000
(Balance) 6,250 units of Z (× 4)   25,000
                                                                                                  40,000

COMMENTS

Question

21

To produce the budgeted quantity of each component would need 18,000 hours of in-house machine time, which is exactly the amount of the shortfall.

	W	X	Y	Z
	£	£	£	£
Unit variable cost	13	8	15	7
External purchase cost	41	23	42	20
Difference in cost	28	15	27	13
	÷ 4	÷ 3	÷ 4½	÷ 2
Difference per machine hour	£7	£5	£6	£6.5
Priority for external purchase	1st	4th	3rd	2nd

22

Year	Total costs	Minus dep'n and allocated overheads	Cash costs	Revenue	Net cash flow	Cumulative net cash flow
	£	£	£	£	£	£
1	120,000	30,000	90,000	150,000	60,000	60,000
2	132,000	30,000	102,000	180,000	78,000	138,000
3	132,000	30,000	102,000	180,000	78,000	
4	120,000	30,000	90,000	150,000	60,000	

Payback is in year 2. Assuming even cash flows throughout year 2, the £100,000 outlay is paid back

$\frac{40,000}{78,000}$ = 0.5 of the way through year 2.

23

Year	Cash flow	Discount factor at 20%	Present value
	£		£
0	(100,000)	1.000	(100,000)
1	60,000	0.833	49,980
2	78,000	0.694	54,132
3	78,000	0.579	45,162
4	60,000	0.482	28,920
		NPV	78,194

Question

24

Annual depreciation = $\frac{(30,000 - 5,000)}{5}$ = £5,000 per annum

Year	Profit/(loss) £	Add back depreciation £	Cash flow £	Cumulative cash flow £
1	(3,000)	5,000	2,000	2,000
2	15,000	5,000	20,000	22,000
			Payback	£30,000
3	20,000	5,000	25,000	47,000
4	20,000	5,000	25,000	
5	10,000	5,000	15,000	

Payback of the £30,000 outlay occurs during year 3, and with even cash flows throughout the year, it will occur

$\frac{£8,000}{£25,000}$ or 0.3 of the way through the year.

25

Year	Cash flow £	Discount factor at 10%	Present value £
0	(30,000)	1.000	(30,000)
1	2,000	0.909	1,818
2	20,000	0.826	16,520
3	25,000	0.751	18,775
4	25,000	0.683	17,075
5	15,000	0.621	9,315
Disposal 5	5,000	0.621	3,105
		NPV =	36,608

9: MARKING SCHEDULE

Question	Correct answer	Marks for the correct answer	Question	Correct answer	Marks for the correct answer
1	C	1	7	C	1
2	A	1	8	D	1
3	D	1	9	B	2
4	C	1	10	B	2
5	A	2	11	B	2
6	B	1			

YOUR MARKS

Total marks available **15**   Your total mark [ ]

GUIDELINES - If your mark was:

0 - 6 You haven't yet properly understood this topic. Revise it carefully.

11 - 15 A very good mark in a topic area that some student cost accountants find quite confusting.

7 - 10 Good, but there may be one or two aspects of this topic that you still need to know.

COMMENTS

Question

1

	£
Opening stock	40,000
Materials	80,000
Conversion costs	100,000
	220,000
Closing stock	20,000
Cost of production	200,000

Production costs are apportioned on the sales value of units *produced*.

Product	Units produced	Sales value	Apportionment of costs	Cost per unit
		£	£	£
W	20,000	80,000	(2) 50,000	2.50
X	20,000	120,000	(3) 75,000	3.75
Y	40,000	120,000	(3) 75,000	1.875
			200,000	

2

When by-product revenue is credited to the process account, this has the effect of reducing the cost of production by the amount of the revenue earned.

	£
Raw materials plus conversion costs	160,000
less by-product revenue	4,000
Net process costs	156,000

Product	Units	Apportioned costs
		£
J	2,500	(5) 48,750
K	3,500	(7) 68,250 *
L	2,000	(4) 39,000
	8,000	156,000

COMMENTS

Question

3

By-products are not costed. The by-product revenue is credited to the sales account, and so does not affect the process costs.

Joint product	Kilos	Sales value £		Apportioned costs £	Cost per kilo £
JP1	4,000	44,000	(44%)	22,880	5.72
JP2	3,000	30,000	(30%)	15,600	5.20
JP3	1,000	26,000	(26%)	13,520	13.52
		100,000		52,000	

4

		Sales value at split-off point £	Apportioned Process 1 costs £
Product X	(3,750 x 8)	30,000	(5) 22,500
Product Y	(4,500 x 4)	18,000	(3) 13,500
			36,000

	£
Process 3: Input transferred from Process 1	13,500
Added materials	6,000
Conversion costs	30,000
	49,500

Cost per unit of product YY (÷ 4,000) = £12.375

5

	Product XX		Product YY	
	£	£	£	£
Sales value of units produced	(3,000 x 14)	4,200	(4,000 x 12.5)	50,000
Sales value of product X/Y at split-off point		30,000		18,000
Added sales value from further processing		12,000		32,000
Added materials costs of further processing	10		6,000	
Variable conversion costs of further processing	5,000		7,500	
Fixed costs saved by shutting down	10,000		15,000	
Relevant costs of further processing		15,000		28,500
Extra profit/(loss) from further processing		(3,000)		3,500

9: JOINT PRODUCTS AND BY-PRODUCTS

Question

6

Variable costs for 4,500 units of YY in April

	£
Process 1 materials	16,000
Variable conversion costs	5,000
	21,000
Process 3 materials	6,000
Variable conversion costs	7,500
	34,500

1,000 units of YY are the equivalent of one quarter of the April output.

Extra cost of 1,000 units of YY = £34,500 ÷ 4 = £8,625.

Note. *All* the extra costs of Process 1 would be incremental costs of making the extra units of Y, since the extra output of X or XX could be sold.

7

Process costs	£
Direct materials	60,000
Direct labour	8,000
Variable overhead (2,000 x 1)	2,000
Variable costs	70,000
Fixed overhead (2,000 x 4)	8,000
Total production cost	78,000

Output quantities 80% of 30,000 kg = 24,000 kg
Full cost per kilogram £78,000 ÷ 24,000 = £3.25
Sales price per kilogram (X,Y and Z) = 120% of £3.25 = £3.90

(*Note.* The 20% loss is normal loss, and so the 'good' output should bear all the process costs, with no direct write-off for loss to the P & L account).

8

To obtain 1 kilo of X, there has to be input of 2.5 kilos of raw materials. To produce 300 kilos of X needs 750 kilos of raw materials. Since the variable cost of processing 30,000 kilos of raw materials is £70,000, the incremental cost of producing 300 kilos of X is

$$\frac{750}{30,000} \times £70,000 = £1,750$$

There will be unwanted output of 120 kilos of Y and 180 kilos of Z.

COMMENTS

Question

9

	Total units	Equivalent units
Opening stock - to complete	1,000	400
Other finished output	2,000	2,000
Total output (1,800S + 1,200T)	3,000	2,400
Normal loss (10% of 5,000)	500	0
Closing stock	2,000	600
Abnormal loss (balancing figure)	500	500
	6,000	3,500

Cost per equivalent unit = £51,800 ÷ 3,500 = £14.80

Total cost of finished output

	£
Opening stock b/fwd	8,400
2,400 equivalent units x £14.8	35,520
	43,920

	Units	Sales value £	Apportioned costs £	Cost per unit £
S	1,800 (x 30)	54,000 (3)	32,940	18.30
T	1,200 (x 15)	18,000 (1)	10,980	9.15
			43,920	

10

Diagram of the processes

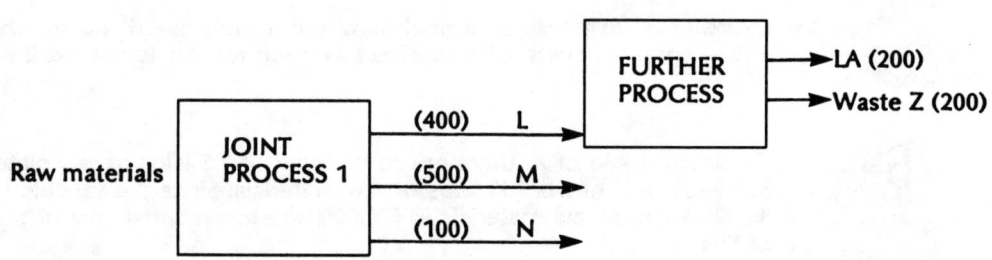

To produce 50 extra units of LA will involve an increase in production activity of 25%

	£
Sales value of 500 units of M (x £30)	15,000
Sales value of 125% of 500 units of M (x £25)	15,625
Extra sales revenue from selling extra units of M	625

266

Question

	£	£
Extra revenue from LA (50 x £160)		8,000
Extra revenue from M		625
Extra revenue from N (25 x £2)		50
		8,675
Extra (variable) costs: joint process (25% of 6,000)	1,500	
further process (25% of £12,000)	3,000	
Extra disposal costs of Z (50 x £10)	500	
		5,000
Increase in profit		3,675

11

	Kilos
Process 1	
Input	6,000
Normal loss (10%)	600
Expected output (equivalent units)	5,400

Cost per expected unit of output £14,850 ÷ 5,400 = £2.75
Total cost of output transferred to Process 2 (x 5,500) = £15,125

Process 2 costs	£
Transfers from Process 1	15,125
Conversion costs	14,675
	29,800
less: By-product revenue (500 x £2)	1,000
	28,800

Product	Kilos	Sales value £	Apportioned costs £	Profit £	Profit per kilo £
X	2,500	40,000	(2) 19,200	20,800	8.32
Y	2,500	20,000	(1) 9,600	1,400	4.16
		60,000	29,800		

10: MARKING SCHEDULE

Question	Correct answer	Marks for the correct answer	Question	Correct answer	Marks for the correct answer
1	A	1	11	A	1
2	A	1	12	B	1
3	B	1	13	D	1
4	D	1	14	C	1
5	A	1	15	A	1
6	C	1	16	C	1
7	D	1	17	B	1
8	C	1	18	B	2
9	A	1	19	D	1
10	D	1			

YOUR MARKS

Total marks available 20   Your total mark ☐

GUIDELINES - If your mark was:

0 - 6 Disappointing. Your mark suggests that there is still some way to go before you have grasped the principles of costing.

7 - 10 Fair, but there will be a few topic areas that you ought to look at again.

11 - 15 Good. You are getting to grips with much of this subject but check whether there is any particular error that you were making consistently.

16 - 20 Very good. You appear to have a good understanding of ratios, and costing in general.

COMMENTS

Question

1

A responsibility centre might be an investment centre, a profit centre or a cost centre, with performance measured primarily by return on capital employed, profits and cost variances respectively. In some organisations, such as charities, there are also revenue centres.

2

	Operating efficiency		Activity efficiency	
	19X1	19X2	19X1	19X2
Department 1	$\frac{146}{2,700} = 5.4\%$	$\frac{142}{2,845} = 5.0\%$	$\frac{525}{8,100} = 6.5\%$	$\frac{525}{8,800} = 6.0\%$
Department 2	$\frac{58}{999} = 5.8\%$	$\frac{67}{1,008} = 6.6\%$	$\frac{406}{5,800} = 7.0\%$	$\frac{488}{6,090} = 8.0\%$

Operating efficiency improves when there is a *lower* ratio of holding costs to operating level (value of issues). Activity efficiency improves when the average stock value as a % of sales turnover becomes *lower*.

3

		19X1	19X2
(1)	Shelf turnover rate	$\frac{£5,000,000}{4,000}$	$\frac{£6,000,000}{4,400}$
	Sales =	£1,250 per cubic ft pa	£1,363.6 per cubic ft pa
(2)	Costs per cubic foot	$\frac{£240,000}{4,000}$	$\frac{£280,000}{4,400}$
		= £60	£63.6

4

The new direct labour cost at the old rate of pay would be

2 hrs × $\frac{100}{120}$ × £3 per hr = $1\frac{2}{3}$ hrs × £3 per hr = £5 per unit of T

This would increase the contribution and profit per unit by £1. Of this, one half should go to the work force, with the work force receiving £5.50 for each unit produced.

Hourly rate = £5.50 ÷ $1\frac{2}{3}$ hrs = £3.30 per hour.

COMMENTS

Question

5

	£	£
Budgeted fixed overhead (200,000 x £8)		1,600,000
Expenditure variance (10%)		160,000
Actual fixed overhead		1,760,000
Expenditure variance	160,000 (A)	
Variance caused by shortfall in hours worked (20% of 200,000 hrs x £8 per hour)	320,000 (A)	
Total under-absorbed overhead		480,000 (A)
Absorbed fixed overhead		1,280,000

Alternatively, absorbed overhead = £480,000 ÷ 37½ %
= £1,280,000

6

Standard hours produced	X	4,000 x 6	24,000
	Y	2,000 x 4	8,000
	Z	6,000 x 2	12,000
			44,000

Efficiency ratio = $\frac{44,000}{42,000}$ x 100% = 104.8%

7-9

Actual production

Product	Units	Standard hours	
W	12,000	(x 0.2)	2,400
X	25,000	(x 0.4)	10,000
Y	16,000	(x 0.5)	8,000
Z	5,000	(x 1.5)	7,500
			27,900

Budgeted production = 3,000 + 8,000 + 7,000 + 9,000
= 27,000 standard hours

Capacity usage ratio = $\frac{\text{Actual hours worked}}{\text{Budgeted hours}}$ = $\frac{29,000}{27,000}$ = 107.4%

Production volume ratio = $\frac{\text{Standard hours produced}}{\text{Budgeted production}}$ = $\frac{27,900}{27,000}$ = 103.3%

Efficiency ratio = $\frac{\text{Standard hours produced}}{\text{Actual hours worked}}$ = $\frac{27,900}{29,000}$ = 96.2%

Note that the production volume ratio = the efficiency ratio multiplied by the capacity usage ratio. (103.3% = 107.4% x 96.2%).

Question

10

Efficiency ratio $= \dfrac{\text{Standard hours produced}}{\text{Actual hours worked on production}}$

$= \dfrac{1,050}{830} \times 100\% = 126.5\%.$

11

Diverted hours are the available hours of direct labour employees that are spent on indirect labour work, such as machine cleaning. It is expressed as a percentage of their available hours.

$\dfrac{325}{1,155} \times 100\% = 28.1\%$

12

Production volume ratio $= \dfrac{80,000}{90,000} \times 100\% = 88.9\%$

13

Idle capacity ratio $= \dfrac{120,000 - 90,000}{120,000} = 25\%$

14

Actual direct labour cost £400,000
Actual sales (x 100/20) £2,000,000
Budgeted sales = £2,000,000 ÷ 1.25 £1,600,000
Budgeted = actual fixed production overhead
= 150% of 20% of £1,600,000 = £480,000

	Actual results £
Sales	2,000,000
Direct materials cost	(500,000)
Direct labour cost	(400,000)
Production overhead absorbed	(600,000)
Other overhead incurred (15% of £1,600,000)	(240,000)
Total costs	(1,740,000)
Over-absorbed production overhead (600,000 - 480,000)	120,000
	(1,620,000)
Profit	380,000

COMMENTS

Question

15

	£
Contribution budgeted (35% of £3.3m)	1,155,000
Profit budgeted (15% of £3.3m)	<u>495,000</u>
Budgeted fixed costs	<u>660,000</u>

Actual sales = £3,000,000

	£
Actual contribution (35% of 3,000,000)	1,050,000
Fixed costs	<u>660,000</u>
Profit	<u>390,000</u>

16

Algebra can help to solve this problem.

Let the price of product Y = Y
and the price of product X = 2Y

Profits are the same at 150,000 units, which is where

$$150,000 \times (60\% \text{ of } 2Y) - 240,000 = (150,000 \times 80\%Y) - 120,000$$
$$180,000Y - 240,000 = 120,000Y - 120,000$$
$$60,000Y = 120,000$$
$$Y = 2$$

If product Y sells for £2, product X sells for (×2) £4.

17

Budgeted sales		100,000 units
Margin of safety (20%)		<u>20,000</u> units
Breakeven volume of sales		<u>80,000</u> units

Let selling price = £P
Contribution = £(P-6) per unit and 0.25P
0.25P = P - 6
P = 8

At the breakeven volume of sales

		£
Sales revenue	(80,000 × 8)	640,000
Variable costs	(80,000 × 6)	<u>480,000</u>
∴ Fixed costs		<u>160,000</u>

10: RATIOS AND PERFORMANCE MEASUREMENT

Question

18

Note Remembering the principles behind a statement of sources and applications of funds should help you to sort out a solution to this question.

Balance sheets

	Start of year £		Year end £	Change £
Current liabilities				
Direct materials creditors	46,000	$(360,000 \times 1\frac{1}{2} \div 12)$	45,000	(1,000)
Direct labour-accrued wages	10,000	$(300,000 \times \frac{1}{2} \div 12)$	12,500	2,500
Other creditors	12,000	$(180,000 \div 12)$	15,000	3,000
Current assets				
Debtors	225,000	$(1,200,000 \div 4)$	300,000	(75,000)
Stocks	<u>32,000</u>	$(360,000 \div 6)$	<u>60,000</u>	<u>(28,000)</u>
				<u>(98,500)</u>

Funds generated from operations in the year should be profit + depreciation = £360,000

The cash position should therefore improve from £20,000 at the start of the year by (+ £360,000 - £98,500) £261,500 at the year end.

19

Reducing unit costs of production would reduce cash expenditures *for a given volume of output*, but if the company increases production volumes without increasing sales volumes, unit costs might fall, but there will be a build-up of stock levels and the company's cash position would not improve.

Further information

The Password series includes the following titles:

	Order code	
Economics	P01X	EC
Basic accounting	P028	BA
Financial accounting	P036	FA
Costing	P044	CO
Foundation business mathematics	P052	FB
Business law	P060	BL
Auditing	P079	AU
Organisation and management	P087	OM
Advanced business mathematics	P095	AB
Taxation	P109	TX
Management accounting	P117	MA
Interpretation of accounts	P125	IA
Financial management	P133	FM
Company law	P141	CL
Information technology	P15X	IT

Password is available from most major bookshops. If you have any difficulty obtaining them, please contact BPP directly, quoting the above order codes.

BPP Publishing Limited
Aldine Place
142/144 Uxbridge Road
London W12 8AA

Tel: 01-740 1111
Fax: 01-740 1184
Telex: 265871 (MONREF G) - quoting '76:SJJ098'